Feminist Theory and Literary Practice

Feminist Theory and Literary Practice

Deborah L. Madsen

Pluto  **Press**

LONDON • STERLING, VIRGINIA

First published 2000 by Pluto Press
345 Archway Road, London N6 5AA
and 22883 Quicksilver Drive,
Sterling, VA 20166–2012, USA

www.plutobooks.com

British Library Cataloguing in Publication Data
A catalogue record for this book is available from
the British Library

ISBN 0 7453 1602 6 hardback
ISBN 0 7453 1601 8 paperback

Library of Congress Cataloging in Publication Data applied for

09   08   07   06   05   04   03   02   01   00
10   9   8   7   6   5   4   3   2   1

Designed and produced for Pluto Press by Chase Production Services
Typeset from disk by Stanford DTP Services, Northampton
Printed in the European Union by TJ International, Padstow

For my girls, Selene, Dana and Aurora

Contents

vii

Preface

Women's writing and feminism have always been closely related because 'women's writing' is a critical category – a product of discourse about the texts women have written – and not the intention of the writers themselves. Women's writing is a critical, not an authorial, category. There are some exceptions (an increasing number) in the late twentieth century, but it is safe to say that not all female writers are feminist and this is especially true of pre-nineteenth century writers. Feminist theory therefore defines the object of study (women's writing) but the relationship between the two goes deeper than this. Many texts by women express the same concerns as feminist theory: the unique experience of women in history; the notion of female consciousness; the definitions of gender that limit and oppress; and the cause of women's liberation from those restrictions.

In the chapters that follow, I offer a survey of the diversity of feminist theories together with a selected history of American women's writing: my aim is to show how the issues of feminism have been engaged by women writers – reflected, supported, challenged – throughout America's history. The book then offers an exploration of American women's writing that focuses upon the synergism that exists between literary texts and the feminist theories that construct those texts as 'women's writing'. Each chapter deals with one of the issues or concepts that have engaged both authors and theorists – Rhetoric, Work, Consciousness, Sexuality, Nature, Class, and Race – offering an analysis of how that concept has been used by feminists to theorise the feminine condition. This analysis is then applied to the reading of key American women's literary texts in order to highlight the conceptual synergism that exists between feminist theory and literary praxis. The book introduces, explains and applies each of the major trends or movements within contemporary feminist theory: Liberal, Marxist, Psychoanalytic, Radical, Socialist, Third-World and Eco-feminism, providing an accessible account of the varieties of American feminist thought within the context of readings of key American women's texts.

In anthologies and introductory monographs, feminist literary theory is frequently explained in terms of how theorists deal with the concepts of 'Woman' or 'the Feminine'. But readers just as often encounter feminism as a bewildering diversity of theoretical practices, distinguished each from the other only as 'isms'. Consequently, many popular introductions to feminism do not do much to clarify the confusion experienced when readers attempt to relate particular schools of feminist thought to the diverse political agenda of feminism. My intention is to describe as clearly and succinctly as possible the main principles, practitioners, and analytic methods of the seven most influential approaches to contemporary feminism. Each theoretical model is exemplified in its application to literary study. Each chapter opens with an analytical survey of theorists working within a particular field of feminist theory. This theory is then exemplified by the practical application of the style of feminist analysis that follows. In each chapter I have selected well-known texts that occupy a canonical place within the American women's literary tradition as the subject for inter-pretation and discussion. Thus, the book offers an account of American women's literary history, from the colonial period to the present, while at the same time introducing the most influential of contemporary feminist theoretical practices.

These literary texts have been chosen with care, to include both well-established texts such as Kate Chopin's *The Awakening* and newly-canonised texts like the writings of Maxine Hong Kingston and Leslie Marmon Silko. As these last few names indicate, I have attempted to represent the diversity of the American women's literary tradition as it is read and studied today. Women of colour are represented extensively both as writers of theory and of literature. It should be noted that not only is the erosion of traditional distinctions between these types of discourse exemplified by the writers themselves who are discussed in this book but the breakdown of the clearly defined categories of 'theory' versus 'literature' emerges as the dominant theme. In the chapter devoted to radical feminist theories, for example, the key writers highlighted here – Adrienne Rich and Audre Lorde – are quite rightly as famous for their incisive contribution to contemporary theoretical debate as for their imaginative work in the fields of poetry and prose. In this case, a close synergism exists between theory and literary practice, where the theorists are also the literary practitioners. In other chapters, however, I have deliberately chosen to discuss literary works that seem indifferent or even hostile towards the feminist approach I have adopted. For example, I use a Marxist feminist approach to Charlotte Perkins Gilman's *The Yellow Wallpaper*, a text that is most frequently discussed in terms of psychological theoretical paradigms. Similarly, I use the principles of Socialist feminism to approach Ann Beattie's short stories, texts that have been criticised for bearing little obvious relation to political and social realities. Perhaps most hostile to contemporary feminist approaches are texts written in a predominantly 'pre-feminist' era, such as the colonial American seventeenth century. I have chosen to open my discussions here with the analysis of Mary Rowlandson's captivity narrative in order to do two things. First, these writers in some ways signify the beginnings of women's writing in America, and so it is appropriate to start a book which claims to cover the chronological breadth of American women's writing with a consideration of their work. Secondly, these texts – like the others I have named above – demonstrate the ways in which literary texts that appear to be removed from specific feminist principles do in fact respond powerfully to analysis when approached in terms of contemporary feminist concerns. These texts maybe more than others show how the issues of feminism have been engaged, reflected, supported and challenged by women writers throughout America's history.

The structure of the book follows a broadly chronological pattern, beginning with a chapter on writers of the colonial period; this is followed by two chapters on nineteenth-century women's writing, three chapters on twentieth-century women's writing, and a concluding chapter devoted to contemporary American ethnic women's writing. In addition to including women of colour with white writers, I have opted to conclude with a chapter that considers ethnic women's writing on its own terms, in order to give full consideration to what I consider to be the most powerful challenge to contemporary feminist theoretical models. The vocabulary I have used deliberately avoids complex theoretical terminology but, to avoid the twin dangers of misrepresentation and oversimplification, I do use the terms deployed by the theorists I discuss. Some of the key terms that recur throughout the discussion here are: 'gender', as opposed to 'sex', which refers to the socio-cultural characteristics attributed to the different biological sexes; 'misogyny', which refers to the systematic practice of woman-hating and usually describes the institutionalised subordination of women and all that is designated 'feminine'. Anti-feminine practices found in misogynistic cultures include: foot-binding, genital mutilation, female slavery, female infanticide, concubinage, forced marriage and child marriage. 'Patriarchy' is another recurrent term, referring to government by men (viz. 'the Father'); patriarchy is a cultural (ideological) system that privileges men and all things masculine, and a political system that places power in the hands of men and thus serves male interests at the expense of women.

These are terms that are common currency in feminist theoretical and literary debates and yet they are worth rehearsing here, if only for the sake of clarity. Clarity is what I have sought throughout this book – clarity of structure and terminology, but I have also sought to clarify the relations that characterise the intellectual fields of contemporary feminist theory and American women's writing. These are fields marked by a diversity that gives rise to bitter controversy as well as immense vitality and dynamism. It is a pressing issue at this time, to negotiate the diversification of feminism into various movements and interest groups that are organised around specific issues (such as class or race or ecology), and to negotiate this diversity in such a way as to maintain a recognition of differences while at the same time recovering a sense of the concerns which women share. To embrace this diversity while mapping shared concerns is the task I have set myself in this book, and I have hoped to achieve this with clarity of purpose and expression, so that all who read the book may come to a better appreciation of the richness of the American women's tradition.

Introduction

Feminism in America

This chapter introduces the primary historical and theoretical contexts for the detailed discussions that follow in subsequent chapters. Here I set out the major historical periods of the American women's movement, with brief analysis of the key texts produced by the theorists of those times. It is important to underline the fact that feminism in America has a long history and is not the invention of the twentieth century. Without this fundamental historical understanding, debates that continue today cannot be fully appreciated in all their intellectual complexity. It is essential that American feminism is seen not only on its own terms but fully in those terms. Thus, I begin with the pre-National and Revolutionary periods, focused upon the revolutionary decade of the 1770s, when women equated domestic tyranny with monarchical tyranny and demanded that the inalienable rights of women as well as men be addressed and inscribed in the foundational documents of the new Republic. I then move to the first wave of American feminism – the period leading up to and following the Seneca Falls Convention in 1848. Key thinkers and texts of this period include Margaret Fuller's *Woman in the Nineteenth Century* (1845), the essays and speeches by Elizabeth Cady Stanton and Susan B. Anthony, and Charlotte Perkins Gilman's *Women and Economics: A Study of the Economic Relation Between Men and Women as a Factor in Social Evolution* (1898), which are discussed in chapter one.

The second wave of American feminism dates from the 1960s, and marks the establishment of the modern Women's Movement. Key texts of second wave feminism include: Betty Friedan's *The Feminine Mystique* (1963), discussed in chapter one, Shulamith Firestone's *The Dialectic of Sex* (1970), discussed in chapter five, Kate Millett's *Sexual Politics* (1971) and Gloria Steinem's *Outrageous Acts and Everyday Rebellions* (1983). Developments within American feminism since the 1970s have been characterised first by the critique of mainstream 'white' feminism, most notably by Angela Davis in *Women, Race and Class* (1981) and bell hooks's *Ain't I a Woman?* (1981), which are both discussed in chapter seven. This same feminist mainstream has been criticised by lesbian feminists, such as Adrienne Rich and Audre Lorde (whose work is discussed at length in chapter five), for failing to confront the politics of 'compulsory heterosexuality' that is one of the major linchpins of the patriarchal power structure. Then the impact of French feminist theory in the 1980s considerably diversified the feminist agenda in America, perhaps exemplified by the cultural or postmodern feminism represented by Judith Butler's *Gender Trouble: Feminism and the Subversion of Identity* (1990); and in the 1990s the emergence of so-called 'post-feminist' debates were taken up in very different ways by such women as Susan Faludi in *Backlash: The Undeclared War Against Women* (1992) and Camille Paglia in *Vamps and Tramps* (1994). It is this historical and intellectual terrain that I want to map out in this introductory chapter.

The Historical Contexts of American Feminism

The position of women in colonial America was determined by the hierarchical worldview of the Puritan colonists. As men deferred to God and His ministers, so women should defer to men. Puritans believed that the inferiority of women was a mark of original sin, manifest in physical weakness, smaller stature, intellectual limitations and a tendency to depend upon emotions rather than the intellect. Women should be confined to the domestic sphere, nurturing children, maintaining the household and serving their husbands. John Winthrop, the first governor of the Massachusetts Bay colony, held that 'A true wife accounts her subjection [as] her honor and freedom', finding contentment only 'in subjection to her husband's authority'. Though the position of women was marginally better in the New World than the Old, due to more liberal property laws, the availability of divorce and legal protection from physical abuse, the principle of female subordination was the foundation of women's position in America as the nation developed. Calls for political equality during the Revolutionary era went largely unheard; the notion of women's rights was ignored by the Constitutional Convention. This, despite the condemnation in 1775 by Thomas Paine, theoretician of the Revolution, of the position of women 'even in countries where they may be esteemed the most happy, constrained in their desires in the disposal of their goods, robbed of freedom and will by the laws, the slaves of opinion ...' (quoted by Friedan, 1963, p. 84).

So, in the nineteenth century a woman in America was unable to vote, and after marriage had no control of her property (in some states the law compelled employers to pay a woman's wages directly to her husband) or her children. Nor could she make a will, sign a contract or instigate legal proceedings without her husband's consent. Her status was akin to that of a minor or a slave. It was in connection with slavery that the organised movement for women's rights had its origin, when the American abolitionist movement split over women's right to participate. A group of women then determined to fight for their own freedom. It should be noted in passing that this also marks the beginning of the problematical relationship between women's rights and civil rights movements, because the two groups often found themselves in competition, debating racial versus gender oppression: which should be prioritized? Susan B. Anthony and Elizabeth Cady Stanton both opposed the 15th Amendment, which gave the vote to black men, because it denied the vote to women. This issue is discussed in more detail in chapter seven.

First Wave of American Feminism: 1840s–1920

The so-called 'first wave' of American feminism began in the 1840s and is commonly marked by the first Women's Rights

Convention, held in Seneca Falls in 1848. It was organised by Elizabeth Cady Stanton and other women who had been denied a place at the international anti-slavery convention in London in 1840. In important respects, the tone of the Seneca Falls Convention had been set by the efforts of Margaret Fuller, who is described by Elizabeth Cady Stanton and Susan B. Anthony as having 'possessed more influence upon the thought of American women than any woman previous to her time' (quoted by Dickenson, 1994, p. ix). Perhaps most influential of Fuller's work was *Woman in the Nineteenth Century*, a plea for the abolition of all intellectual and economic restrictions imposed for reasons of gender which, when it was published in February 1845, sold out an edition of one thousand copies within a week. *Woman in the Nineteenth Century* was based upon Fuller's essay 'The Great Lawsuit – Man *versus* Men; Woman *versus* Women' which she published in the Transcendentalist magazine *The Dial* in July 1843. In the preface, Fuller explains that she altered the title of the book-length version because of complaints that the significance of her original title was obscure. Fuller's preference for the original lies in the effort of understanding it requires on the part of the reader: that 'while it is the destiny of Man, in the course of the ages, to ascertain and fulfil the law of his being ... the action of prejudices and passions which attend, in the day, the growth of the individual, is continually obstructing the holy work that is to make the earth a part of heaven' (Fuller, 1845, p. 3). In this description of her subject, Fuller reveals the Transcendentalist basis of her thought, especially the emphasis upon self-realisation and self-fulfilment as the object of human life. Her indebtedness to Emerson is revealed by assumptions such as that America offers superior opportunities for self-fulfilment and self-reliance; so American women, who are free from the conventions and traditions that constrain the women of other nations, should be able to discover 'the secrets of nature' and the 'revelations of the spirit' (p. 71).

Fuller explicitly includes both men and women in her category of 'Man' and shows how the 'action of prejudices' upon individual lives affects men and women differently. She first illustrates through historical, mythical and literary example, the imperative that man achieves self-knowledge but the subject subtly changes as she observes that 'the idea of Man, however imperfectly brought out, has been far more so than that of Woman' (p. 11). At this point, Fuller suggests that the improvement of women's condition will better prepare them for their task of moral guardianship of men. In this way, women can fulfil their part in the grand national destiny which awaits the Republic. Fuller does not allow the subject to rest, however, with her endorsement of the then popular justification of women's education. She roundly rejects the idea that women should accept the external regulation of their minds and lives rather than pursuing their own needs and suggests that this is the tenor of contemporary women's thought: '[m]any women are considering within themselves, what they need that they have not, and what they can have, if they find they need it' (p. 15). But Fuller goes on to catalogue the obstacles to this self-fulfilment .... The limited rights of married women over their own property, the automatic custody of children to the father in the event of divorce or separation, the symbolic association of women with children and slaves in habits of thought and expression, the enforced frivolity which Fuller sees as a continuum with prostitution at one extreme. Finally, she cites the life of drudgery that afflicts all women, rich and poor, who are limited in their exercise of will and in their capacity for self-reliance, a quality that Fuller values highly. All of these obstacles are examined in turn. These are the obstructions preventing the further development of humanity, in Fuller's description of men and women as two parts of the same thought: 'What woman needs is not as a woman to act or rule, but as a nature to grow, as an intellect to discern, as a soul to live freely and unimpeded, to unfold such powers as were given her when we left our common home' (p. 20). Women need to fulfil their personal and national destinies, but they also need to fulfil the spiritual destiny of humanity and it is men who have historically placed obstacles in their way: from the Christian religion that blames a woman for the Fall and thus condemns her to eternal serfdom, and the Roman conviction that while the human body is inherited from the mother the more valuable, eternal part, the soul, comes from the father, to the contemporary injustices outlined above.

The 1848 Seneca Falls Convention marked the beginning of the political struggle for women's rights; the Declaration of Sentiments, modelled ironically on Jefferson's Declaration of Independence, was drafted primarily by Elizabeth Cady Stanton.

> We hold these truths to be self-evident: that all men and women are created equal ... The history of mankind is a history of repeated injuries and usurpations on the part of man toward woman, having in direct object the establishment of an absolute tyranny over her ... He has never permitted her to exercise her inalienable right to the effective franchise ... He has made her, if married, in the eyes of the law, civilly dead.

Together with Susan B. Anthony, Stanton founded the National Woman's Suffrage Association in 1869, and Lucy Stone established the American Woman's Suffrage Association, to promote a suffrage amendment to the Constitution (this became the 19th Amendment only in 1920). Additional demands such as the reform of divorce laws and improved working conditions for women were added by both organisations to the suffrage platform. The two organisations merged in 1890 to become the National American Woman's Suffrage Association, which later became the League of Women Voters. A number of pro-suffrage groups sprang up in the pre-war years: Elizabeth Cady Stanton's daughter, Harriet Stanton Blatch, founded the Equality League in 1907 and Alice Paul, who had been active in the British suffrage struggle, founded the more militant Congressional Union, which later became the Woman's Party. It was the Woman's Party that first proposed the Equal Rights Amendment to Congress in 1923 – 'Men and women shall have equal rights throughout the United States and every place subject to its jurisdiction' (quoted in Humm, 1992, p. 3) – and although this move was unsuccessful, it did lay some of the intellectual groundwork for the second wave of American feminism in the 1960s when the proposed amendment to the Constitution that would ensure federal equality for women became the focus of renewed efforts on behalf of women's rights.

Women's suffrage was viewed as a matter for state action rather than constitutional change and some states did adopt universal suffrage. Though the female vote provided a point of focus for the women's rights campaign, women did not pursue this as their only political objective. In the latter part of the century, for instance, the women's clubs movement involved women in organised charity and reform activities, and in 1903 the National Women's Trade Union League was founded to protect women workers. In 1923 the Woman's Party introduced in Congress an Equal Rights Amendment, designed to remove all legal distinctions between the sexes. But legislative change was slow. There was some progress in the reform of property laws and gradually educational opportunities became available, although job opportunities were restricted to teaching and nursing – extensions of traditionally feminine domestic and nurturing roles. The Equal Rights Amendment was finally adopted by Congress in 1972 but it fell short of ratification. Civil rights, affirmative action and abortion rights were not introduced until the 1960s and 1970s; successes of the so-called 'second wave' of feminism.

Second Wave of American Feminism: 1960s

The second wave of American feminism emerged in the early 1960s and focused upon an indictment of male sexism and the domestic oppression of women. Betty Friedan's *The Feminine Mystique* (1963) called for women to renew the struggle of the first wave which had culminated in female suffrage in 1920, but now feminist attention was focused on the exclusion of women from the public sphere and sex-based discrimination in the workplace. State and federal provision of childcare and the legalisation of abortion also formed part of the agenda of NOW (the National Organisation of Women, founded by Friedan in 1966). Nineteen seventy-two was a watershed year: the Educational Amendments Act of 1972 made it mandatory for all colleges to instigate affirmative action programmes in relation to admissions, hiring and athletics; Congress approved the Equal Rights Amendment, and the landmark decision by the Supreme Court in Roe v. Wade overruled state laws forbidding abortions during the first three months of pregnancy. By the end of the decade, however, the Equal Rights Amendment expired (in 1982), having failed to gain ratification; feminism was under attack for its failure to extend its sphere of interest beyond the middle classes, and divisions between moderate and radical feminists also undermined the unity of the movement and its ability to force change. Political change has always been fundamental to feminism, but the concept of 'change' articulated by the Women's Movement ranges from cultural revolution to radical separation of the sexes to liberal reforms of the existing socio-economic order.

Early calls were for equal rights, reproductive rights and economic justice, drawing on the relationship between the early Women's Movement, the New Left and the Civil Rights Movement. This relationship is described by Sara Evans in *Personal Politics: The Roots of Women's Liberation in the Civil Rights Movement and the New Left* (1979). She counts the rise of Third World nationalism, the beatnik challenge to middle-class values, and growing racial unrest, as elements that contributed to the weakening of the feminine mystique. The election of the Kennedy administration in 1960 helped to shift attitudes towards change from negative to positive, and the formation of the National Organization of Women instituted a new civil rights group capable of lobbying government to enact and enforce anti-sexual discrimination legislation. But, as Evans points out, important though these civil rights efforts were, the professional women who created NOW tended to accept the existing division between domestic and public spheres, and their activism was directed towards achieving equality in the public world rather than challenging the network of gender roles that supported such a division.

The pressures on most women were building up not on the level of public discrimination but at the juncture of public and private, of job and home, where older structures and identities no longer sufficed but could not simply be discarded either. The growing emotional strains of providing nurture for others with nowhere to escape to oneself, of rising expectations and low self-esteem, of public activity and an increasingly private, even submerged, identity required radical – in the literal sense – response (p. 21).

This radical response came, in Evans's account, from young women who had gained valuable experience, within the Civil Rights Movement and the New Left, of self-respect, of their own capacity to organise especially at a grassroots level. Within these movements they had learned an egalitarian ideology that stressed the connection between political commitment and personal experience within the context of community action and co-operative structures. Despite the valuable lessons learned, these women felt compelled to break away from these political movements which replicated the same gender roles as the mainstream and thrust women into subservient, 'feminine' roles. Activism on their own behalf and on behalf of all women was the new freedom struggle.

The raising of women's consciousness of gender oppression and raising as a political issue the personal experience of that oppression were central to the efforts of early second-wave feminism. Characteristic of these early efforts is Gloria Steinem's *Outrageous Acts and Everyday Rebellions* (1983) which collects various of her journalistic pieces written throughout the decade from the early 1970s to the early 1980s. What emerges from these stories is a powerful sense of women occupying a distinct social and cultural class. What defines this class is the shared experience of oppression based upon the stereotypical definition of feminine sexuality. For example, in the now famous exposé of Hugh Hefner's Playboy empire, 'I Was a Playboy Bunny', Steinem uncovers the commonality of female sexual exploitation. Contrary to the advertised profile of a Playboy Bunny as college educated, middle class, highly paid, glamorous and sophisticated and also in contradiction to the reality of the characterless young women who are recruited –

'We just want you to fit the Bunny image', Steinem is repeatedly told (Steinem, 1983, p. 35) – she finds that women of all kinds are recruited as Bunnies only to be moulded, quite literally, by the punitively close-fitting costumes they must wear, into a clearly defined sexual stereotype. White women and women of colour, young and older women, married and single women, women with children and those without, all are treated as the objectified images of the Playboy 'brand'.

Any doubt as to the sexual categorisation of these women is dispelled when Steinem is told about the prohibition against dating customers because a clear distinction must be maintained between the Bunnies' legal employment and prostitution. Steinem quotes a memo from Hugh Hefner which states, 'We naturally do not tolerate any merchandising of the Bunnies' (p. 41), yet 'merchandising' is precisely the process upon which Heffner's organisation is based. The women are all required to pose repeatedly for photographs, which remain the property of the Playboy organisation; Steinem also discovers that while the Bunnies are prohibited from dating customers, there are some privileged patrons, 'Number One keyholders', who are exceptions, and promotional parties which girls fail to attend at the risk of losing their jobs. Sexual coercion and exploitation are the reality of a Bunny's life, as Steinem discovers during her own few weeks as a Playboy Bunny and in the years following. She tells how for the next 20 years she would receive occasional telephone calls from Bunnies, 'with revelations about their working conditions and the sexual demands on them. ... One said she had been threatened with "acid thrown in my face" when she complained about the sexual use of the Bunnies. Another quoted the same alleged threat as a response to trying to help Bunnies unionize' (p. 69). But what Steinem describes as perhaps the most powerful realisation to come out of this experience was the awareness that all women are Bunnies, all women are coerced and exploited and objectified through their sexuality.

It is the material, bodily basis of female sexual oppression that contributes a unifying theme to Steinem's writing. She analyses the way women talk, in terms of the low volume and high pitch of their speech as well as the willingness to allow a man to interrupt their speech or to dominate discussion, which reflects feminine passivity and weakness. She points to the way that cultures manipulate women's access to food, remarking that '[f]or much of the female half of the world, food is the first signal of our inferiority. It lets us know that our own families may consider female bodies to be less deserving, less needy, less valuable' (p. 191). Steinem exposes the myth that patriarchy expresses no consistent attitude towards females by showing that women function consistently as the symbol of masculine power and privilege. So in a poor and deprived culture, powerful men will fatten their wives to represent their superior wealth; in a wealthier society where poor women become fat on a diet of starch and sugar, powerful men will favour lean and delicate women. Steinem remarks, 'Nonetheless, the common denominators are weakness, passivity, and lack of strength. Rich or poor, feminine beauty is equated with subservience to men' (p. 195).

Pornography is the cultural production that focuses Steinem's arguments about the connection between feminine sexuality, masculine dominance and violence as a strategy of control. In the piece entitled 'Erotica vs. Pornography' she makes a distinction between images of free, mutual sexuality and the violence or unequal power relationship that is an essential ingredient of pornography; yet she remarks that in our patriarchal society erotica and pornography are categorised indistinguishably as 'obscenity': 'because sex and violence are so dangerously intertwined and confused. After all, it takes violence or the threat of it to maintain the unearned dominance of any group of human beings over another' (pp. 219–220). All women are subject to the influence of pornography, all women are surrounded by pornographic images of women's bodies on display, violated, tortured, even murdered, and appearing to enjoy the sexual thrill of it all. In 'The Real Linda Lovelace' Steinem describes as the most disturbing aspect of this woman's experience of sexual enslavement, forced prostitution, rape and beatings, the fact that her story is not believed and that she is blamed, despite several unsuccessful attempts at escape for which she was severely punished, for failing to escape earlier. This story attacks the myth of female masochism that insists women enjoy sexual domination and even pain, but prostitution and pornography are big businesses built on that myth.

> When challenged about her inability to escape earlier, Linda wrote: 'I can understand why some people have such difficulty accepting the truth. When I was younger, when I heard about a woman being raped, my secret feeling was *that could never happen to me*. I would never *permit* it to happen. Now I realize that can be about as meaningful as saying I won't permit an avalanche (original emphasis, p. 248).

Steinem's point is that all women are subject to the threat represented by her degradation and the sexual violence she suffered both in private and also in the prostitution and pornography industries.

The use of sexual violence by men as a strategy for sustaining patriarchal control of women rose to prominence as a major feminist issue in the 1970s and was the subject of Susan Brownmiller's ground-breaking analysis of rape in *Against Our Will: Men, Women and Rape* (1975). Brownmiller shares the radical position that all women constitute a single class with the same experience of oppression. All women are victimised by rape because the threat of rape is directed towards all women in patriarchal culture and therefore benefits all men in that culture. The rapist is not defined in Western legal culture as a specific criminal type, and thus rape is regarded as a general masculine characteristic.

> Once we accept as basic truth that rape is not a crime of irrational, impulsive, uncontrollable lust, but is a deliberate, hostile, violent act of degradation and possession on the part of a would-be conqueror, designed to intimidate and inspire fear, we must look toward those elements in our culture that promote and propagandize these attitudes which offer men, and in particular, impressionable, adolescent males, who form the potential raping population, the ideology and psychologic [sic] encourage-

ment to commit their acts of aggression *without awareness, for the most part, that they have committed a punishable crime,* let alone a moral wrong. (Brownmiller's emphasis, in Humm, 1992, p. 72)

It is this status of rape as a masculine characteristic that leads Brownmiller to investigate historical, anthropological, military and criminal cases of rape as instances where patriarchy is linked directly to male aggression, an aggression that is biologically based but culturally defined. Pornography, prostitution, male aggression, militarism and rape are connected, in Brownmiller's critique, in a network of meanings and practices that support the exercise of male power in both private and political terms. Brownmiller argues that this masculine aggression is twinned with feminine passivity and lack of will that is the result of the deliberate and powerful conditioning of women in the meaning of 'femininity' under patriarchy. Susan Brownmiller drew attention to rape specifically and sexual violence in general as feminist issues that escape the reformist energies of liberal feminist organisations such as NOW (National Organization of Women). In a series of books published after Brownmiller's ground-breaking study Susan Griffin set out her view of the cultural nature of male aggression and hatred of women and relates the use of violence as a mechanism of social and psychological control to the differential gender development of men and women. In *Woman and Nature: The Roaring Inside Her* (1978), *Rape: And the Power of Consciousness* (1979), and *Pornography and Silence: Culture's Revenge Against Women* (1981) Griffin explores the representation of sexual violence in western culture and traces a connection between the domination of 'feminine' nature and a dominating and aggressive 'masculine' science. The reproductive capacity of women, together with the emphasis upon connectivity and nurturing in feminine gender development, lends women a greater understanding of nature but also leaves 'feminised' nature vulnerable to the exploitative power of men under patriarchy. In this way, Griffin opens up an area of feminist analysis that is developed by ecofeminist theorists, such as

Ynestra King and Carol Adams, whose work is discussed in chapter four.

Perhaps the most prominent feminist activist against institutionalised male sexual violence and pornography in particular is Andrea Dworkin who, with the feminist legal scholar Catherine MacKinnon, created a landmark when they sought legal means to have pornography designated a civil offence, in the Minneapolis Anti-Pornography Ordinance. Dworkin argues, in works like *Pornography: Men Possessing Women* (1981), that pornography victimises all women, who are objectified and their meaning fixed within a network of violent sexual imagery. In this way, pornography serves to legitimate and to perpetuate the structures of male power. 'The major theme of pornography as a genre is male power, its nature, its magnitude, its use, its meaning. Male power as expressed in and through pornography, is discernible in discrete but interwoven, reinforcing strains: the power of self, physical power over and against others, the power of terror, the power of naming, the power of owning, the power of money, and the power of sex. ... The valuation of women in pornography is a secondary theme in that the degradation of women exists in order to postulate, exercise, and celebrate male power. Male power, in degrading women, is concerned first with itself, its perpetuation, expansion, intensification, and elevation' (in Humm, 1992, pp. 83–84).

The Rise of American Feminist Literary Theory

At this time, feminist activism saw the rise of feminist theory in the areas of literary study, political theory, philosophy and history. This development culminated in the emergence of Women's Studies programmes in the United States and globally. The first full Women's Studies programme was set up at San Diego State College in 1970 (Leitch, 1989, p. 325). The preferred method of organisation has been interdepartmental and the preferred methodology interdisciplinary with a strong emphasis upon the historical. Feminist literary theory had three main aims: to expose the workings of the ubiquitous patriarchal power structure; to promote the rediscovery of women's historical achievements (including literary history); and to establish a feminine perspective on critical, literary, political, scientific, philosophical (and other) theories of the cultural forces that shape our lives. The intended aim was to change the sexist bias of traditional educational and social practices.

In literary critical circles, pre-feminist or 'traditional' criticism came under attack for its blindness to gender. Traditional approaches to the text assume that texts are not gendered, 'great' works of literature express timeless and immutable truths that are not affected by such worldly issues as sex. Feminists charge that this kind of approach institutionalises male prejudice by refusing to acknowledge that 'great' works of literature often endorse masculine values and interests. Early feminist theory, which developed from the Women's Liberation and Civil Rights movements, focused upon points of continuity between the reading experience and personal experience (including family, society, networks of relationships, power structures, systems of value learned and lived and perpetuated in 'private' life).

One of the pioneering literary studies was Kate Millett's *Sexual Politics* (1971) which offered an analysis of authoritative male writers and revealed a pattern of masculine dominance and feminine submission that Millett identified as misogyny. *Sexual Politics* exposed the patriarchal prejudice and sexual violence celebrated in classic modern texts such as D.H. Lawrence's *Sons and Lovers* and *Lady Chatterley's Lover*, or Norman Mailer's *The Naked and the Dead*. Millett's basic insight was that all writing is marked by gender; this fact is suppressed by traditional non-feminist theory which claims for literature immunity from such worldly experiences as the experience of one's sexuality. The aim of feminist literary critics such as Millett was to promote a positive image of women in art and therefore in life, and also to raise the consciousness of women to their own oppression. The method pursued by Millett is to look at how female characters are portrayed and in what positions/situations they are placed in 'great' literary works. From this, she builds up a picture of the attitudes towards women that characterise the work of a particular author or genre or period. The purpose is to show how women are placed culturally within a scheme of male values. At the same time, she draws attention to the complexity of female characters, a complexity that is obscured by the overwhelming stress on the 'hero' and other male characters. By dividing characters into categories of male and female, and proceeding from there to criticise the exclusion of women from an active part in the male-dominated reading process, this kind of feminist criticism raises questions of how gender is defined in terms of 'maleness' and 'femaleness'. The concept of a cultural process of exclusion, through representation, suggests that women's inferior social status is a cultural phenomenon, not a biological condition. If this is so, reading is a culturally conditioned activity, so women will not necessarily read in a 'female' way just because they are biologically female. Women who are taught to read as men *will* read as men, according to masculine standards and values. Women are taught to identify with men against their own interests, in the reading of literary works as in the rest of culture, and this is what produces the contradictions of the female condition and the anxieties that were identified by second wave feminists. Gender is not a biological given but a theoretical position. Before feminism offered an alternative, we all read as men and that style of reading was our theory. Literary feminism tried to awaken a sense of the value of the feminine by promoting a revaluation of the image of women in literature.

Early deconstructive work, such as Millett's, was followed by the effort to discover and define a tradition of women's writing. This involved finding and publishing the work of neglected writers as well as the theoretical effort to define the nature of feminine lives, creativity, styles, genres, themes, images, genius or sensibility, and the like. Prominent literary critics working in this area include: Ellen Moers, Elaine Showalter, Patricia Meyer Spacks, Sandra Gilbert, Susan Gubar, Nina Baym, among others. Gender identity is assumed to be the determinant of women's lives and therefore their writing – society shapes women's language, consciousness, education and careers – through powerful social-historical conditioning ('socialisation'). With the development of a cultural understanding of gender came the effort to promote a 'resisting' style of reading, described most influentially by Judith Fetterley in *The Resisting Reader* (1976). The resistance her title referred to focuses upon how women are led to identify and sympathise with those forces represented within the text that conspire to oppress women by obscuring their complexity and neutralising any attempt to question the text's sex-bias. From this basis, feminists began to analyse the political and literary assumptions involved in reading. They questioned how 'universal' values are defined, how 'truth' is distorted in directions that serve male interests. The aim of this kind of analysis was to create a genuinely female reader who would practice a female style of interpretation: someone who would have rid herself of the 'male reader' role that was created for her. This female reader is a woman who refuses to co-operate in her own oppression, who refuses to accept her conditioning into patriarchal society, who refuses to collude with the male power structure.

Cultural analysis and criticism, then, took on equal stature with the formal analysis of the literary qualities of individual texts. The perceived danger of this style of analysis is the risk of treating woman as a universal category and thereby re-establishing restrictive stereotypes based on gender 'essence'. The issue of essence is of great importance to the question: can men be feminists? Many women argued No! Men are the 'carriers of patriarchy'. As authority figures and role models intellectual men cannot but intimidate and repress women. Other women argue that whilst men cannot share feminine experience they can study, analyse and come to understand women's experience as different to their own. The desire to keep feminism exclusively for women reinforces the biological identification of gender but also sustains the esprit de corps so important to the continued motivation of the women's movement; the generalisation of feminist insight broadens the scope of feminism and increases the number of people liable to be influenced by feminist analysis but threatens to dissipate the political activism that is at the heart of the feminist enterprise. The concept of female solidarity that propelled the Women's Movement is now seen as controversial: perhaps it embodies a false universalism that denies the diversity of women's experience in favour of an oppressive gender category that reproduces the effects of masculine gender stereotypes; alternatively, female solidarity can provide the basis for activism and for pro-women legislation, a numerical basis (if nothing else) that is undermined by attacks on the meaning of 'woman' as a political category. Some point to the coincidence of such attacks at a time when pro-female legislation is beginning to have perceptible effects on Western society and suggest that the attack on female commonality itself serves male interests.

The main difference between American feminism and Continental (specifically French) feminism also depends upon this debate over gender 'essence'. American feminist approaches tend to be grounded in cultural and historical analysis; French feminism of the kind that became increasing influential throughout the 1980s is grounded in Freudian psychoanalysis. There are enormous differences between these kinds of feminism but an American 'compromise', a psychoanalytically informed feminism, did emerge in the work of Nancy Chodorow. Crudely, where American feminism is concerned with feminine history, French feminism is concerned with the 'feminine' as a category of discourse, a definition constructed in language, philosophy, psychoanalysis and elsewhere. Psychoanalysis helps in the effort to understand how it is that a woman can be taught to think and read like a man, with a man's view of the world, and why it is that this male view is so powerful. Psychoanalysis attempts to discover in the subconscious, and in the linguistic determinants of consciousness, the reasons for female oppression. Theorists ask how specific cultural values are tied to male interests: such as the oppositions between rational (male) and emotional (female), nature (female) and civilisation (male) – which position woman as the defining opposite or 'Other' of man. Women are defined as 'other' or they are ignored, rendered invisible and silent, if they do not fit the patriarchal scheme. Outside the dominant definitions of male-dominated culture women exist only as insane, inarticulate or irrelevant.

Influential French feminists like Hélène Cixous, Julia Kristeva and Luce Irigaray separate 'the feminine' from 'women as people' and are concerned to analyse how a specific kind of writing, designated feminine (écriture féminine), subverts the linguistic and metaphysical conventions of Western discourse. The repressions of a patriarchal society create silences, things that cannot be said, and these silences are disrupted by the avant-garde feminine practice of writing – which is produced equally by men and women (Mallarmé, Joyce, Artaud, Duras, Lispector). It is this insistence that feminine writing is entirely independent of gender, that men can create écriture féminine, that poses French feminism's most radical challenge to gender 'essence'. Gender is treated as a style, a kind of expression, that has little to do with political activism and the daily experience of oppression. The 'feminine' then becomes not the sex of individual women but instead the symbol of otherness, alterity, the unconscious, the unspoken, the 'Imaginary' of Jacques Lacan's revision of orthodox Freudian thought. The opposition between male and female is characterised by Cixous and Kristeva as a symptom of the hierarchical and binary patriarchal thought that écriture féminine subverts. To escape these repressive binaries, one must escape the masculine metaphysics, the logic of essences, that binds the feminine to a particular biological identity. So French feminists have attacked male systems and values that support misogyny but they also have left intact the traditional canons of male literature.

This escape has been described by some critics as an escape into androgyny or bisexuality. The Imaginary – opposed to the Symbolic realm of rationality and masculine discourse – is the pre-Oedipal period before the child becomes aware of separation from its mother and consequent assimilation into the society dominated by the father. Entrance into the Symbolic Order is entry into language, society and the unconscious as well as alienation, loss and desire for a return to undifferentiated identity. The primeval realm of the Mother is, then, identified with undifferentiated sexuality (androgyny or bisexuality), limitless creativity and imagination, but it is also psychotic when viewed from the

Symbolic. The space of the Imaginary offers a refuge from oppressive patriarchy but it is a recourse to madness; the special discourse available there is 'écriture féminine'. Chodorow does not use Lacan but instead she adopts a Marxist-Freudian approach to the Oedipal experience. Chodorow argues that boys and girls experience this separation differently: boys are encouraged to seek autonomy and independence whilst girls remain in a more dependent relationship with their mothers until adulthood. Consequently, men and women approach adult relationships quite differently; the path to sexual equality which Chodorow recommends is equal parenting, where both fathers and mothers mother their children, thus avoiding the creation of overly-independent sons and overly-dependent daughters – precisely the gender stereotypes that best suit the organisation of labour in an industrial capitalist society. The separation of the sexes described by French feminism appears to Chodorow to serve conservative political and economic ends. Resistance to the feminist separation that is the conclusion of French feminism, with the écriture féminine that is its subject, has been found both in France and in the work of influential American feminists.

Among the most influential of these American feminists is Judith Butler, whose 1990 book *Gender Trouble: Feminism and the Subversion of Identity* set out an approach that has since become known as 'cultural' or 'postmodern' feminism. Butler begins by explaining the significance of the term 'trouble' in her title. For men, as the subject of desire, 'trouble' is represented by the female 'object' of desire who unexpectedly returns and answers the masculine gaze, who refuses the passive position of the feminine object and thereby 'contests the place and authority of the masculine position' (Butler, 1990, p. vii). In this situation, the dependence of male authority upon the acceptance by the female of the passive subject position (the Other) in relation to a position of male dominance exposes the lack of the very autonomy that men assume under patriarchy. Taking this relation as a starting point, Butler asks, 'What configuration of power constructs the subject and the Other, that binary relation between "men" and "women," and the internal stability of those terms?' (p. viii). That the relation is based upon the presumption of heterosexuality – a male subject desiring a female object – and that knowing this relation as an instance of heterosexuality causes us to assume that the 'beings' involved 'are' male and female prompts Butler to ask what happens when the female position is occupied by a female impersonator? This upsetting of the opposition between the natural and the artificial divorces women's 'natural' reproductive capacity from the cultural gestures that are the markers of, that carry the meanings of, gender and in this way 'implicitly suggests that gender is a kind of persistent impersonation that passes as the real' (p. viii). She goes on to observe that the performance of the female impersonator:

> destabilizes the very distinctions between the natural and the artificial, depth and surface, inner and outer through which discourse about genders almost always operates. Is drag the imitation of gender, or does it dramatize the signifying gestures through which gender itself is established? Does being female constitute a 'natural fact' or a cultural performance, or is 'naturalness' constituted through discursively constrained performative acts that produce the body through and within the categories of sex? ... What other foundational categories of identity – the binary of sex, gender, and the body – can be shown as productions that create the effect of the natural, the original, and the inevitable? (p. viii).

It is in this concept of gender identity as a cultural performance, a matrix of signifiers that enables members of a cultural group to 'read' the signs of gender and to be read as a gendered subject, that the basic principle of cultural feminism resides. Butler takes as one of her key assumptions the idea that the vocabulary of gender should be seen as a series of relational terms, having little meaning outside a network of social relationships – outside 'the gaze'. Thus, Butler suggests that feminism should refuse 'to search for the origins of gender, the inner truth of female desire, a genuine or authentic sexual identity that repression has kept from view' (p. viii). This timeless, universal, gender 'essence' shared by all women of all times and places is an illusion, and a distracting one. It distracts feminist inquiry from investigating 'the political stakes in designating as an *origin* and *cause* those identity categories that are in fact the *effects* of institutions, practices, discourses with multiple and diffuse points of origin' (Butler's emphasis, p. ix). What Butler does in this work is to investigate these institutions that define the terms of gender identity: compulsory heterosexuality, mentioned above, and phallogocentrism – that discourse of power that designates the phallus as the defining centre of all systems of value and knowledge. Thus, all that is designated masculine is highly valued both in itself and as an object of knowledge – ultimately, it is what enables knowledge by dictating the cultural terms upon which understanding takes place – and all that is designated feminine, lacking the value of the phallus, is rendered invisible, unknowable, mysterious outside the terms of masculine knowing. In three chapters dealing with the status of 'woman' as the subject of feminism Butler draws heavily upon Continental theories of deconstruction and sexual difference: the incest taboo as represented in structuralist, psychoanalytic and feminist accounts; the maternal body represented by Julia Kristeva in relation to Foucault's critique, and Monique Wittig's theory of bodily disintegration. It is this emphasis upon difference that makes cultural or postmodern feminism controversial. The postmodern challenge to the idea that there is a single and coherent feminine experience to which feminism can appeal is grounded in the perception that to seek such a unitary viewpoint is to adopt the patriarchal preference for singularity, coherence and unity. Such a viewpoint would deny the class, race, cultural and ethnic distinctions that divide women; it would also confine women to one of a range of possible gender identities or ways to be women and to experience their femininity. But too great an emphasis upon difference and diversity can shatter the grounding of feminist activism against forms of oppression that affect women as a class. Thus, the challenge is to reconcile the awareness of difference with the need for rigorous grounding of feminism in women's common experience.

Contemporary Feminism and the Post-Feminism Debate

Feminism at the present time is, then, characterised by a diversity of practice, though that very diversity makes feminism vulnerable to the conservative backlash mounted by the New Right, the anti-abortion and pro-life campaign, and the whole notion that we have entered a 'post-feminist' era, when the aims of the Women's Movement have been realised and further efforts to extend women's rights are needless. This is the subject of Susan Faludi's study, *Backlash: The Undeclared War Against American Women* (1992). Other recent critics, such as Camille Paglia in *Vamps and Tramps* (1994), take the feminist movement itself as the subject of their critique and the object of their condemnation.

Camille Paglia explains the title of *Vamps and Tramps* as evoking 'the missing sexual personae of contemporary feminism' (Paglia, 1994, p. ix). The vamp inhabits the world of the night and is excluded from and repressed by 'today's sedate middle-class professionals in their orderly, blazing-bright offices' (p. ix). Paglia continues, '[t]he prostitute, seductress, and high-glamour movie star wield women's ancient vampiric power over men' (p. ix). In order to re-vamp feminism, as Paglia claims to do, the sexual and sensual must be reintroduced. Paglia criticises the advances made by feminist campaigning for equality for taking women out of the home and placing them in the office but never disturbing the quiet bourgeois reality of their lives. The tramp, who complements the vamp is not only a sexually available woman, a whore, but also a displaced person who, in Paglia's use of the term, is displaced from the safety of the nuclear family and let loose in a kind of spiritual homelessness. The tramp is of the same spiritual kin as the hippies of the 1960s, the spiritual questers in search of meaning outside the American mainstream. By excluding vamps and tramps from its ideological constituency, Paglia asserts, contemporary feminism has overregulated sexuality, confused career advancement with true personal liberation, and put at risk fundamental civil liberties.

This issue of civil liberties and of liberty as a social and moral concept is at the heart of Paglia's criticism of contemporary feminism. Paglia chooses the term 'libertarian' to describe her particular stance on this issue. The brand of libertarianism that Paglia represents is based upon a radical individualism that denies the legitimacy of social intervention in any area of life that would constrain the right of the individual to pure self-determination. What this means is that the individual should be granted the freedom to do anything that does not restrict the freedom of any other individual to do anything they wish. To this idea, Paglia adds her own commitment to the pagan tradition in Western civilisation. She argues that the history of Western civilisation, especially in its art, represents the unconquered power of nature and the sexualised body. This pagan power has been constantly under threat from the rationalising forces of Judeo-Christianity, and civilisation represents both this conflict and the powerful residual traces of paganism. Paglia's aim is to reinstate paganism as a substantial force in contemporary culture and she does this by attacking all attempts to repress the power of nature and sexuality that are represented by the pagan. Paglia describes contemporary feminism, stereotypically, as a white middle-class movement, and identifies it with the reactionary forces of Judeo-Christianity.

This combination of libertarianism and paganism is behind Paglia's scornful rejection of the feminist denunciation of pornography, for example. In her essay on the anti-pornography writings of Catherine MacKinnon and Andrea Dworkin, Paglia claims that 'pornography must continue to play a central role in our cultural life'. She goes on,

> Pornography is a pagan arena of beauty, vitality, and brutality, of the archaic vigor of nature. It should break every rule, offend all morality. Pornography represents absolute freedom of imagination, as envisioned by the Romantic poets. In arguing that a hypothetical physical safety on the streets should take precedence over the democratic principle of free speech, MacKinnon aligns herself with the authoritarian Soviet commissars (p. 111).

So pornography represents freedom and democratic free speech while feminism is authoritarian and invasive of individual rights. Unlike the anti-pornography campaigners, such as Gloria Steinem, discussed above, Paglia does not make distinctions among different types of pornography. Steinem carefully distinguished 'erotica' which she described as characterised by mutuality and consent, from pornography which is characterised by violence and domination – precisely the kind of sexualised power relationship that feminism seeks to transform. Paglia makes no such distinction – in her account, all pornography is equal in its representation of elemental, untamed lust, 'the dark truth about nature, concealed by the artifices of civilization' (p. 110); and all pornography is equal in its symbolic status of the right of the individual to free self-expression. She does, however, concede that child pornography should be restricted, but only in that the legal sanctions against child labour should be observed and the posing for pornographic photographs and videos constitutes labour. But sketches and paintings of children engaged in pornographic acts, she approves. In the article 'On Censorship' she explains, 'Anything that can be imagined should be depicted' (p. 124).

This is also the foundation of Paglia's criticism of what she calls the 'date-rape hysteria' afflicting contemporary America. In the essay 'No Law in the Arena' she attributes blame for rape and sexual harassment to white middle-class women who send out 'mixed signals'; these are 'young women unable to foresee trouble or to survive sexual misadventure or even raunchy language without crying to authority figures for help' (p. 27). This claim is characteristic of Paglia's thought in several ways: first, there is the dismissal of 'authority figures' as irrelevant, and contempt for those who appeal to the authority of others for assistance. Second, the tendency to rely on false authority is nurtured as part of the sexual psycho-drama that is Paglia's description of the middle-class white nuclear family. Paglia holds up as superior specimens those individuals born into the urban working-class, who thereby become 'streetwise', and those born into rural farming communities because they grow up with an intensified awareness of the power of nature. These urban and rural children are better off than suburban middle-class children, according to Paglia, because they able 'to foresee trouble or to survive sexual misadventure or even raunchy language' and this ability comes from their own individual self-determination. The sovereignty of the individual, self-reliance and self-fulfilment are the linchpins of Paglia's denunciation of contemporary feminism which she represents as having transformed women into victims who refuse to take responsibility for the quality of their own lives.

More than this, feminism is denounced as a powerful reactionary force that works within the Judeo-Christian tradition to repress and destroy the pagan heritage that celebrates nature and resists the forces of civilisation. In Paglia's view, this is the true motivation of contemporary feminism and the reason why feminism has failed to achieve substantial change. By fighting nature, by contesting the power of the irrational, sexual pagan tradition, feminism has taken on too much and must, therefore, condemn itself to failure. In the conclusion to 'The Culture Wars' Paglia claims: 'Women will never know who they are until they let men be men. Let's get rid of Infirmary Feminism, with its bedlam of bellyachers, anorexics, bulimics, depressives, rape victims, and incest survivors. Feminism has become a catch-all vegetable drawer where bunches of clingy sob sisters can store their moldy neuroses' (p. 111). It is to a collection of victims that Paglia reduces second-wave American feminism. The legislative reforms sought so passionately by the National Organization of Women and other lobbying organisations are perceived by Paglia as so many dangerous restrictions upon individual liberty. Rather than appeal to such social authorities as the law, Paglia suggests women would better look to themselves for sources of strength, legitimacy and power.

This shift of emphasis away from corporate or social change towards individual responsibility is characteristic of the trend in contemporary Anglo-American society that Susan Faludi has termed 'the backlash'. In her 1992 book, *Backlash: The Undeclared War Against Women*, Faludi situates the current reactionary trend within the context of a history of anti-female activity that has followed close upon the achievement of limited rights for women. What Faludi observes is that similar strategies are used in the 1980s to frighten women out of the public arena and back into the home as were used in the latter part of the nineteenth and early twentieth centuries: warnings of a man shortage and inevitable spinsterhood for educated women; an infertility epidemic; the loss of femininity and 'career burn-out' or 'exhaustion of the feminine nervous system' among women who worked (Faludi, 1993, p. 69). Then, as now, a number of cultural myths concerning the ill-effects of equality upon the female population were propagated with the aim of discred-iting the efforts of feminist reformer movements. Faludi's introduction is sub-titled 'Blame it on Feminism' and in a series of chapters she shows how false images of unhappy liberated women have been attributed to the feminist movement. She notes that '[b]y the end of the 1980s many women had absorbed the teachings of the media and were bitterly familiar with various "statistical" developments, most notably a "man shortage"; a "devastating" plunge in economic status for women divorcing under new "no-fault" laws; an "infertility epidemic"; and a "great emotional depression" and "burn-out" attacking, respectively, single and career women' (p. 21). Faludi documents the promotion of these myths in the media, the movies, on TV, in fashion and standards of feminine beauty and the effects of these myths: on women's minds, in terms of popular psychology, on women's jobs, and on women's bodies, in terms of repro-ductive rights. At the same time, she reveals a more likely source of gender discontent. Faludi suggests that it is not women who are suffering as a consequence of the gains made by the women's movement, rather it is men who are suffering. She shows that various cultural indicators point to the incomplete success of the struggle for women's rights as the true source of feminine discontent. It is men, as a class, who resent the Women's Movement and the myths of the suffering that afflicts professional and single women serve the interests of that male resentment. Faludi suggests that the myths which comprise the cultural component of the backlash in important ways project male discontent and resentment on to women and on to the feminist movement specifically. Citing the 1988 American Male Opinion Index, Faludi observes: 'By the eighties, as the poll results made evident, men were interpreting small advances in women's rights as big, and complete, ones; they believed women had made major progress toward equality – while women believed the struggle was just beginning' (p. 81).

In Faludi's terms, the contemporary 'backlash' she describes is what others have termed 'post-feminism'. Post-feminism is a term that has been used in diverse ways to mean a whole range of things: to Faludi, post-feminism is the backlash against the gains made by the Women's Movement; others use the term to describe 'feminism without women', a brand of feminism that responds to the separatist challenge of radical feminism by attempting to assimilate men and their needs into a feminist framework. There is also the feminism espoused by Hélène Cixous which, she claims, does not belong solely to women; for still others post-feminism describes a political climate in which feminism has yet to recognise the gains that have been made and so the Women's Movement continues to campaign for women's rights but in a political vacuum. What all of these 'post-feminisms' share, however, is a common transference of responsibility to individual women and away from social, legislative, gender-based reforms. Thus, a few favoured issues keep appearing in post-feminist discussions: date-rape and sexual violence generally, sexual harassment, pornography – all the subject of Camille Paglia's post-feminist attention – recur throughout the discourse of post-feminism. One of the more controversial of these post-feminist works is Katie Roiphe's 1993 book, *The Morning After: Sex, Fear, and Feminism*. Roiphe compares the feminism experienced by her mother in the early 1960s with her own encounter with feminism as dogma, first as an undergraduate at Harvard and later as a graduate student at Princeton. What emerges from this comparison is Roiphe's view of contemporary feminism as promoting an image of woman as a passive victim of male domination – the very image that feminists of her mother's generation tried to destroy:

The image that emerges from feminist preoccupations with rape and sexual harassment is that of women as victims, offended by a professor's dirty joke, verbally pressured into sex by peers. This image of a delicate woman bears a striking resemblance to that fifties ideal my mother and the other women of her generation fought so hard to get away from. They didn't like her passivity, her wide-eyed innocence. They didn't like the fact that she was perpetually offended by sexual innuendo. They didn't like her excessive need for protection. She represented personal, social, and psychological possibilities collapsed, and they worked and marched, shouted and wrote, to make her irrelevant to their daughters (Roiphe, 1993, p. 6).

Here are repeated the same characteristics that Camille Paglia attributes to the contemporary feminist: the passivity and delicacy of the perpetual victim. The opposing qualities of agency, streetwise maturity and chutzpah are the characteristics that Paglia recommends for her liberated, self-reliant individuals of both sexes. Both Paglia and Roiphe hold up an image of the 1960s in America not as a period of radical women's activism but as an idealistic time of free love, psychedelic experience and carefree self-fulfilment. It is against this image of the 1960s that they measure the condition of women in the 1980s and 1990s. Complaining about the culture of fear and disease that is promoted by on-campus warnings about the dangers of rape and AIDS, Roiphe compares this to 'stories from older brothers, sisters, cousins, and aunts about sleeping around and not caring, and feeling free and pretending to feel free' (p. 14). Like Paglia, Roiphe casts her discussion in individualistic terms. Rather than analyse the political structures that support and legitimate a culture of feminine fear, Roiphe blames the women who expose the strategies by which that fear is created and sustained. In a series of chapters on date-rape, sexual harassment, the 'Take Back the Night' campaign, the profeminist man, and pornography Roiphe condemns the legal remedies for which women have fought as the makers of feminine victims. She reveals her sympathies when she compares Catherine MacKinnon with Camille Paglia and wonders why Paglia, 'with her dramatic views and her courageous articulation of the unpopular, is always portrayed as crazy, hysterical, while MacKinnon is not' (p. 155). Like Paglia, Roiphe revels in the unpopularity of her libertarian views. But from the perspective of Susan Faludi and others like her who perceive in the current political climate a powerful backlash against women's civil rights, the 'unpopularity' of libertarians like Paglia and Roiphe is more apparent than real. To blame the victim without asking questions about the process of victimisation and the socialisation of domination is to serve the interests of reaction and conservatism rather than the history of feminism in America.

References and Selected Further Reading

Banner, Lois W., 1974. *Women in Modern America: A Brief History*, New York: Harcourt Brace Jovanovich.

Brownmiller, Susan, 1975. *Against Our Will: Men, Women and Rape*, London: Secker & Warburg.

Buel, Joy & Richard Buel, 1984. *The Way of Duty: A Woman and her Family in Revolutionary America*, New York: W. W. Norton & Co., 1995.

Butler, Judith, 1990. *Gender Trouble: Feminism and the Subversion of Identity*, New York: Routledge.

Chafe, William Henry, 1972. *The American Woman: Her Changing Social, Economic, and Political Roles, 1920–1970*, New York: Oxford University Press.

Chodorow, Nancy, 1978. *The Reproduction of Mothering: Psychoanalysis and the Sociology of Gender*, Berkeley: University of California Press.

Cixous, Hélène & Catherine Clement, 1986. *The Newly Born Woman*, trans. Betsy Wing. Minneapolis: University of Minnesota Press.

Cott, Nancy F., 1977. *The Bonds of Womanhood: 'Woman's Sphere' in New England, 1780–1835*, New Haven: Yale University Press, 1997.

——, 1987. *The Grounding of Modern Feminism*, New Haven: Yale University Press.

Davis, Angela, 1981. *Women, Race and Class*, London: The Women's Press, 1982.

Demos, John, 1970. *A Little Commonwealth: Family Life in Plymouth Colony*, New York: Oxford University Press.

Dickenson, Donna, ed., 1994. *Margaret Fuller, Woman in the Nineteenth Century and Other Writings*, Oxford & New York: Oxford University Press.

Eagleton, Mary, ed., 1986. *Feminist Literary Theory: A Reader*, Oxford & Cambridge, MA: Blackwell, 1987.

Eisenstein, Hester, 1983. *Contemporary Feminist Thought*, Boston: G. K. Hall.

Eisenstein, Hester & Alice Jardine, eds, 1980. *The Future of Difference*, New Brunswick, NJ: Rutgers University Press, 1980.

Ellman, Mary, 1968. *Thinking About Women*, New York: Harcourt.

Evans, Sara, 1979. *Personal Politics: The Roots of Women's Liberation in the Civil Rights Movement and the New Left*, New York: Vintage.

Feder, Ellen K., Mary C. Rawlinson & Emily Zakin, eds, 1997. *Derrida and Feminism: Recasting the Question of Woman*, New York: Routledge.

Flexner, Eleanor, 1959. *Century of Struggle: The Women's Rights Movement in the United States*, rev. ed. Cambridge, MA: Belknap Press, 1975.

Firestone, Shulamith, 1970. *The Dialectic of Sex: The Case for Feminist Revolution*, London: Jonathan Cape.

Friedan, Betty, 1963. *The Feminine Mystique*, New York: Dell, 1983.

——, 1981. *The Second Stage*. Cambridge, MA: Harvard University Press, 1998.

——, 1985. *It Changed My Life: Writings on the Women's Movement*, Cambridge, MA: Harvard University Press, 1998.

Fuller, Margaret, 1845. *Woman in the Nineteenth Century*, ed. Donna Dickenson, Oxford & New York: Oxford University Press, 1994.

Gatlin, Rochelle, 1987. *American Women Since 1945*, Jackson: University Press of Mississippi.

Gilman, Charlotte Perkins, 1898. *Women and Economics: A Study of the Economic Relations Between Men and Women as a*

Factor in Social Evolution, Mineola, NY: Dover Publications, 1998.

Greene, Gayle & Coppelia Kahn, eds, 1993. *Changing Subjects: The Making of Feminist Literary Criticism*, New York & London: Routledge.

Griffin, Susan, 1978. *Woman and Nature: The Roaring Inside Her*, London: The Women's Press, 1984.

——, 1981. *Pornography and Silence: Culture's Revenge Against Women*, London: The Women's Press.

Guerin, Wilfred, Earle Labor, Lee Morgan, Jeanne C. Reesman & John R. Willingham, eds, 1992. *A Handbook of Critical Approaches to Literature*, 3rd ed, New York & Oxford: Oxford University Press.

Hartmann, Susan M., 1983. *The Home Front and Beyond: American Women in the 1940s*, Boston: G. K. Hall.

Hartsock, Nancy, 1983. *Money, Sex and Power*, London: Longman.

hooks, bell, 1981. *Ain't I a Woman: Black Women and Feminism*, Boston: South End Press.

——, 1984. *Feminist Theory: From Margin to Center*, Boston: South End Press.

Hull, Gloria T., Patricia B. Scott & Barbara Smith, eds, 1982. *All the Women are White, All the Blacks are Men, But Some of us are Brave: Black Women's Studies*, New York: The Feminist Press.

Humm, Maggie, ed., 1992. *Feminisms: A Reader*, London & New York: Harvester Wheatsheaf.

Irigaray, Luce, 1985. *Speculum of the Other Woman*, trans. Gillian C. Gill. Ithaca, NY: Cornell University Press.

Jaggar, Alison, 1983. *Feminist Politics and Human Nature*, Totowa, NJ: Rowman & Allanheld.

Jefferson, Ann & David Robey, eds, 1982. *Modern Literary Theory: A Comparative Introduction*, 2nd ed. London: B. T. Batsford Ltd., 1986.

Karlsen, Carol, 1989. *The Devil in the Shape of a Woman: Witchcraft in Colonial New England*, New York: Vintage.

Kerber, Linda K., 1980. *Women of the Republic: Intellect and Ideology in Revolutionary America*, Chapel Hill: University of North Carolina Press.

Kristeva, Julia, 1980. *Desire in Language: A Semiotic Approach to Literature and Art*, ed. Leon S. Roudiez, trans. Alice Jardine. New York: Columbia University Press.

——, 1986. *The Kristeva Reader*, ed. Toril Moi, Oxford: Blackwell.

Langley, Winston E. & Vivian C. Fox, eds, 1994. *Women's Rights in the United States: A Documentary History*, New York: Greenwood Publishing Group.

Leitch, Vincent B., 1989. *American Literary Criticism from the 30s to the 80s*, New York: Columbia University Press.

MacKinnon, Catherine, 1989. *Toward a Feminist Theory of the State*, Harvard, MA: Harvard University Press.

Marks, Elaine & Isabelle de Courtivron, eds, 1981. *The New French Feminisms: An Anthology*, London & New York: Harvester Wheatsheaf.

Millett, Kate, 1971. *Sexual Politics*, London: Abacus.

Moi, Toril, 1985. *Sexual / Textual Politics: Feminist Literary Theory*, London: Routledge.

Morgan, Robin, ed., 1970. *Sisterhood is Powerful: An Anthology of Writings from the Women's Liberation Movement*, New York: Vintage.

Newton, K.M., 1988. *Twentieth-Century Literary Theory: A Reader*, London: Macmillan.

Norton, Mary Beth, 1980. *Liberty's Daughters: The Revolutionary Experience of American Women, 1750–1800*, Ithaca, NY: Cornell University Press.

——, 1996. *Founding Mothers and Fathers: Gendered Power and the Forming of American Society*, New York: A. A. Knopf.

Paglia, Camille, 1994. *Vamps and Tramps: New Essays*, London: Viking, 1995.

Rich, Adrienne, 1976. *Of Woman Born: Motherhood as Experience and Institution*, London: Virago, 1979.

Roiphe, Katie, 1993. *The Morning After: Sex, Fear, and Feminism*, London: Hamish Hamilton.

Rylance, Rick, ed., 1987. *Debating Texts: A Reader in Twentieth Century Literary Theory and Method*, Milton Keynes: Open University Press.

Ruthven, K.K., 1984. *Feminist Literary Studies: An Introduction*, Cambridge: Cambridge University Press.

Scharf, Lois. 1980. *To Work and to Wed: Female Employment, Feminism, and the Great Depression*, New York: Greenwood Publishing Group.

Scharf, Lois & J. M. Jensen, eds, 1983. *Decades of Discontent: The Women's Movement, 1920–1940*, New York: Greenwood Publishing Group.

Showalter, Elaine, ed., 1985. *The New Feminist Criticism: Essays on Women, Literature and Theory*, London: Virago.

——, 1994. *Sister's Choice: Tradition and Change in American Women's Writing*, Oxford & New York: Oxford University Press.

Steinem, Gloria, 1983. *Outrageous Acts and Everyday Rebellions*, London: Jonathan Cape, 1984.

Tallack, Douglas, 1991. *Twentieth-Century America: The Intellectual and Cultural Context*, London: Longman.

Tindall, George B., & David E. Shi, 1989. *America: A Narrative History*, 2nd ed. New York & London: W. W. Norton & Co.

Tuana, Nancy & Rosemarie Tong, eds, 1995. *Feminism and Philosophy: Essential Readings in Theory, Reinterpretation and Application*, Boulder, CO: Westview Press.

Ulrich, Laurel, 1982. *Good Wives: Image and Reality in the Lives of Women in Northern New England, 1650–1750*, New York: Vintage, 1991.

Walby, Sylvia, 1990. *Theorizing Patriarchy*, Cambridge: Polity.

Ware, Susan, 1981. *Beyond Suffrage: Women in the New Deal*, Cambridge, MA: Harvard University Press.

Warhol, Robyn R. & Diane Price Herndl, eds, 1997. *Feminisms: An Anthology of Literary Theory and Criticism*, New Brunswick, NJ: Rutgers University Press.

1
Gender and Rhetoric: Liberal Feminism and Mary Rowlandson

This chapter begins with a survey of liberal feminist theorists, focusing upon the work of Elizabeth Cady Stanton, Charlotte Perkins Gilman's *Women and Economics* (1898) and Betty Friedan's *The Feminine Mystique* (1963). The primary theoretical concepts explored here include: the origins of liberalism; the limits of liberal theory, particularly in terms of the liberal desire to reform patriarchy rather than to achieve structural social change; the relevance of liberal theory, in terms of liberalism's focus upon (gendered) exclusions from power and economic rights, liberalism's critique of strategies of disempowerment, and liberalism's structural contrast between the individual and socio-economic classes. In the section that follows this theoretical survey, I turn to the liberal feminist analysis of Mary Rowlandson's captivity narrative, *The Sovereignty and Goodness of God* (1682).

Survey of Liberal Feminist Theory

Summary of Liberal Feminist Principles

The liberal emphasis on the individual (in contrast with movements such as Marxist feminism that emphasise collectivity) stresses the importance of the individual and individual autonomy which are protected by guaranteed rights, economic justice and equality of opportunity. Liberalism arose in the seventeenth century with the call for reform of oppressive socio-economic practices and structures; such as the feudal privileging of nobles over peasants and the system of absolute monarchy. Liberalism motivated the American Revolution and shaped the key documents of the new Republic – the Bill of Rights and the Constitution – both of which assumed that the American citizen was a rational self-determining individual who was to be served by the social, economic and political institutions described by these documents. Liberal individualism and the primacy of personal freedom only applied to men, and white men specifically, at that time.

Liberal feminist theory is limited in various ways and has been extensively critiqued by feminist scholars. First, the concept of domestic tyranny is kept separate from liberal theorising about public, political tyranny. One might ask, is this separation of the private and the public a necessary part of liberalism? The liberal emphasis upon nature, natural rights and self-evident truths, suggests a biological essentialism that leads inevitably to a basic distinction between the sexes which is founded in a distinction between the public masculine world and the private feminine world. Second, an unwillingness to direct efforts towards transforming the capitalist basis of Western society means an unwillingness to confront the patriarchal bias of capitalism itself, where structural inequities and a pool of available labour are integral parts of the economy. Together, this toleration of the capitalist economic structure of patriarchy and the separation of the domestic from the public has drawn criticism from feminists, who identify deep structural causes of women's oppression: causes that are not addressed by liberal feminist theory. When combined with the liberal commitment to freedom of speech as a basic individual right, this has led liberal feminists into conflict with socialist feminists and others over the issue of pornography and censorship – liberal feminists argue in favour of complete freedom of expression and such strategies as women-centred pornography to overcome the demeaning effects of pornographic images of women, rather than legislation to ban or restrict pornography.

The efforts of liberal feminism are directed towards the reform of patriarchy rather than the structural change of a male-dominated society. Liberal feminists support the Equal Rights Amendment and other legislative acts to abolish sexual discrimination and to erode oppressive gender roles.

But beyond legal and educational barriers to equality there do exist these deeper structural obstacles to gender equality: obstacles such as the lack of adequate child care provision, woman's 'double day', the lack of comparability between the sexes within the economy (exemplified by the concept of 'women's work'). The deeper separation between male and female economies is not accounted for in liberal assumptions about the single economy. Reform, generally, benefits only middle-class women who have the money to circumvent some of these obstacles (by the use of paid domestic help, for example). Critics like Seyla Benhabib have addressed the difference between the category of 'woman' postulated by liberal feminist theory and the reality of women's experiences. What Benhabib calls the 'generalized other' in her critique is equated with some theoretical middle-class white woman (a rational being with predictable rights and duties), but she is prioritised in liberal feminist thinking at the expense of what Benhabib calls the 'concrete other': individual women with specific histories, identities, affective-emotional constitutions and desires, needs and motivations that must be understood rather than assumed (see Benhabib, 1987). The basic issue revolves around the fact that equality or 'equal with' has, in the past, meant implicitly that women should be equal with white men, or that women should have the opportunity to live as men do; but do all women (and men) want to become white, middle-class men in order to benefit from equal rights? This kind of 'equality' carries with it racial and class prejudices that are inimical to the egalitarian commitment of feminism.

Liberal feminist perspectives focus upon how women's writing attempts to create a feminist consciousness of the oppression and injustice suffered by women. A liberal feminist approach to critical interpretation allows us to see how women writers seek to make us recognise women's exclusion from economic rights because of their membership of a sexual class. The liberal feminist interpretation of texts promotes a respect for rights – of all individuals, regardless of class – and arouses condemnation of the practices and social structures that deny those rights. Three prominent liberal feminist thinkers are Elizabeth Cady Stanton, Charlotte

Perkins Gilman and Betty Friedan; in what follows I look more closely at their work.

Elizabeth Cady Stanton

The work of Elizabeth Cady Stanton is in important respects inseparable from that of Susan B. Anthony, Stanton's friend and collaborator. They wrote together, travelled together, Anthony even lived periodically in the Stanton household to help with housework and the raising of the seven Stanton children, and so release time for her friend to write and to continue the cause. Stanton once wrote: 'In thought and sympathy we were one, and in the division of labor we exactly complemented each other. I am the better writer, she the better critic. She supplied the facts and statistics, I the philosophy and rhetoric, and, together, we have made arguments that no one has answered. Our speeches may be considered the united product of our two brains' (quoted in Gilbert & Gubar, 1996, p. 465). Stanton's feminism, and Anthony's as well, arose initially from her commitment to the abolitionist movement. At the World Anti-Slavery Convention in London in 1840 she objected to the exclusion of the women delegates and from that experience determined to organise the women's rights meeting which became the 1848 Seneca Falls Convention. The liberal idea of emancipation informs both Stanton's feminism and her abolitionism; in both cases (slavery and women's oppression) the state has withheld fundamental rights held by the individual. The basic liberal tenets of individual freedom and social equality were denied by the denial of citizenship to women and slaves; these then are the principles Stanton demands in her call for women's suffrage and the enfranchisement of slaves. On the basis of race and gender, these classes of people were denied the equality of opportunity that is enshrined in the founding documents of the Republic. However, the sexism of the abolitionist movement, with which Stanton was confronted in London, gave rise to a critical distancing between feminism and abolitionism in Stanton's thought.

This was exacerbated by Stanton's growing suspicion that black men would be enfranchised before women, to the detriment of the women's movement, and that the position of black women would not be improved at all. She wrote to the prominent abolitionist Wendell Phillipps in 1865 to point out that 'if the two millions of Southern black women are not to be secured in their rights of person, property, wages, and children, then their emancipation is but another form of slavery' (Stanton & Blatch, 1969, vol. 2, p. 110). Enfranchised black men would join with their white brothers to continue the patriarchal oppression of women, Stanton suspected; the enfranchisement of black men alone would not ensure the equality of opportunity that Stanton wanted for all – men and women, black and white, as sovereign and independent individuals.

Her writings on marriage, maternity and divorce recognise the oppressed status of women as belonging to a subordinate sexual class. The separation of women as a class into a female sphere of experience which is identified with the private and the domestic, while the public sphere is reserved exclusively for the sexual class of men, informs Stanton's writings on family and marriage and motivates her commitment to individualism and women's independence from men. The rights of the individual are natural rights which the individual brings into the world at birth; these rights cannot be taken away because they are constitutive of the individual. Stanton and her collaborators open the 'Declaration of Sentiments and Resolutions', drawn up at the Seneca Falls Convention, with a deliberate echo of the Declaration of Independence: 'We hold these truths to be self-evident: that all men *and women* are created equal ...' (my emphasis; Schneir, 1972, p. 77). Stanton's political struggle was directed towards realising the promises made in documents like the Constitution and the Declaration of Independence; she demanded citizenship rights for all citizens of the Republic and the reform of laws that denied women their full human rights. And it was the oppressive legal machinery of the state that she held responsible for women's subordination: 'It has taken the whole power of the civil and canon law to hold woman in the subordinate position which it is said she willingly accepts' (Anthony & Harper, 1970, vol. 4, p. 41).

This legal or state oppression is mirrored in private relations within marriage which Stanton represents as relations of power, of domination and control. In marriage, husband and wife become legally a single defined unit, which is male; women surrender themselves entirely in the marriage relation. In her 1860 address to the New York State Legislature, Stanton makes precisely this point: 'Blackstone declares that the husband and wife are one, and learned commentators have decided that that one is the husband. In all civil codes, you will find them classified as one' (Gilbert & Gubar, 1996, p. 467).

The unwillingness of men to share an equal partnership with their wives is Stanton's primary explanation for the unwillingness of men to grant political equality to women. Yet marriage is only one of a range of choices men may make about how to live their lives; and although Stanton counsels against marriage, an institution within which women have no individual sovereignty, she recognises that women are educated and socialised to expect only marriage as the structuring principle of their lives. 'Personal freedom is the first right to be proclaimed, and that does not and cannot now belong to the relation of wife, to the mistress of the isolated home, to the financial dependent' (Stanton & Blatch, 1969, vol. 2, p. 70). The married woman surrenders all her rights, including the right to control her own body, though her husband gives up nothing; she becomes an unpaid domestic drudge, robbed of her labour; and when women are paid to work outside the home they are paid not according to the value of their labour but according to the value of their gender. The lack of legal status as a citizen is identified by Stanton as the root cause of women's dependence within marriage; and reform of the laws governing the rights of married women and access to divorce is, in large part, the remedy. By changing the laws that regulate social relations, transformation of those relations – economic and sexual – that oppress women, can follow.

Charlotte Perkins Gilman, Women and Economics *(1898)*

Gilman preferred to call herself a 'sociologist' rather than a feminist. Gilman's achievement is distinct from that of many of her female contemporaries in that she was not exclusively concerned with the vote but considered suffrage important only as part of an entire revolution in gender relations. The very public struggle for women's suffrage marginalised her work and this was the case even more after the vote was won in America in 1920, when the issue of women's rights was reduced to insignificance in the popular mind. Only when the full equality of women in industrial society was seen once more as an urgent social issue was interest in Gilman's work revived. Gilman focused her writing upon the demonstration that men and women share a common humanity; the notion that women actually want to be dependent on men, that their ambitions and aspirations are less than men's, that women do not want education or professional attainment or a life outside the home. These fallacies are exposed as the products of social conditions that work to transform individual people into sexual stereotypes. Female economic and psychological dependence is revealed as a cultural or ideological construction in Gilman's writing – both her fiction and her prose.

In Gilman's view, capitalism and patriarchy work together in the economic and sexual exploitation of women. What Gilman called the 'sexuo-economic relation' is extensively analysed in *Women and Economics* (1898). Under capitalist patriarchy, 'the economic relation is combined with the sex-relation' (Gilman, 1898, p. 3) and the consequence is women's dependence and subordination. Gilman uses the concept of evolution to point out that under these conditions a particular type of woman is bred – men choose women for marriage and reproduction who suit the prevailing patriarchal view of femininity. 'We have trained and bred one kind of qualities into one-half the species, and another kind into the other half. … For instance, we have done all we could, in addition to natural forces, to make men brave. We have done all we could, in addition to natural forces, to make women cowards' (p. 163). In marriage, a man becomes the woman's 'food supply' (p.11); Gilman comments, that '[w]e are the only animal species in which the female depends upon the male for food, the only animal species in which the sex-relation is also the economic relation' (p. 3). Because of this close relationship between marriage and economic survival, the 'marriage market' becomes a woman's whole world and not just one aspect of the social environment. The economy is perverted away from important priorities by woman's insatiable demand for domestic consumption; that is, her role as 'the limitless demander of things to use up'. Gilman continues, 'To consume food, to consume clothes, to consume houses and furniture and decorations and ornaments and amusements, to take and take and take forever, – from one man if they are virtuous, from many if they are vicious, but always to take and never to think of giving anything in return except their womanhood, – this is the enforced condition of the mothers of the race' (p.59). It is to this role of consumer rather than creative producer of economic wealth that women are confined. Gilman exposes the economic basis of women's oppression by bringing the language of economics to bear upon the description of private experience.

> Our general notion is that we have lifted and ennobled our eating and drinking by combining them with love. On the contrary, we have lowered and degraded our love by combining it with eating and drinking; and, what is more, we have lowered these habits also. ... She must consider what he likes, not only because she loves to please him or because she profits by pleasing him, but because he pays for the dinner, and she is a private servant (pp. 116–117).

Gilman is quite brutal in pointing to the fundamental condition of women under capitalist patriarchy: because men control the economic structure of life, women must please men in order to survive. There is no realistic alternative for them, save madness and death.

But Gilman proposes an alternative which is grounded in women's economic independence. Only when women have achieved autonomy in the economic sphere will it become

economic independent

possible to break down the sexual division of labour (p. 111).
Thus, Gilman's feminist efforts are directed toward reforming
the barriers that limit women's access to economic opportunities. The liberal emphasis of Gilman's thought becomes
apparent in this connection; she is not concerned with the
revolutionary overthrow of the capitalist economy nor does
she address the sexual basis of patriarchal oppression.
Gilman proposes that marriage and 'the family' should be
seen as separate institutions, one based upon a sexual
relation and the other based upon social and economic
relations. Rather, she suggests that the domestic labour in
which women engage for little or no pay should be fully professionalised and transferred from the family context to a
business situation. Cleaning, shopping, housekeeping and
cooking, childcare – all these should be seen as specialised
activities requiring the paid services of trained professionals.
Gilman does not challenge the primacy of women in the
sphere of reproduction and motherhood; in her descriptions
she does not show men engaged in domestic 'women's work'
though she does point out the obstacles that prevent women
from doing 'men's work'. Gilman's emphasis is upon reform
of the existing economic structure to open up equal opportunities for women by freeing them from restrictive inherited
gender roles.

Betty Friedan, The Feminine Mystique *(1963)*

Gilman's warnings about the consequences for women's full
liberation through the reform of oppressive patriarchal social
structures are realised in Betty Friedan's description of
American women's lives in the post-war years. Gilman had
expressed her apprehension that a single focus upon the issue
of women's suffrage would divert attention away from the
many ways in which women suffered from discriminatory
legal and economic practices. Friedan comments, 'It is a
cliché of our own time that women spent half a century
fighting for "rights" and the next half wondering whether
they wanted them after all' (Friedan, 1963, p. 83). Gilman
was afraid that the granting of the vote would be seen as the

'solution' to the 'woman problem'. The situation that Friedan describes is where the 'woman problem' has not been solved, has not gone away, but what has disappeared is a language or vocabulary capable of representing women's experience of oppression. This lack is what Friedan termed 'the feminine mystique' or, in her opening chapter, 'the problem that has no name'.

> The problem laid buried, unspoken, for many years in the minds of American women. It was a strange stirring, a sense of dissatisfaction, a yearning that women suffered in the middle of the twentieth century in the United States. Each suburban wife struggled with it alone. As she made the beds, shopped for groceries, matched slipcover material, ate peanut butter sandwiches with her children, chauffeured Cub Scouts and Brownies, lay beside her husband at night – she was afraid to ask even of herself the silent question – 'Is this all?' (p. 15).

The entrapment within the private sphere that Friedan describes here is matched by a powerful exclusion of women from the public world and, importantly, a crippling sense of guilt among women who feel ungrateful and selfish for wanting more. The source of this guilt is what Friedan reveals as the feminine mystique. She documents the pressure upon women to leave school or college early, to marry young, to produce families of five or six children, to nurture and to satisfy the every need of their husband and children, to conform to an image of sexual attractiveness promoted throughout the American media; in short, women were under pressure to believe that 'they could desire no greater destiny than to glory in their own femininity'(p. 15). In the late 1950s, Friedan notes, the only women who engaged in paid work outside the home were young women in part-time jobs who were assisting the family finances (to pay college fees or mortgages) or widows supporting families. The shortage of staff in the traditionally female-dominated professions such as nursing and teaching was critical, while women pursued the ideal image of the American suburban housewife: 'freed by science and labor-saving appliances from the drudgery, the dangers of childbirth and the illnesses of her grandmother. She was healthy, beautiful, educated, concerned only about her husband, her children, her home. She had found true feminine fulfillment' (p. 18).

Friedan documents the manifold ways in which this image of feminine fulfilment pervaded American culture and worked to keep women isolated both from their own feelings of dissatisfaction and frustration, and also from sharing their common awareness that something was deeply wrong with their lives. She describes her own discovery of a shared set of problems experienced by women widely separated by geography, age, social and economic background: 'in college dormitories and semi-private maternity wards, at PTA meetings and luncheons of the League of Women Voters, at suburban cocktail parties, in station wagons waiting for trains, and in snatches of conversation overheard at Schrafft's' (p. 20). Underlying the apparent problems with marriages, children, houses, communities, Friedan identified the real problem of feminine entrapment, the desire for something more than the domestic ideal that was identified with 'true' femininity. Friedan takes the example of an early 1960s issue of the women's magazine, *McCalls*, to exemplify both the feminine mystique and its exclusions. After detailing the contents of this magazine she comments,

> The image of woman that emerges from this big, pretty magazine is young and frivolous, almost childlike; fluffy and feminine; passive; gaily content in a world of bedroom and kitchen, sex, babies, and home. The magazine surely does not leave out sex; the only passion, the only pursuit, the only goal a woman is permitted is the pursuit of a man. It is crammed full of food, clothing, cosmetics, furniture, and the physical bodies of young women, but where is the world of thought and ideas, the life of the mind and spirit? (p. 36).

It is the silent, unspeakable, desire for these exclusions that afflict those women who most desperately try to conform to the demands of the feminine mystique; as Friedan points out, ironically, the 'career women' who resist the mythology of

American femininity are not afflicted by this 'problem that has no name'.

The women's magazines and the fictional stories, as well as the features, that they offered to women were one powerful representation of the feminine mystique. Friedan shows how the character of the fictional heroine of these magazine stories shifted during the post-war years from strong, capable career-oriented woman to idealised housewife, committed to home, husband and family. These stories and the magazines that published them form one aspect of the powerful public image of femininity. Television and advertising also present American women with influential external images of what women should be. When the question then arises, why so many women should accept and conform to the feminine mystique, Friedan's answer is bound to the mystique itself: the 'feminine mystique permits, even encourages, women to ignore the question of their identity. The mystique says they can answer the question "Who am I?" by saying "Tom's wife ... Mary's mother" (p. 71). It is not only the media, however, that Friedan identifies as the source of images of femininity. More influential in terms of social and cultural attitudes and practices is the psychoanalysis of Sigmund Freud, the anthropology of Margaret Mead, the gender-orientation of the educational system, all mutually-reinforcing systems that prescribe woman's biology as her destiny and dictate that a woman's life and identity are fated to be confined by her reproductive capacity.

Friedan's answer to the dilemma posed by the feminine mystique is couched in the individualistic terms of liberal discourse: 'To face the problem is not to solve it. But once a woman faces it, ... she begins to find her own answers' (p. 338). Rejecting the biological determinism she finds in the feminine mystique and the various cultural practices and belief systems that support it, she believes that self-help, though on a massive scale, is the answer that recommends itself most strongly for the women who are excluded from American public life, and from whom opportunities for self-determination and self-realisation are withheld. Access to education, and specifically higher education, equal rights in family and in law: the denial of these civil liberties are the obstacles that continue to trap women in the feminine mystique. But the impulse for freedom must come from each individual woman who must find her own answers and her own strategies for liberation.

Liberal Feminism in Praxis

In the following section, Mary Rowlandson's *The Sovereignty and Goodness of God* is analysed in liberal feminist terms. The discussion of this text focuses first upon patriarchal attitudes towards women in the period before the Enlightenment, especially the emerging conflict between patriarchal and liberal social theories. I then turn to issues of literary style and rhetoric: Puritan women at this time were forbidden to participate in public oratory; therefore we see the development of a peculiarly female 'voice' or style of rhetorical expression emerge out of the dominant masculine and patriarchal form of discourse, which in colonial New England was Puritan typology. This context is then used to highlight such themes as: individual versus class identity, or woman as individual versus 'woman' as a sexual class; personal versus public elements or the opportunities for psychological, as opposed to spiritual, expression within the constraints imposed by typological rhetoric; and the economic subtext or the financial dependence of women on men.

My primary context for discussing Rowlandson's work, then, is the position of American colonial women under Puritan patriarchy. In patriarchal theory, women's inferior position in family, state and society is sanctioned by divine decree: the Bible (Genesis 1:28) was interpreted to mean that God had placed in Adam's power all of creation, including women and children. As God's agent, man as a sexual class has absolute power; this is traditionally exercised through the absolute monarch who has power over all his subjects; in turn, husbands have complete power over their wives, as do fathers over their children and masters over their servants. As the agents of God's will, only men had property rights and only the propertied class could vote. Thus, according to patriarchal theory, those who were best able to rule legislated on behalf of the entire community. In Puritan thought, each class had certain responsibilities, obligations and duties, the fulfilment of which resulted in a harmonious and godly society. To shirk one's responsibilities or to fail in one's duties was to risk God's displeasure, which would bring suffering to the whole community. This dire penalty (famine, pestilence, Indian attack, etc.) was the consequence of betraying the 'federal covenant', or community agreement with God, into which New England Puritans had entered. The federal covenant was an agreement between God and the Massachusetts Bay settlers that, as reward for the establishment of a perfect godly society and perfectly reformed church, all members of the community would be saved. Thus, Puritans referred to themselves as a community of 'visible saints'; that is, individuals who would collectively find salvation after death. But this agreement depended crucially upon every member of the community maintaining a high standard of conduct.

Mary Rowlandson, The Sovereignty and Goodness of God

Mary Rowlandson was emphatically *not* a feminist; in the colonial society in which she lived notions of democracy, equality and women's rights were anathema. However, her narrative does express the situation of women in colonial Puritan society and the systematic exclusion of even privileged women from the public sphere. Rowlandson unintentionally shows us how women were excluded from participation in colonial politics (even while they were vulnerable as pawns in colonial politics, as was Rowlandson herself) and she offers us a basis for criticising the strategies whereby women are disempowered in traditional patriarchal society. In her narrative, Mary Rowlandson describes her captivity as punishment for her failings as a Puritan, a woman, a wife and a mother. She has failed because she has lost her sense of identification with a sexual class (Puritan women) in favour of her own individualism. The narrative describes her gradual understanding of the 'true' nature of her dilemma and her struggle to regain that sense of herself as a member of a distinct sexual class which will enable her to rejoin her community. We begin then with the interlocking themes of individual versus family versus society, and Rowlandson's treatment of the conflict between her perceptions of 'woman as an individual' and of 'woman as a sexual class'.

Mary Rowlandson was taken captive by the Narrangansett Indians, who attacked her frontier town of Lancaster, Massachusetts, in February 1676. In her narrative she is brought to the gradual awareness of her special destiny as a Puritan woman while, through the sufferings and pain and deprivation of Indian captivity, she renounces her earlier selfish and complacent ways and surrenders herself to the knowledge of God's absolute power and sovereignty. Her physical redemption thus comes to mirror her spiritual redemption, and her eventual restoration to the community of visible saints in Boston prefigures, in her representation, the future destiny of her soul among the saints of heaven. Further, Rowlandson claims for her experience an exemplary significance as an indication of the special destiny reserved for God's chosen people of New England. Mary Rowlandson's liberation from suffering, her rescue from the moral and geographical wilderness prefigures, in her account, the future liberation of the community of saints from the bondage of worldly sin into the freedom of heavenly bliss.

Mary Rowlandson and other Puritan women like her – Hannah Swarton and Hannah Dustan, for instance – who otherwise could not speak publicly found a voice in the typological rhetoric of the captivity narrative. Granted, this was a deeply compromised voice: Rowlandson's narrative was bound together with her husband's last sermon, entitled 'The Possibility of God's Forsaking a People that have been Visibly Near and Dear to him, together with the Misery of a People thus Forsaken', in the first edition. Other returned captives, such as Hannah Swarton, had their stories appropriated by Cotton Mather: a prime representative of the Massachusetts elite. Neal Salisbury, commenting on the preface to Rowlandson's narrative, which was presumably written by Increase Mather, observes that 'when Mary finally does become the center of discussion, the preface never directly names her but refers to her sometimes as Joseph's "precious yokefellow" and "dear consort," but mostly as "Gentlewoman." The author, whether Mather or another, seems to have hoped that an emphasis upon Rowlandson's marital status and social rank and an avoidance of her individuality would in some measure obviate the fact of her gender' (Salisbury, 1997, p. 45). Puritan women were in an anomalous position: as Puritans they were members of an elite but as women they were members of a powerless class. The dependence of such women upon the male theocracy thus provided an image of man's spiritual dependence upon God. The intrinsic worthlessness of women (made plain by the ransom demanded for the return of female captives) outside the boundaries of Puritan culture also mirrored the worthlessness of men apart from the value bestowed upon them by God. The experience of women therefore highlighted the importance of perceiving oneself in terms of a class and dramatised the dangers of individualism. Individuals are worthless, in patriarchal terms; only as a member of a class can an individual enjoy the comforts and benefits patriarchal society is willing to offer its members. So the captivity experiences of women, who have gone beyond the bounds of Puritan society but have been brought back, are expressed in highly conventional terms so that they express the ideology of patriarchy even as they warn of the dangers of dissent. 'Typology' is the name given to this style of expression and whilst typology allowed Puritan women a public voice which they were otherwise denied, the pronounced patriarchal bias of typology severely limited what these women could express.

The experience of captivity is thus interpreted in terms of a complex typological significance. Under the influence of typology, Rowlandson's suffering in the wilderness becomes the 'type' of personal uncertainty regarding the ultimate destiny of the soul. Her eventual redemption, through the efforts of the magistrates in Boston and the will of God, signifies the final redemption of the always-already redeemed soul of the visible saint. More than this, however, Rowlandson's experience assumes a communal significance as a typological repetition of the Babylonian captivity and

her eventual release signifies the glorious future destiny of God's newly chosen people in the New World. Like Mary Rowlandson, if the community of visible saints can keep to their faith despite the vicissitudes of temporal history then, like the redeemed captive, they too will be released from bondage to the physical into the freedom of salvation. As Annette Kolodny has noted, Rowlandson is not unaware of the communal interpretation invited by her ordeal and this typological significance motivates her use of the Judea capta motif. It is during the journey to King Philip's encampment that Rowlandson describes how she surrenders her inability to weep before her captives and there by the side of the river she gives herself over to weeping. She creates then a parallel between her experience and the captivity of Israel in Babylon: 'now I may say [she writes] as Psal. 137:1, "By the rivers of Babylon there we sat down; yea, we wept when we remembered Zion" ' (Rowlandson, pp. 46–47). The victory of the heathen over the settlers of New England appears to her as a typological repetition of the sufferings of God's chosen people. Through this typological logic, the narrative offers its contemporary readers the opportunity to experience, as Kolodny phrases it, 'their community's spiritual vulnerability through the biblical type, and then, more dramatically, their own individual vulnerability through identification with an actual captive woman who exemplifies the type' (Kolodny, p. 21).

Mary Rowlandson develops the typological parallel between her destiny and that of the Puritan community by creating a pattern of biblical reference which serves to generalise the significance of her experiences. When she first catches sight of the Indian town of Wenimesset and sees the large number of Indians gathered there she likens her feelings of dismay to the experience of David: 'I had fainted, unless I had believed' (Psalms 27:13). She finds some comfort in the biblical parallel between the taking of her own children by Indians and Jacob's loss of his sons (Genesis 42:36). When she is forbidden to see her daughter in a nearby Indian village, Rowlandson prays that God will show her some sign of His goodwill and will give her reason to hope that her trials will end; shortly after this her son Joseph (whose

whereabouts had been unknown to her) unexpectedly appears. She exclaims that 'indeed quickly the Lord answered in some measure my poor prayers' (p. 40). The very next day Rowlandson acquires a Bible, taken by an Indian in the raid on Medfield, and there she finds a scriptural passage which describes both her experience of despair and the hope of ultimate redemption:

> in that melancholy time [she tells us,] it came into my head to read first the 28 chapter of Deut., which I did, and when I had read it, my dark heart wrought on this manner, that there was no mercy for me, that the blessings were gone and the curses come in their room, and that I had lost my opportunity. But the Lord helped me still to go on reading till I came to chapter 30, the seven first verses, where I found there was mercy promised again if we would return to him by repentance, and, though we were scattered from one end of the earth to the other, yet the Lord would gather us together and turn all those curses upon our enemies (p. 41).

Rowlandson concludes, 'I do not desire to live to forget this scripture and what comfort it was to me' (p. 41). This passage encapsulates the orthodox interpretation of Puritan experience: that in return for genuine repentance and a faithful heart, God will show mercy to his people and redemption will finally be theirs. This dispensation applies equally to individuals and to the community of saints. Despite any backsliding that may have occurred among the visible saints of New England, God remains willing to keep to the terms of the federal covenant. He will show mercy where there is true repentance but where there is none His power will be manifest instead through His wrath.

Gradually, she realises that what she is witnessing is a battle for the bodies and souls of the captives, including her own. God preserves them through the temptations of loss of faith and despair even as He causes them to be tested for the good of their souls. The Indians, as the agents of Satan, struggle with the chosen people of God and try to lead them away from the path of redemption. But the Indians in

Rowlandson's account are primarily controlled by God as agents within His typological history. The typological signif- icance of the heathen, as she calls them, becomes clear to Rowlandson during their fifth remove. There, she describes how the Indians threaten her with physical violence ('they answered me they would break my face' (p. 44)) when she refuses to work on the Sabbath. She has learned the error of her earlier ways when she did not observe the Sabbath and now that she realises what is at risk in incurring God's displeasure she will not be intimidated by physical threats. She remarks upon 'the strange providence of God in preserving the heathen'; despite the difficulties of travelling with the very young and very old and particularly when carrying all their belongings with them, still the Indians are able to elude the pursuit of the English army. The Indians are able to cross the Bacquag (now Miller's) River by building rafts from material they find by the river bank. The English army, however, is unable to find a way to cross the river and, despite the sight of smoke from the Indian encampment, the army turns back. Rowlandson accounts for this as an instance of God's preservation of the Indians so they can continue to test the faith and spiritual resolve of the captives who 'were not ready for so great a mercy as victory and deliverance' (p. 44). Many Indians contribute food or the warmth of their fire and in this way preserve her through the ordeal until her final redemption.

Any sense of spiritual comfort is, however, punctuated with episodes when she feels keenly the possibility that she might lose the favour so recently gained. So when she is threatened with blindness after a squaw throws hot ashes into her face, Mary is reduced again to a state of uncertainty concerning her spiritual welfare and asks, 'upon this and the like occasions I hope it is not too much to say with Job, "Have pity upon me, have pity upon me, oh, ye my friends, for the hand of the Lord has touched me" ' (p. 52). Rowlandson moves from a passive acceptance of God's will to an awareness of her own sinfulness and the justice of her punishment. The prime vehicle for this understanding has been the Bible which so providentially found its way into her hands. But in the next stage of spiritual self-knowledge the

Bible is of no help to her. She must now acknowledge that God is, ultimately, mysterious to His creatures. She cannot know the divine will and it is impertinent of her to attempt to discover that which she cannot understand. The continual disappointments that Rowlandson suffers, when she becomes convinced that God does intend eventually to redeem her, contribute to her development of this understanding.

At first she hopes to be rescued by the English army, but that hope is frustrated; then she hopes that the Indians will do as they said they might and take her to Albany for ransom, but they do not; then, when her master promises to sell her to her husband she is obliged to stay with her mistress at the encampment while her master, the only Indian who is consistently kind to her, leaves instead. Her distress at this series of disappointments leads her first to her Bible but there she finds no comfort for the comfort she seeks lies, as finally she discovers, in the awareness recorded in Isaiah 55:8, that ' "my thoughts are not your thoughts, neither are your ways my ways", saith the Lord' (p. 53). Rowlandson is brought to the realisation of the fundamental uncertainty that lies at the heart of her understanding of her spiritual destiny. This uncertainty destroys for ever the complacency which she describes as characteristic of her earlier life. And it is in the shadow of this knowledge of contingency that a new selfhood is born, a self that embraces uncertainty and rejects the easy assurance that arises from spiritual myopia.

> I have seen the extreme vanity of this world. One hour I have been in health and wealth, wanting nothing, but the next hour in sickness and wounds and death, having nothing but sorrow and affliction. Before I knew what affliction meant, I was ready sometimes to wish for it. ... I should sometimes be jealous lest I should have my portion in this life, and that scripture would come to mind, Heb. 12:6, 'For whom the Lord loveth he chasteneth and scourgeth every son whom He receiveth'. But now I see the Lord had His time to scourge and chasten me (p. 75).

She is brought to a heightened self-consciousness which marks the distance she has travelled from the person she was before her capture and ordeal. And this new self-awareness empowers her to hope, as she writes, that 'I can say in some measure, as David did, "It is good for me that I have been afflicted" ' (p. 75). So Mary is brought from a 'sinful' self-reliance and independence through her suffering and abasement to an acute consciousness of her subjection to God's will. Only as a member of God's elect (the community at Boston) does she have any value – to her fellow Puritans, to her Indian captors and, finally, to herself.

This reassessment of her self-worth involves a shift from individual identity to a class identity; Rowlandson must cease thinking of herself as an individual and consider herself only as a member of a class. Typology helps her to do this. Typology describes the ways in which God intervenes in her life to bring about the promises He has made. Thus, typology treats not individuals but classes of individuals who are distinguished by the similarities they share throughout sacred history. Thus, God punishes and preserves Rowlandson not for any special quality possessed by her as an individual but because she belongs to the class of visible saints. Mary Rowlandson's description of her ordeal is punctuated with lengthy exclamations about the power and mercy of God, demonstrated by His constant renewal of her strength and stamina. When she thinks she must surrender to despair and give up the struggle to survive, God preserves her spirit 'that [she] might see more of His power' (p. 37).

God's power over all aspects of temporal life is made clear to Rowlandson, as is her relative insignificance. The Indians are represented as Satanic agents through whom God warns and chastises His people. It is only when she is prevented from observing the Sabbath that she remembers how many Sabbaths she misspent or let pass unremarked. This recollection brings with it the guilty awareness that God could justifiably cast her from His sight but Rowlandson is surprised and impressed by the extent of God's mercy that He does not. This guilty realisation is soon recognised as a crucial step in her chastisement and repentance; only now does Rowlandson see clearly the error of her earlier ways and resolve to reform her conduct: 'as He wounded me with one hand, so He healed me with the other' (p. 38). God's chastisement is not only justified but also merciful, she realises. The proximity of God in her suffering is enough to preserve her. Paradoxically, the nearness of death signifies the new life to which God is leading her. Rowlandson's acceptance of the fact that she must leave the body of her dead child in the wilderness where the Indians have buried it, and her awareness that she simply has no choice in the matter, symbolise for her a rediscovered knowledge of her dependence upon God. 'There I left that child in the wilderness', she tells us, 'and must commit it and myself also in this wilderness condition to Him who is above all' (p. 39). The brutal realisation that the Indians have complete control over her physical body gives way in her account to the knowledge that God has a similarly absolute power over her spiritual being. She must, therefore, suffer her ordeal passively while attempting to discover how her own experience fits into God's redemptive plan. As an individual she is powerless; only as God's subject can she participate in her own future.

The precise nature of her spiritual trial is made clear only slowly, through the interpretation and reinterpretation of her own sufferings and through her witness to the experiences of others. She gains the assurance that God travels with her, though she laments that her chastisement was ever necessary: 'Oh that my people had hearkened to me, and Israel had walked in my ways, I should soon have subdued their enemies and turned my hand against their adversaries' (Psalms 81: 13–14). At this stage, Rowlandson speaks less as an individual and more as a representative of God's chosen elite. She surrenders the voice of the individual woman whose domestic life was shattered by the sudden violence of the Indian attack and instead she speaks as a member of her sexual and spiritual class. Towards the end of her narrative she repeats the significance of her captivity for the entire Puritan community. She blames the conflict between the colonists and the Indian tribes upon the failure of the New Canaan to keep to its scriptural, typological, potential.

If the community of saints in New England were true to the terms of the federal covenant, Mary Rowlandson suggests, then God would destroy all its enemies among the heathen. As it is, God must use the Indians to chastise His people and to lead them back to the way of righteousness. It is in this connection that Rowlandson justifies her own text and the public voice it articulates. As Scripture spoke to her at crucial moments in her distress to comfort her with the true significance of her suffering and with hope of redemption, so her narrative is intended 'even as the psalmist says to declare the works of the Lord and His wonderful power in carrying us along, preserving us in the wilderness while under the enemy's hand and returning of us in safety again' (p. 46). Rowlandson intends her story to draw attention to the merciful aspect of the chastisement that all of the colonists have experienced in the varying forms of famine, disease, Indian attack, or the extreme trauma of captivity. She has had impressed upon her as a result of her experience the transient nature of the things of this world. As a result, she seeks in her narrative to communicate this sense of vanity to her peers and to encourage them to reassess the priorities in their lives, to look to the spiritual rewards that await them rather than to the physical and material aspects of everyday life.

The acceptance of God's supreme power and her own dependence upon that power bring to her an awareness of God's mercy and justice. Once she has learned how to hear it, the Bible speaks to her of God's intentions towards her. First she must surrender her own will to God's and then as a further stage of reformation she must not only accept but embrace as just God's chastisement of her. By the end of the eleventh remove Mary finds that her understanding of the nature of her ordeal is expressed in the passage from Psalm 119: 'I know, O Lord, that Thy judgments are right, and that Thou in faithfulness hast afflicted me' (p. 50). The knowledge that her sufferings are not arbitrary but are punishment for her past sins and past impiety brings a new and comforting appreciation of God's loving chastisement of her. It is the punitive aspect of typological rhetoric that characterises Rowlandson's narrative. And the sins for which she is punished are sins that apply both to her personally and to her entire community. The particular transgression for which she is being punished, the sin of her earlier life to which her commentary returns, is her failure to observe the Sabbath. When she is prevented by her captors from observing the Sabbath, Rowlandson recalls 'how careless I had been of God's holy time' (p. 38). This carelessness returns to bother her conscience later in the narrative when she studies her previous life to discover how she has incurred God's wrath.

> My conscience did not accuse me of unrighteousness toward one or the other, yet I saw how in my walk with God I had been a careless creature. ... On the Sabbath days I could look upon the sun and think how people were going to the house of God to have their souls refreshed and their bodies also, but I was destitute of both and might say as the poor prodigal, 'He would fain have filled his belly with the husks that the swine did eat, and no man gave unto him', Luke 15:16. For I must say with him, 'Father I have sinned against heaven and in thy sight', ver. 21 (p. 56).

Spiritual and physical refreshment – she is deprived of both as punishment for her earlier complacence. She had placed herself alone in a spiritual desert by failing to keep God's holy day and her physical trial in the wilderness is a fitting punishment, a punishment that symbolises the nature of her transgression and points the way for her repentance. This is a common theme in Puritan captivity narratives.

Hannah Swarton, who was taken captive from the frontier settlement of Casco Bay, Massachusetts, in May 1690, explains the nature of her ordeal as God's just punishment for her neglect of religion. The Swarton family had recently moved from the town of Beverly to the frontier outpost which had as yet no church and, as Swarton admits, their removal had been for worldly and not spiritual reasons. She therefore concludes that her trial is a fitting punishment: she is taken deep into the howling wilderness where she is surrounded by heathen and Catholic idolaters. Rowlandson is not alone in interpreting her suffering as the punishment of her own sinfulness but this sinfulness is common to many in her community. It is after her release and in the knowledge that she has been scourged for the sake of her own and her community's salvation that Mary Rowlandson is able to write that there are 'many scriptures which we do not take notice of or understand till we are afflicted' (p. 57). The ordeal of her captivity enables her to develop a deeper and more complete understanding of God's will in relation to His chosen people. Consequently, the narrative concludes with Mary Rowlandson's expression of gratitude that she has been chastised and set aright on the path to salvation. And her conclusion invites also the gratitude of the community of saints. For the typological significance of her experiences makes clear that God is aware of their backsliding and her example offers a warning of what God's wrath might entail if His people forget the glorious destiny that God intends for them as the elite class.

What Rowlandson is able tell in her narrative is determined by the typological style which emphasises the public and the spiritual at the expense of the personal and the psychological. Consequently, Mary's sufferings, and especially her sufferings as a woman, punctuate the narrative but are never the focus of the story. Rowlandson's regeneration and restoration are not without psychological cost to her: she suffers the lingering after-effects of trauma in the form of sleeplessness and anxiety caused by her constant awareness of the uncertainty of all things, the omnipresence of God's providential power and her vulnerability and powerlessness as a woman. She has been subject to both personal and communal admonition. She reminds us of the scriptural warning that there cannot 'be evil in the city and the Lord hath not done it' (p. 58). Through providence God manipulates the agents of evil for the scourging of his chosen people so that they might realise the glorious destiny that awaits them. Rowlandson is convinced of the operations of this punitive aspect of typology in her personal history. She asks us, 'Hear ye the rod and who hath appointed it' (p. 58): she has undergone trial and penance and knows fully who controls the 'rod' of divine chastisement, yet she cannot predict when that rod will fall again and upon whom.

Rowlandson's experience conforms to what Alden T. Vaughn and Edward W. Clark, in the introduction to their collection of colonial captivity narratives, term the 'abasement-salvation theme' (Vaughn & Clark, 1981, p. 6). The narrative of her captivity and restoration follows a pattern of degradation and awareness of worthlessness which is gradually supplanted by a growing sense of new self-worth but now within God's covenant of grace. Certainly Mary Rowlandson finds that she is abased by her life as a captive slave. She is thoroughly terrorised by the experience. She is kept in a state of near starvation and want so dire that in order to survive she must accept food, clothing and shelter from those she would shun under any other circumstances. More importantly, from the point of view of her soul, Rowlandson discovers that she is capable of committing the very sins of which she accuses her captors. She complains that Indians steal her food. During the seventh remove she turns her back upon two ears of corn that she has found and turns only to find that one has been stolen; at that time also she obtains a piece of horse liver but before she can cook it properly 'they got half of it away from me so that I was fain to take the rest and eat it as it was with the blood about my mouth' (p. 45). But she does exactly the same thing during the time of the nineteenth remove when, having devoured her own piece of boiled horse's hoof, she takes from an English child its share and claims divine authority for this act of theft: 'I took it [the morsel] of the child and ate it myself and savory it was to my taste. ... Thus the Lord made that pleasant refreshing which another time would have been an abomination' (p. 60). Her overwhelming hunger leads her to eat all manner of things which during the fifth remove she thinks of as 'filthy trash' (p. 44) but which, by the time of the ninth remove, were 'savory to me that one would think was enough to turn the stomach of a brute creature' (p. 49). By the time of her release she is willing to eat that which before would have appeared inedible, like the bark of trees.

Through the use of the abasement-salvation structure, and Rowlandson's representation of her sufferings as significant for the entire Puritan community, her narrative conveys hope for those who are uncertain of their own spiritual destiny. By emphasising the representative nature of her merciful chastisement, Rowlandson assures the members of the Massachusetts elite that any suffering they may undergo will be compensated. At the same time, however, her reassurances only apply to those who accept the patriarchal assumptions that underpin typology. Merciful chastisement is God's strategy for ensuring that His elite will fulfil their divine mission. Those who choose to resist identification with the elite, who choose to see themselves as individuals rather than as members of a class, can expect no mercy. Mary Rowlandson understands fully what will be their lot: starvation, enslavement and torture perhaps leading to death at the hands of Indian captors. Rowlandson's experience has shown her the stark alternatives for a woman in her place and time: conformity to Puritan gender roles or banishment (and almost certain death). That this realisation may also contribute to her sleeplessness she is prevented from saying.

Typology leads us to identify God as Rowlandson's 'true' liberator from the bondage of sin but in fact it is her husband and the magistrates in Boston who are responsible for paying her ransom and ensuring her release. If Rowlandson's 'redemption' is twofold (a physical release and spiritual salvation) so too her experience of 'worthlessness' has two dimensions: she reaches an understanding of how she may appear worthless in the eyes of God but she also discovers how much she is worth in cash terms (£20) and what she is worth in the sexual economy (nothing). The only other class of people in Boston who could claim to know exactly what they were worth were, of course, slaves. And through the experience of captivity Mary comes to realise that, apart from the privileges bestowed upon her by virtue of her religion, her condition is largely indistinguishable from that of a slave. She is liable to be bought and sold by her captors, she is treated as a commodity with no control over her destiny or her future, she cannot prevent having her children taken from her, she has no remedy for the injustices done to her (the assaults and thefts) and, although she claims she was not sexually abused, she is vulnerable to rape and sexual exploitation. Life among the Indians offers Mary a shocking glimpse of what life is like without the protection of patriarchal society. The cost of that protection may be high, in terms of sexual conformity, but the alternative is terrifying. Mary's economic dependence upon her husband and the male-dominated society he represents then can be seen to underlie her typological representation of the choices dramatised in her narrative. The choice between salvation and damnation finds a more worldly parallel in the choice between patriarchal protection and lonely destitution in the wilderness of the world.

References and Selected Further Reading

Anthony, Susan B. & Ida Husted Harper, 1970. *History of Woman Suffrage*, New York: Source Book Press.

Benhabib, Seyla, 1987. 'The Generalized and the Concrete Other: The Kohlberg-Gilligan controversy and Feminist Theory', in Seyla Benhabib & Drucilla Cornell, eds, *Feminism as Critique: On the Politics of Gender*, Minneapolis: University of Minnesota Press.

Bercovitch, Sacvan, ed., 1972. *Typology and Early American Literature*, Amherst, MA: University of Massachusetts Press.

Castiglia, Christopher, 1996. *Bound and Determined: Captivity, Culture-Crossing, and White Womanhood from Mary Rowlandson to Patty Hearst*, Chicago: University of Chicago Press.

Davis, Margaret H., 1992. 'Mary White Rowlandson's Self-Fashioning as Puritan Goodwife', *Early American Literature*, vol. 27 no. 1, pp. 49–60.

Derounian, Kathryn Zabelle, 1987. 'Puritan Orthodoxy and the "Survivor Syndrome" in Mary Rowlandson's Captivity Narrative', *Early American Literature*, vol. 22, pp. 82–93.

Eisenstein, Zillah, 1981.*The Radical Future of Liberal Feminism*, New York: Longman.

Betty Friedan, 1963. *The Feminine Mystique*, (rpt. New York: Dell, 1983).

Gilbert, Sandra M. & Susan Gubar, eds, 1996. *The Norton Anthology of Literature by Women: The Traditions in English*, 2nd edn. New York: W. W. Norton.

Gilman, Charlotte Perkins, 1898. *Women and Economics: A Study of the Economic Relations Between Men and Women as a Factor in Social Evolution*, Mineola, NY: Dover Publications, 1998.

Jaggar, Alison M., 1983. *Feminist Politics and Human Nature*, Totowa, NJ: Rowman & Allenheld.

Kolodny, Annette, 1984. *The Land Before Her: Fantasy and Experience of the American Frontiers, 1630–1860*, Chapel Hill: University of North Carolina Press.

Logan, Lisa, 1993. 'Mary Rowlandson's Captivity and the "Place" of the Woman Subject', *Early American Literature*, vol. 28 no. 3, pp. 255–277.

Mill, John Stuart, 1869. *The Subjection of Women*, New York: Dover, 1997.

Namias, June, 1993. *White Captives: Gender and Ethnicity on the American Frontier*, Chapel Hill: University of North Carolina Press.

Okin, Susan Moller, 1979. *Women in Western Political Thought*, Princeton: Princeton University Press.

Pateman, Carole, 1979. *The Problem of Political Obligation: A Critique of Liberal Theory*, Berkeley: University of California Press.

Salisbury, Neal, ed., 1997. *The Sovereignty and Goodness of God by Mary Rowlandson, with Related Documents*, Boston: Bedford Books.

Schneir, Miriam, ed., 1972. *Feminism: The Essential Historical Writings*, New York: Vintage.

Shea, Daniel, 1968. *Spiritual Autobiography in Early America*, Princeton: Princeton University Press.

Stanton, Theodore & Harriet Stanton Blatch, eds, 1969. *Elizabeth Cady Stanton*, New York: Arno and The New York Times.

Steinem, Gloria, 1983. *Outrageous Acts and Everyday Rebellions*, New York: Holt, Reinhart & Winston.

Tong, Rosemarie, 1989. *Feminist Thought: A Comprehensive Introduction*, Boulder, CO: Westview Press.

Toulouse, Teresa A., 1992. ' "My Own Credit": Strategies of (E)valuation in Mary Rowlandson's Captivity Narrative', *American Literature*, vol. 64, pp. 655–676.

Rowlandson, Mary, 1682. *The Sovereignty and Goodness of God, Together with the Faithfulness of His Promises Displayed, Being a Narrative of the Captivity and Restoration of Mrs Mary Rowlandson*, ed. Neal Salisbury. Boston: Bedford Books, 1997.

Vaughn, Alden T. & Edward W. Clark, eds, 1981. *Puritans Among the Indians: Accounts of Captivity and Redemption, 1676–1724*, Cambridge, MA & London: Belknap Press.

Wollestonecraft, Mary, 1792. *A Vindication of the Rights of Women*, New York: Dover, 1996.

2

Gender and Work: Marxist Feminism and Charlotte Perkins Gilman

This chapter begins with a survey of Marxist feminist theorists, focusing upon Emma Goldman's *The Traffic in Women* (1970), Michèle Barrett's *Women's Oppression Today* (1980) and Lillian Robinson's *Sex, Class and Culture* (1978). The primary theoretical concepts explored here include: capitalism versus patriarchy, in terms of the relationship between class and gender oppression; the economics of publishing; the sexual division of labour; and Marxist feminist analysis as the identification of the structural elements that determine the quality and nature of our experience. In the section that follows this theoretical survey, I turn to the Marxist feminist analysis of Charlotte Perkins Gilman's 'The Yellow Wallpaper' and various of her short stories.

Survey of Marxist Feminist Theory

Summary of Marxist Feminist Principles

Marxist feminism is organised around the basic conflicts between capitalism versus patriarchy and class versus gender oppression. Marxist feminism combines the study of class with the analysis of gender. Capitalism is viewed as both sexually and economically exploitative; capitalist patriarchy is seen as the source of women's oppression: their alienation from labour (through the necessary creation of a pool of available labour), the patriarchal ownership of the means of production and reproduction, the construction of women as a class of passive consumers, and the exploitation of women's

65

work. The latter constitutes a common perspective that unites all women and allows them to expose the ways in which capitalism requires that men dominate women, through a political analysis of the ideology of patriarchy. So gender is a more profound and basic cause of oppression than is class, and gender oppression structures all our social relationships. 'Though class society appears to be the source, the cause of the oppression of women, it is rather its consequence', Nancy Hartsock observes, in her rewriting of Marx. She continues, 'Thus, it is "only at the last culmination of the development of class society [that] this, its secret, appear[s] again, namely, that on the one hand it is the *product* of the oppression of women, and that on the other it is the *means* by which women participate in and create their own oppression' [Hartsock's emphasis and ellipses, 1983, p. 86). Personal and cultural identities are viewed as ideological products. One of the contradictions of capitalism revealed by a feminist analysis is that capitalism trivialises what it most needs – female labour. Marxist feminists find themselves in conflict with socialist feminists over the question: does class or sex underpin the primary division between men and women? Marxist feminists substitute sex for the role taken by class in classical Marxist analyses and attend to the conditions of the sexual division of labour.

The material conditions of the household prescribe various gendered oppositions, like the separations analysed by Marx as by-products of the class struggle: among these oppositions are those formed between body and mind, nature and culture, real and ideal. The dominance of the masculine side of each dichotomy and the corresponding devaluation of the female is a powerful characteristic of patriarchy. When the political relationships within the domestic sphere are seen as in a microcosm, it becomes apparent that similar relationships in the public world produce the systematic devaluation of 'women's work' which structures social relations and public political life.

In terms of literary theorising, Marxist feminists focus upon the relationship between reading and social realities. Art, including literature, is seen to be prescribed by the forms of economic production. The conditions of the production of literary texts are determined by the economics of publishing and distribution, marketing and profit-making. Marxist feminists question the effect of gender on the manner in which authorship is received and canons are formed. Textual meanings are assumed to be produced by their socio-economic context and the ideology of the reader rather than existing in some transcendent apolitical realm. Marxist analysis concerns itself with the identification of the structural determinants of experience. This involves analysing the ways in which private experience is prescribed by public political conditions and, correspondingly, how public experiences are shaped by personal relationships. Three prominent Marxist feminist thinkers are Emma Goldman, Lillian Robinson and Michèle Barrett; in what follows I look more closely at the work of these three women.

Emma Goldman, The Traffic in Women and Other Essays *(1970)*

This volume reprints some of Emma Goldman's essays on prostitution, marriage and woman suffrage, which were written out of her Marxist-inspired anarchism, in the early part of the century. I want to focus here upon the title essay of this collection in which Goldman presents an early analysis of the subordination of women as a class through the conjunction of class and sexual relations. Emma Goldman opens this essay by forging a link between sexual prostitution and economic prostitution – wage slavery as opposed to sexual slavery; both part of what Goldman calls 'the white slave traffic' (Goldman, 1970, p. 19). She goes on to propose that in fact the economic subordination of women is the cause and origin of prostitution: 'the merciless Moloch of capitalism that fattens on underpaid labor, thus driving thousands of women and girls into prostitution' (p. 20). Why work long, exhausting hours for very poor pay, she asks, when prostitution offers a more lucrative opportunity? Goldman cites examples of women working in factories in New York City for a wage of six dollars a week in payment for 48 to 60 hours of work. From this specific economic condition of working women, Goldman moves to a consideration of the related social determinants of women's behaviour as a distinct class.

> Nowhere is woman treated according to the merit of her work, but rather as a sex. It is therefore almost inevitable that she should pay for her right to exist, to keep a position in whatever line, with sex favors. Thus it is merely a question of degree whether she sells herself to one man, in or out of marriage, or to many men. Whether our reformers admit it or not, the economic and social inferiority of woman is responsible for prostitution (p. 20).

In order to emphasise that it is the economic dependence of women as a sexual class and not the circumstances, moral, personal and social, of particular women that causes them to turn to prostitution, of one sort or another, Goldman points to the diverse reasons why women become prostitutes: financial need, escape from an abusive home, physical disablement that excludes them from other forms of labour. Goldman is also careful to point out that married women comprise a significant proportion of the community of prostitutes, thus negating the power of moral explanations of prostitution. For Goldman, the reason for prostitution is based on the relation between economic class and the status of woman as a sex commodity. So working class women become prostitutes while bourgeois women become de facto prostitutes within marriage. 'To the moralist prostitution does not consist so much in the fact that the woman sells her body, but rather that she sells it out of wedlock. That this is no mere statement is proved by the fact that marriage for monetary considerations is perfectly legitimate, sanctified by law and public opinion, while any other union is condemned and repudiated' (p. 25). The sexual relation is determined by the class relation; the status of individual women is dependent upon their class position, but the economic status of women as a sexual class is the shared condition of dependence. Indeed, Goldman suggests that paid prostitution offers some advantages over the unpaid sexual and domestic labour of marriage: for '[t]he prostitute never signs away the right over her own person, she retains her freedom known, by whose status she will be defined, the man who will rescue her from emptiness and loneliness by filling "the inner space"' (p. 12). So for women, the process of establishing intimacy is part of the development of identity, while for men identity precedes intimacy and separation is a constitutive part of identity. Thus, 'male identity [is] forged in relation to the world and ... female identity [is] awakened in a relationship of identity with another person' (p. 13). Gilligan treats these theories of masculine versus feminine identity formation not as wrong in themselves but she does point out that the theories carry gendered values that are not acknowledged. The development of male identity and moral values is represented as universal and objective rather than particular and masculine. The values articulated by men and women may vary enormously but only the male values are clearly represented. Feminine experience is presented as characterised by weakness, confusion, self-doubt, uncertain judgments but Gilligan suggests that these qualities need not necessarily be seen as signs of weakness. 'Sensitivity to the needs of others and the assumption of responsibility for taking care lead women to attend to voices other than their own and to include in their judgment other points of view' (p. 16). So rather than a sign of moral weakness, what appears as confusion and a reluctance to judge others can, when seen from the perspective offered by feminine rather than masculine values, appear to be moral strength. Feminine judgments should, therefore, be interpreted within the context of feminine nurturance and care. The difference between male and female approaches to morality Gilligan distinguishes by referring to a masculine 'morality of rights' and a feminine 'morality of responsibility'. She does not contest the fact that male and female identity formation and moral development are different; what she does contest is the psychological evaluation of these distinct moral voices: '[t]he elusive mystery of women's development lies in its recognition of the continuing importance of attachment in the human life cycle. Woman's place in man's life cycle is to protect this recognition while the developmental litany intones the celebration of separation, autonomy, individuation, and natural rights' (p. 23).

and personal rights, nor is she always compelled to submit to man's embrace' (pp. 26–27). The wife, however, finds herself in a condition akin to slavery in that she is bound by her entire person to the man she has married. Thus, the commodity status of women under capitalism and the dependent status of women under patriarchy produce a set of social relations that transform all sexual relations into forms of prostitution.

Goldman can envision the transformation of these relations only if prostitution is recognised as a product of social conditions (as a social rather than moral issue), and only when we achieve 'a complete transvaluation of all accepted values ... coupled with the abolition of industrial slavery' (p. 32). Only the transformation of all exploitative relations can abolish the sexual class to which women have been assigned, along with the commodification of sexual labour represented by prostitution. Emma Goldman's analysis of prostitution is indicative of the nature of her Marxist feminist thought, in that the essay brings into relation class and gender oppression, within the context of the sexual division of labour under capitalist patriarchy, and in terms of Goldman's own revolutionary activism.

Michèle Barrett, Women's Oppression Today: Problems in Marxist Feminist Analysis *(1980)*

Barrett's concern in this book is to bring together the analysis of gender relations with the materialist analysis of contemporary capitalist society. She begins by acknowledging that there is little common ground shared by Marxist theory and feminism: Marxism deals with relations of appropriation and exploitation, generated by the primary contradiction between capital and labour, and not, as Barrett points out, with 'the gender of the exploiters and that of those whose labour is appropriated' (Barrett, 1980, p. 8). And Barrett further acknowledges that the gender divisions that produce sexual discrimination and oppression precede the transition to capitalist economies and so cannot be abolished by the further transition away from capitalism within the context of a socialist revolution alone. Despite its gender-blindness, there is a job for Marxism to perform within the context of the feminist movement. Marxist feminism can 'identify the operation of gender relations as and where they may be distinct from, or connected with, the processes of production and reproduction understood by historical materialism' (p. 9). It is significant that Barrett qualifies her use of the term 'reproduction' by placing it explicitly in an historical materialist context, drawing on Louis Althusser's concept of the reproduction of the relations of production. This is important because Barrett wants to distinguish her use of the term from that of radical feminists who define reproduction as the experience of maternity which is grounded in the biological difference between men and women, and which is the origin of women's oppression (see the discussion of Shulamith Firestone's *The Dialectic of Sex*, in chapter five). Barrett is very critical of Firestone's biologistic arguments, for their reductionism, for the elision of definitions of sex as a biological category and gender as a social category, for the potential reassertion of separate spheres (public versus private) for men and women respectively. Instead, Marxist feminism would focus upon 'the relations between the organization of sexuality, domestic production, the household, and so on, and historical changes in the mode of production and systems of appropriation and exploitation' (p. 9).

Consequently, Marxist feminism approaches the concept of patriarchy not in terms of the biological basis of power relations but in terms of class analysis, to allow a more properly materialist understanding of women's oppression. Barrett cites the example of the divorced wife of a bourgeois man; this woman is a member of the bourgeoisie only by virtue of her marriage, in effect she is an honorary member of the middle class. But outside the relation of marriage, this woman must earn her own living and take her place in the working class to which she has essentially belonged all along. This is a powerful example of marriage as a domestic mode of production, involving the husband's appropriation of his wife's unpaid labour, but it does not indicate how the concept of patriarchy relates to this particular mode of production. Rather, patriarchy is represented as an ahistorical and universal principle of oppression. The difficulty of constituting patriarchy as a system of male domination in relation to the capitalist mode of production in some ways crystallises the difficulty of formulating an effective Marxist feminist analysis. This difficulty is emphasised when considering the relations of reproduction as patriarchal relations that can be said to exist independently of capitalist relations of production. Unpaid domestic work, for example, falls outside the parameters of Marx's analysis of exploitation under capitalism, which looks to the exploitative wage-contract and which obviously does not apply to the situation of the unpaid housewife. However, the housewife's labour can be said to reproduce the worker's labour at the same time as she reproduces capitalist ideological relations of domination and submission within the context of the family. In this way, the unpaid domestic labourer and the low-paid worker share the same class interests. In this respect, the analysis is reductionist and further, it does not take account of the sexual division of labour in pre-capitalist and socialist societies. Barrett concludes that in fact the oppression of women is not necessary to the functioning of capitalism but this mode of oppression 'has acquired a material basis in the relations of production and reproduction of capitalism today' (p. 249).

The difficulty of accounting for the social reproduction of capitalist class relations in connection with the patriarchal reproduction of the species depends in part on the importance or primacy assigned to class or to gender. This same conflict between the claims of class and gender to be the original basis of oppression emerges in debates over women's location within the class structure. Radical feminists claim that women constitute a patriarchal 'sex class' apart from but enmeshed within the capitalist class system. So women experience oppression *as women* in ways that are more immediate and more powerful than their oppression by virtue of their economic class affiliation. The gendered experience of oppression within a class context can be approached in terms of Louis Althusser's revision of the concept of ideology as lived experience, 'the imaginary relationship of individuals to their real conditions of existence'

(Althusser, 1971). Barrett does point out that, despite the usefulness of this concept which retains a connection with material conditions of life, ideology alone cannot explain women's oppression under capitalism; economic processes as well as ideological determinants contribute to the specific nature of the oppression women experience. It is crucial, as Barrett explains, to define closely the concept of ideology; first, she limits the idea of the relative autonomy of ideology: we should be able to specify what range of possibilities exist for the ideological processes of a particular social formation; and then she goes on to limit the concept to describing mental rather than material phenomena:

> the concept of ideology refers to those processes that have to do with consciousness, motive, emotionality; it can best be located in the category of *meaning*. Ideology is a generic term for the processes by which meaning is produced, challenged, reproduced, transformed. Since meaning is negotiated primarily through means of communication and signification, it is possible to suggest that cultural production provides an important site for the construction of ideological processes (p. 97).

In this way, literature and literary study as material forms of cultural practice, are open to the Marxist analysis of ideology in specific social formations. The analysis of ideology in historical and material terms would then enable identification of the mechanisms which operate to oppress women, such as the mythology of the ideal family, the ideological construction of gendered subjectivity, and so on.

Lillian S. Robinson, Sex, Class and Culture *(1978)*

Inspired by the New Left politics of the 1970s, Lillian Robinson provides just this historical materialist analysis of canonical literary works. The essay that opens the collection, 'Dwelling in Decencies: Radical Criticism and the Feminist Perspective' (1971), sets out the difficulty of constructing an effective relationship between feminism and inherited modes of literary criticism: 'feminist criticism cannot become simply bourgeois criticism in drag [Robinson claims]. It must be ideological and moral criticism; it must be revolutionary' (Robinson, 1978, p. 3). The effectiveness of feminist criticism is not to be measured in terms of the contribution that can be made to academic literary criticism as such but by what this effort of feminist ideological analysis can do for the women's movement. In her indication of what this ideological analysis might do, Robinson comes close to taking up in the literary realm the concept of ideology set out by Michèle Barrett. Robinson observes:

> Many books about women concentrate on the moral and social 'choices' they make; their authors almost always show us how little material scope for choosing they really have. This is clearly more than just telling us how much money someone has or can get – although writers, when speaking of women, are astonishingly explicit about these facts. It is a matter of relating the economic and cultural experience of class to someone's sense of herself and to what happens in her life. It also means understanding the extent to which sexual identity itself is a material fact (pp. 9–10).

Robinson is not referring here exclusively to texts written by and about women; the representation of women in the male literary works that comprise the great tradition can also reveal a great deal about the mechanisms of women's oppression. But this can only happen if feminist literary critics surrender their learned assumptions of objectivity and disinterestedness and textual value. A book cannot be sexist and still 'great' as a work of literature, in feminist terms. The evaluation of a text in feminist terms requires that the critic go beyond the limits of textual form to ask what is the relation between form and moral or ideological content. Both the aesthetic and the ideological aspects of a text must be engaged if feminism is to function as an 'engaged' mode of criticism; that is, as criticism with a political cause.

What Robinson wants those professing to 'do' feminist criticism to resist is adopting a gender inquiry as part of traditional, bourgeois, scholarship. In the 1974 essay 'Criticism – and Self-Criticism' she identifies the kind of feminist literary criticism that fails to resist this approach as proceeding 'as if gender functioned as a natural, rather than a social category' (Robinson, 1978, p. 65). By failing to move beyond the recognition that sexism is a social constraint, this kind of limited feminist analysis fails to identify the forms taken by this constraint in a particular society. And so this criticism fails to contribute to the cause of women's liberation; it 'does not help us use literature to understand an urgent issue that literature is uniquely fitted to illuminate – the peculiar forms sexism has assumed in *capitalist* society' (Robinson's emphasis, p. 65). What feminist criticism should be analysing is the social history that motivates the meanings of works of art, both those produced in the present and in the past. Robinson does make a distinction in terms of the issues that must be addressed by contemporary as opposed to historical works of art:

> For our own period, it means taking mass culture seriously – examining the art addressed to working people, the forms it uses, the myths it creates, the influence it exerts, and seeking a new audience for criticism among those people who are the chief actors in history. For the past, it means looking at the recognized masterpieces as historically alive: conditioned by historical forces, produced in specific material circumstances, serving certain interests and ignoring, threatening or repressing others. And it means considering how popular culture coexisted and sometimes overlapped with those monuments (p. 67).

In the essays that make up the bulk of *Sex, Class, and Culture*, Robinson does precisely what she describes here. Essays like 'Who's Afraid of a Room of One's Own?' about Virginia Woolf, 'Woman Under Capitalism: The Renaissance Lady' about the cult of courtly love, 'Why Marry Mr. Collins?' about Jane Austen, are juxtaposed with essays like 'On Reading Trash', about precisely the 'overlap' between popular and literary romances, 'Working/Women/Writing' which is about working class women's writing, and 'What's My Line?

Telefiction and Women's Work'. The literary forms, the myths, the influences these texts exert, and the audiences they potentially reach are all defined in terms of gender; the historical forces by which the texts are conditioned, the specific material circumstances that have produced the texts, and the historical interests with which they deal, are all engaged but in gender terms in Robinson's analyses. The focus of her Marxist feminist analyses is not so much patriarchy or even capitalism as such, but rather the relationship between class and gender oppression and the structural elements that determine the quality and nature of our experience as gendered beings. For example, in 'Who's Afraid of a Room of One's Own?' Robinson explores the ways in which chastity and sexual behaviour are related to socio-economic class, both historically in Virginia Woolf's writing and in her own contemporary American experience. The relation between class and sexuality only superficially obscures the common experience of women in society – sexual availability and a capacity for sexual enjoyment characterise working class women who are also often identified with prostitution, whereas sexually indiscreet bourgeois or upper class women (Robinson uses the examples of Edith Wharton's Lily Bart and the heroines of the later Henry James) are just as financially dependent upon men as working class whores, and the sexual indiscretion of these 'ladies' can be similarly traced to financial need.

It is men who legislate between 'respectable' women and whores, yet it is the dependence of women as a subordinate class that determines feminine sexual behaviours (both chastity and promiscuity). That tag of 'respectability' carries with it a class identification – respectable women can join by association the middle-class of their husbands and fathers – and the hierarchy of class relations thus constructs the experience of gender as it determines the experience of sexuality. Women do not gain power through these identifications but they do gain proximity to and material benefits from their proximity to those who control the means of production. Robinson notes, 'It is in this sense that forms of sexual behavior create material barriers best understood as class-based' (p. 108).

Marxist Feminism in Praxis

In the following section, Charlotte Perkins Gilman's novella 'The Yellow Wallpaper' and various of her short stories are analysed in Marxist feminist terms. The discussion of Charlotte Perkins Gilman's work is set within the context of Gilman's feminism. The conjunction of gender and materialism in Gilman's representation of the condition of nineteenth-century women's lives provides the terms for the Marxist feminist analysis of her work and the themes she explores there: capitalism and patriarchy, or the relationship between economic dependence and female sexual identity; political analysis in terms of the structural determinants of experience and the destruction of female individuality; and the sexual division of labour which, in 'The Yellow Wallpaper', Gilman explores in terms of writing and communication. The style in which this text is constructed is discussed in terms of the conditions of its production and consumption: at the time of its initial publication, this text was unpopular because the Gothic style in which it is written expresses a feminine sensibility which contradicted the dominant realistic style that was popular among Gilman's contemporaries (especially that arbiter of late nineteenth-century literary taste, William Dean Howells).

Charlotte Perkins Gilman, 'The Yellow Wallpaper' and Stories

Gender roles form the focus of Gilman's social criticism. A Marxist feminist approach to Gilman's writing can enhance our appreciation of Gilman's exposure of the ideological construction of the self under patriarchy and the conditions of necessity (the social coercion) that make women conform to these oppressive gender roles. She does this in her literary work in three primary ways: first, she shows how social forms work to reduce the potential of women (in texts such as 'The Yellow Wallpaper', 'The Cottagette', and 'Making a Change'); secondly, she shows what women can achieve when they are liberated from these social forms (such as in 'Turned', 'What Diantha Did', and 'An Honest Woman'); thirdly, she represents the world in a utopian fashion, as it should be rather than as it is, with women in possession of equal rights and responsibilities and the dignity that comes from realising their full human potential, though this latter strategy was only available to Gilman as a reversal of gender roles, in texts like *Herland*, *With Her in Ourland*, and 'Moving the Mountain', where women are represented as dominant and men as marginal. It is worth pausing to consider in some detail the significance of Gilman's representation of these aspects of women's oppression.

Capitalism invariably provides the economic context for Gilman's writing, as patriarchy provides the sexual context. Capitalism is represented not as the root cause of women's oppression but as a consequence of patriarchy. Especially in relation to the economics of housework, Gilman reveals the enormous financial debt owed to women for their unpaid domestic labour. The existence of a pool of cheap (or free) female labour is a necessary part of the capitalist economy. This is made quite clear by the heroine of 'What Diantha Did' (1912), who presents her father with an account of precisely how much she has cost to raise. This he receives with an amused air as Diantha's response to his challenge that she owes him a duty of care as his daughter. What does not amuse him at all is her account of what he owes her in payment for her domestic labour – housework and care of her mother and younger siblings. 'Mr. Bell meditated carefully on these figures. To think of that child's labor footing up to two thousand dollars and over! It was lucky a man had a wife and daughters to do this work, or he could never support a family' (Gilman, in Lane, ed., 1980, p. 133). The ironic setting for this realisation is the domestic labour of his wife, who is darning socks throughout this encounter between her daughter and husband, and of Diantha herself, who must cook her father's dinner and wash up after him before he will even listen to her.

The motivation for this accounting is Diantha's justification of her decision to leave home in order to work. Her parents and her sister all object that the only respectable work for a woman is in the home; her sister can leave in order to marry and her brother can leave in order to work but

Diantha, a woman, cannot leave to find paid work outside the home without incurring the displeasure of all those around her. In financial terms, her family will miss her unpaid labour and Diantha must arrange to pay for domestic help to take her place. In the public world of paid work, Diantha discovers a similar division between men's and women's work. She succeeds as a businesswoman not so much by challenging this sexual division of labour but by working with it. She professionalises the business of housework by arranging cleaning services and the delivery of cooked meals, for example. But her success as a woman maintains the sexual class division separating men and women. In Gilman's fiction this pattern is repeated. Women succeed in business but the business in which they engage is an extension into the public world of the domestic work women perform, unpaid, in their own home: cooking, cleaning, childcare, and so on. Thus, in Gilman's work the sexual class divisions of capitalist society are seen to be a consequence and not a cause of patriarchy. The two work together but the liberation of characters like Diantha takes place within a capitalist economy. Gilman shows that patriarchy precedes capitalism, which is its consequence and not its cause. A Marxist analysis of texts like 'What Diantha Did' would not then penetrate beyond the economic context but a Marxist *feminist* analysis is able to reveal the relationship between capitalism and the sexual division of labour under patriarchy.

Narratives like 'What Diantha Did' and 'An Honest Woman' (1911) explore the implications of the sexual division of labour. The exploitation of women's work under patriarchy and the necessity of female labour as a structural component of capitalist economics both become apparent when Gilman reveals what women can achieve when they are liberated from repressive economic and social forms. The heroine of 'An Honest Woman' transforms herself from a 'fallen woman', abandoned by the father of her child, into a successful business woman who runs a respectable hotel and is a pillar of the local community. When her seducer finally returns and hopes to share in her financial success she is able to reject him for the liar and cheat he is. When he threatens to reveal her past to the community, she is able to respond to his blackmail by informing him that the details of her past are known to the town yet she is judged an 'honest woman' because of her exemplary behaviour, and so his threat has no substance. Mary resists the patriarchal demand that she make herself available to this man; he attempts to claim his child, his name, and her as his wife, but she has no need of him in any of these respects because neither she nor her child is financially dependent upon him. This independence, however, depends upon her conformity to the expectations of what is a patriarchal society. She is praised for sending her daughter away to school rather than have her live in the hotel, which would not be socially acceptable; her own work is an extension of woman's traditional domestic work rather than a challenge to the category of 'men's work'. Her success is that of the individual entrepreneur and her liberation represents the success of which a woman is capable if she is free to make her way in the capitalist economy.

Gilman's stories expose the hidden structural or class determinants of feminine experience, especially the social and economic forces that constrain women to a sexual class: in the story 'Turned', for example, the betrayed wife, Marion, realises that her husband's seduction of the young servant girl Gerda is not only a personal betrayal. After her shock and grief have subsided she is able to reflect, 'This is the sin of man against woman … . The offense is against womanhood. Against motherhood' (p. 94), she tells herself. Her husband has taken advantage of the passivity, obedience, and respect of the servant. The class relationship of master to servant is reflected in the sexual relationship of man to woman. Seen in these terms, Marion realises that her initial reaction to banish Gerda from her home is wrongly conceived. That reaction serves the class and sexual distinctions that have enabled her husband to exploit the girl. Rather, Marion recognises her husband as the perpetrator and Gerda as the victim in these circumstances and together the women leave to establish an independent life for themselves and Gerda's child. The title of the story, then, represents not only the 'turning' of the women against this faithless man but also suggests the way in which these women turn to each other as members of the same sexual class, subject to the same kinds of exploitation and betrayal.

Gilman exposes the construction of women as a class of passive consumers and the destruction of feminine individuality that is part of the creation of a class consciousness. By prescribing the meaning of femininity and constraining feminine consciousness through concepts such as duty, social formulations operate to reduce the potential of individual women. Stories such as 'The Cottagette',(1910) and 'Making a Change' (1911) reveal the process by which individual women are reduced by their dependence upon men to conform to specific gender roles. 'The Cottagette', for example, portrays the transformation of an artist into a domestic drudge as she adopts the domestic roles she believes are necessary to find a husband. In 'Making a Change' the wife is again an artist but in this story she is driven to attempt suicide because of the domestic and maternal pressures to which she is subjected. In this story the wife and her mother-in-law, both of whom are miserable in their conventional roles, devise a plan whereby Julia can resume teaching music while her husband works and her baby is cared for by his grandmother along with all the other babies who attend her nursery. In this way, the two women earn sufficient money to pay for a cook and housekeeper while they, rather than live as the passive consumers of Frank's income, are the active producers of paid services. Again, this paid labour is an extension of domestic labour and initially Frank is scandalised by this 'unfeminine' behaviour: his mother's childcare effort should be reserved for his son and his wife's music should be enjoyed only by him. It is only his awareness of the happiness and fulfilment that paid employment brings to each woman that permits him to approve of their work. Masculine resistance to feminine work and financial independence is a recurring theme in Gilman's stories. Concepts such as duty and respectability work with conventional patriarchal gender roles to confine both men and women, but the assault on their individuality is felt most destructively by women. This is the primary subject of Gilman's most famous work, 'The Yellow Wallpaper'.

In 'The Yellow Wallpaper', the relationship between the narrator and her husband John represents the opposed sexual stereotypes that are brought into conflict in the course of the narrative. The husband is defined as rational, scientific, objective and dominant; his wife, in contrast, is passive, irrational, nervous, emotional and subjective, 'superstitious'. But above all, it is the power of her imagination that is identified as dangerous. John is compelled to control his wife and that dangerous impulse that threatens his comfortable view of the world. His fear causes him to become authoritarian, particularly when the object of his fear is 'the weaker sex'. The narrator sees his problem but she is unable to speak of it as a problem. Consequently, her tone is uncertain; insight alternates with naiveté, resistance with resignation.

The story is ostensibly a journal but the confidential tone suggests that the narrator is trying to reach or even create a reader that otherwise she cannot find. Her relationship with her husband is filled with deception because she cannot tell him what he does not want to know and will not acknowledge (hence his repeated refrain that she is getting better). Only in her journal can she confess to the deceit and explain why it is necessary. In writing she can explain what she wants to tell her husband but cannot. The journal itself is her greatest deception but it also represents her most complete attempt at honesty. These contradictions are experienced as personal failures but they are expressed by the narrative as the inevitable consequence of prescribed gender roles; here, that of wife. Individual women are placed in a situation where they must aspire to conform to the artificial stereotype of 'wife' and honestly embrace this role as the avenue to self-fulfilment. But this process inevitably creates a conflict between social and personal perceptions of one's self, a conflict that is experienced as an irresolvable demand for self-deception and, simultaneously, the impulse toward honesty.

The narrator cannot stop deceiving herself about the true nature of her treatment. Thus, her descriptions generate dramatic irony as the reader pieces together meanings she does not quite understand. For example, the description of her room which to her appears as a nursery but to the reader appears as a room designed to confine violent mental patients. The gap between the physical details of her environment and her interpretation of them derives in large part from her desire to believe the things her husband tells her. What she reveals in this way is the extent to which she is trapped in a conception of herself derived from John and the values of the patriarchal society he represents. It is through the medium of these patriarchal values that women are controlled most effectively and while the narrator can object to the terms in which he describes her situation, she does not have the words with which to challenge his authority.

Not only the narrator but her husband also is shown to be a victim of the repressive society in which they live. Her cruel treatment is motivated by love; her husband does not willingly torture her but he has no other solution to her predicament but to insist that she conform to the gender roles prescribed for her. The roles of 'loving husband' and 'devoted wife' lead those who try to live out these roles into disaster. Jenny also shares John's views of the narrator's malady and her dangerously disposed imagination; in this she represents women's complicity in the maintenance of oppressive social roles by dramatising the figure of the male-identified woman. Jenny identifies not with the interests of women but with the vested interests of men; she sides with the powerful, with the oppressors, for there lies her own personal advantage. In the story there is no hint of a community of women beyond the narrator's crazed vision of a hoard of 'creeping women'. Both women are imprisoned by the wifely pattern that society imposes upon them, like the imaginary woman imprisoned behind the patterned wallpaper and the real woman imprisoned behind her barred window. At the end, she is liberated from her confinement but the freedom she discovers is only freedom from the need to deceive herself and others about the true nature of her role. She has sloughed off the trappings of wife and mother; she is left only with her madness and her insight into the true workings of the patriarchy. She is punished for her refusal to embrace and conform to socially conditioned gender roles; she becomes an example to women like Jenny who see that outside the roles instituted for them there is no place for women in her society. The independent woman, the woman without male protection, is shunned and reviled. So sexual identity and economic dependence coexist in a complex relationship that determines every aspect of social life.

Marxist feminist analysis is concerned with identifying the structural determinants of experience, such as the co-existence of female economic dependence and female sexual identity. Nancy Hartsock describes the violence done to the feminine experience of self by the misogynistic organisation of female life in a capitalist patriarchy:

> The organization of motherhood as an institution in which a woman is alone with her children, the isolation of women from each other in domestic labor, the female pathology of loss of self in service to others – all mark the transformation of life into death, the distortion of what could have been creative and communal activity into oppressive toil, and the destruction of the possibility of community present in women's relational self-definition (Hartsock, 1983, p. 84).

This passage describes the essential features of Gilman's story. The narrator resists isolation with her children, she perceives her baby as a threat to her personal autonomy (the child makes her 'tired') and the story suggests that the original cause of her illness is post-natal depression. However, this means simply that Jenny is left to care for the child alone and so a different woman is isolated with the child. Whilst the husband goes to town and participates in the public world, the women are isolated in the house and they are kept separate by their distinct relations with John, the head of the household. Jenny is his silent ally who shares his values and opinions and enacts his judgments; his wife is opposed to him as she struggles to engage him in a dialogue concerning those very values and judgments. Most of all it is the female 'pathology of loss of self in service to others' that is dramatised by 'The Yellow Wallpaper'. Of the two central female characters, Jenny asserts no sense of self; she simply serves the needs and desires of John. The narrator, however, struggles to curb her acute sense of her own individuality and submit to her husband's will. In the contradictory value scheme of this society, it is the failure to suppress feminine identity that is seen as pathological.

This struggle against her sense of self as the narrator tries to conform, but fails, provides the basic structuring principle of the narrative. In 'The Yellow Wallpaper' narrative structure is represented as a process, a process thematised as the process of interpretation. The narrator moves between the demands of her own identity and the demands placed upon her gender by society and as she does so her perception of the wallpaper, and the meaning she finds there, changes. Her interpretation of details in the pattern leads to a complete subjectivity of perception, where the wallpaper and the woman studying it become one. The narrator finds that she can free her rebellious self from the bars that pattern the paper, but self-liberation of this kind becomes the imprisonment of the self in madness as she alienates herself from all that is outside herself. The narrator loses her sense of perspective, she loses her bearings in the world, and so although details are still presented realistically in the narrative, the meaning of them becomes obscured. The narrative questions the decipherability of the external physical world as basic categories of perception break down: real versus fantasy, living versus dead, actual versus imaginary, friend versus foe.

The narrator discovers two layers of reality: a superficial pattern of everyday details and a world of psychic repression that exists beneath this placid surface. Her sense of restriction finds a parallel in the contrasts between the closed room and the open garden view. At first she sees both realistically, but gradually her view becomes more personal and subjective as the figures in the garden become identified with the figure in the wallpaper. Finally, the narrator merges with this figure and, although this identification enables her to release the pent-up anger and frustration she experiences, still the madness that ensues is only another form of imprisonment. This hidden self which she can express only by identifying it with the wallpaper figure is perceived as mad in her society. She cannot articulate her sense of herself to her husband, although she tries, because she does not have a language adequate to counter the patriarchal terms in which he (and she) think. She struggles not only against the people and society around her but also with her own education, her indoctrination in the values of capitalist patriarchy. Consequently, the only outlet for her rebellion is to strip away the structure of illusions, the false and superficial patterns, that have kept her sense of individuality repressed.

From the beginning the wallpaper has been seen as angry and violent – with 'eyes' trying to 'read' her. She realises that the lurking woman is within her but covered and concealed by external patterns; thus the woman appears 'strangled'. As her realistic vision dissolves, she sees a more direct reflection of her own self in the wallpaper. Her emotions are projected on to her surroundings, where they are easier to cope with. Though she may try to elude the guilt she feels, there is no cure available in the world of the story for the emotional disorder she is suffering. The distortion of perception, her stripping away of the impositions of the external world, is a response to the rootlessness, isolation and constriction of her life. Physically and psychically she is destroyed by the impossibility of finding for herself a fixed and meaningful personal identity, embedded in a network of supportive and nurturing family relationships.

The paper on which she writes her journal is replaced by the wallpaper as her objective observations are replaced by subjective imaginings. This substitution indicates that her sense of self is shrinking, becoming uncertain and fragmented. Writing becomes increasing tiring to her and perhaps also threatening to what is left of her self-identity. Later, she withholds from writing down some details of her experience. The reader, like John and Jenny, is shut out of her private world. They have no part in that world for the same reasons that they are responsible for the impossibility of her position: they are the representatives of the patriarchy that has destroyed her. In the eyes of her husband it is she, and not society, who is responsible for her destruction. She has failed to produce conventional responses to experience, the kinds of responses that can be explained according to conventional ideas, and this failure leads to insanity. Yet from the point of view of the narrator – the perspective endorsed by the story itself – insanity follows inevitably from the rejection of those social conventions that are determined by men. Her attempts to resist the cultural mechanisms that reduce individual women to stereotypes by repressing their sense of individuality leads to her total rejection of the social world in favour of the only alternative available to her – a private world of madness.

The narrator's nascent sense of her own self-worth, her sense of herself as a distinct individual, threatens to contradict the fundamental principle of capitalist patriarchy: the coexistence of female economic dependence and female sexual identity. Women are inferior, therefore they are economically dependent upon men; because women are economically dependent upon men, they must be inferior. The image of an independent woman who perceives herself to be the equal of her husband is profoundly subversive and consequently cannot be permitted in a patriarchal society. As the narrator of 'The Yellow Wallpaper' discovers to her enormous cost, under patriarchy an independent woman is made the equivalent of an insane woman.

In *Women and Economics* (1898) Gilman proposed that by abolishing 'women's work', by making *all* labour available to both sexes, women could improve their status and become more productive as members of society. Domestic labour – cooking, cleaning, child-rearing – should be professionalised and socialised. Trained professionals should do the work traditionally done, unpaid, by women in the home and women should then move into the public world to take up the work of their choice. It is women's economic dependence inside marriage, the unpaid and so devalued work they perform in the home, that determines women's subordinate social status. In many of Gilman's short stories she depicts the consequences for individual women who become economically self-sufficient and thus transform themselves into autonomous and dignified individuals. But Gilman was *not* a Marxist feminist. She proposed strategic changes to the economic structure of patriarchy but she did not promote a wholesale restructuring of capitalism. Patriarchy should be reformed in order to allow women access to the capitalist economy, and in her fiction the women who liberate themselves find freedom as entrepreneurs and small-scale capitalists (small businesswomen, etc.). In the utopian novel *Herland*, for example, children are raised collectively by trained specialists, who profit financially from their expertise in child rearing. The notion that the capitalist economy is a gender-neutral arena is naive – women have found that paid work outside the home does not bring liberation or an end to oppression. Separate spheres ensured that the meaning and value of work remained unchanged even as more women than ever entered the work force (17% in 1900, nearly 22% by 1929). But women entered the so-called 'caring professions', clerical and domestic work, and wages were not equal even when the work done was equal. Female employment was specifically targeted during the Depression, with men demanding the few jobs available and legislation to reinforce this demand (according to the Federal Economy Act of 1933 only one member of a family could be employed by the government, for example).

Writing or communication is the only work the narrator is capable of performing and she is rigorously denied the opportunity to do it and, consequently, denied the chance to experience herself as productive. She has produced a child but the psychosis of post-natal depression prevents her fulfilling her prescribed role as mother. Instead, she aspires to perform men's work (writing) in stark contradiction of her social role. This 'unnatural' inversion of sexual roles is what the physicians (the narrator's husband and brother) diagnose as a 'nervous disorder'. John determines what is communicated. Writing is forbidden; he reads to her rather than permitting her to read to herself. The narrator surrenders the 'dead paper' of writing and instead focuses her interpretative energies upon the wallpaper. She becomes obsessed with the problem of meaning, of bringing the imaginative and the actual into relationship. The unacknowledged patterns of her own real life experience are symbolised by the paper patterns, and through the process of interpretation she discovers images of her own unacceptable situation. But this insight is not liberation: by decoding the paper images of her life she re-encodes them in her mind where they are inescapable. The imaginative and the actual become one as she becomes the woman in the wallpaper. She reads as a conventional woman, John as a conventional man; their interpretations are gender-determined. But their very conventionality leads them to a tragic misreading of their situation where the unconventional view would be the healthy perspective. The activity of writing is seen as potentially subversive but this potential to produce real social reactions is used by society to determine the social perceptions of its citizens. Gilman, then, uses writing to expand the perceptual and interpretative horizons of her readers (see her 1913 essay, 'Why I Wrote "The Yellow Wallpaper"').

Gilman encountered great difficulty in publishing 'The Yellow Wallpaper' and the story was neglected for much of this century. Gilman's achievement as a writer of fiction was fully recognised only as a consequence of the recent efforts of feminist literary critics who set out to restore the tradition of women's writing by rescuing such texts from oblivion. When 'The Yellow Wallpaper' *was* read, it was as a horror story; for example, it is included in a 1971 collection entitled *Ladies of Horror: Two Centuries of Supernatural Stories by the Gentle Sex* (Doubleday, 1971). The connection between insanity and the gender of the victim was ignored, as was the absence of the supernatural in the story. The story does belong to the genre of the Gothic novel, popularised by Edgar Allan Poe, but Gilman adapts her narrative to the expression of a feminine sensibility which is in conflict with masculine orthodoxy. The style of the narrative and the kind of psychological realism that Gilman employs so skilfully brought her into conflict with the orthodox forms of realism recommended by influential critics such as William Dean Howells. It is instructive, then, to consider in what ways Gilman's style of writing contradicted the fashionable style and how this relates to the question of gender.

Howells in *Criticism and Fiction* (1891) and *Novel-Writing and Novel-Reading* (1899) describes the characteristics of 'good' fiction:

> We start in our novels with something we have known of life, that is, with life itself; and then we go on and imitate what we have known of life. If we are very skilful and very patient we can *hide the joint*. But the joint is always there,

and on one side of it are real ground and real grass, and on the other are the painted images of ground and grass (Howells, in Baym, et al., 1994, vol.2 p. 241).

This skill involves creating an objective point of view, convincing characters who speak in actual colloquial language, who move in a specific historical and geographical environment, where the values and beliefs are recognisable, and avoiding melodramatic or sentimental effects. The style of realism promoted by Howells, through his very influential magazine pieces, emphasised the 'ordinary'. The novelist, as discussed by Howells, is invariably male, though Howells cites the work of Jane Austen and George Eliot as among the greatest achievements in the novel form. But Howells was blind to the gender bias in his prescriptions for good writing. The objective reality of which Howells writes as the subject of fiction is the world as perceived by men. In *Criticism and Fiction* he writes that the artist's success lies in '*his* relation to human nature, known to us all, which it is *his* privilege, *his* high duty, to interpret'. The 'human nature' which Howells assumes we all recognise is later identified as 'the mass of common *men*' (my italics). Howells is speaking from the male point of view which to him is 'natural' and 'universal'. He is not aware that his definitions preclude women from writing what he judges to be good fiction. Consequently, Howells is unable to see the worth in a form of realism such as 'The Yellow Wallpaper' which represents the world as it appears to a woman.

Writers like Gilman show that reality is not something that we can simply assume is universally understood and universally the same; instead, reality is something created by society through the operations of ideology. Reality is class-based and is different for the rich and the poor, men and women. One's experience of reality depends upon where one is placed in society. Reality resides not so much in the objective world as in the individual's perception. In 'The Yellow Wallpaper' Gilman portrays women's experience of reality as qualitatively different to men's, but assigns the cause of this difference to artificial gender distinctions and culturally-defined sex roles. This experience and the perceptions of the world to which it gives rise are alien to the dominant male reality which is defined as 'ordinary' and 'objective' perception. Gilman represents this conflict by using the Gothic form, adapted to her feminist purposes.

The Gothic form is suited to representing the unconscious, the subjective vision of the world, but where the world is the world of nightmare. The form emphasises separation from what is accepted as the everyday objective world, which Howells considered the only appropriate subject for fiction. The conflict between the values of society and the individual's ability to play a social role can be represented through the gap between subjective and objective realities. The very presence of two realities undermines the idea that a certain world exists. Therefore, by asking the reader to question the authenticity of the world, fiction written in the Gothic style can convey effectively a writer's protest against the constrictions of society.

In 'The Yellow Wallpaper' the conflict between society and the individual or objective and subjective realities is represented by a mind caught in an insanity-generating situation. The treatment to which the narrator is subjected is designed to make her docile and dependent (in conformity with her social role) through the technique of sensory deprivation. But such deprivation leads inevitably to insanity. So, at its most radical, the story asks us to consider whether conformity to gender roles is a kind of madness and whether our patriarchal society is based fundamentally on controlled insanity. Gilman is concerned with the insanity, the illogicality, of social injustice. In this instance she cites the absurdity of treating depression with deprivation strategies that are designed to deal with symptoms of nervous exhaustion. The 'treatment' described is less a form of medical treatment and more a means of controlling the way women relate to themselves, each other and the world. It becomes apparent that it will be when the narrator begins once more to talk and to think in ways that her physician-husband considers appropriate and 'sane' that she will be released from her physical imprisonment. So her perceptions and the way she expresses them are considered the real symptoms of her illness and the treatment prescribed is intended to rectify these symptoms.

Gilman suggests that woman's role in nineteenth-century American culture is linked to dominant ideological constructions of the world. The female perspective is an imaginative view that must be controlled and kept subordinate to the rational, common-sense, practical and objective worldview which supports the interests of nineteenth-century American men. As the story explores the tensions between the subjective and objective worlds it shows not that one is more real than the other but how a supportive set of family and community relationships are necessary for the accurate perception or construction of reality. Gilman exposes just how easy it is for the individual's relationship with the world to become warped. When established social roles are challenged or threatened, one's interpretation of physical surroundings can become distorted. The relationship between the individual and the world depends crucially upon relationships with other people. When a woman is unable to play her socially approved role of wife and mother then her entire network of socially-regulated relationships goes wrong and her perception of reality goes fundamentally awry. The psychological and physical health of individuals and the economic health of their societies depends upon universal justice in all social relationships.

Ultimately, the narrator of 'The Yellow Wallpaper' is not a reliable reporter of her experience; she is not aware of all of her own actions nor is she in control of her thoughts as her reason dissolves into madness. The 'smooch' on the wall is the result of her own crawling; the mark on her bedstead is from her biting. The distance between the image and its meaning foreshadows her own alienation from her wife-self as she increasingly becomes the paper woman. Her alienation from material reality, which has a material and ideological cause, becomes alienation from her self.

Marxist feminism allows us to identify in 'The Yellow Wallpaper' the creation of a distinct sexual class which is dispossessed and kept in a position of inferiority by the use of ideological and economic strategies of oppression. Female inferiority is not simply assumed: society insists upon the subordination of women to men and this gives rise to a social class that is impoverished in mind and body – symbolised in this novella by a horde of 'creeping women' who efface themselves in every conceivable way since only by denying themselves any social presence can they seek to ensure their survival.

References and Selected Further Reading

Althusser, Louis, 1971. 'Ideology and Ideological State Apparatuses', in *Lenin and Philosophy and Other Essays*, London: NLB.

Barrett, Michèle, 1980. *Women's Oppression Today: Problems in Marxist Feminist Analysis*, London: Verso Editions.

Baym, Nina, et al., ed., 1994. *The Norton Anthology of American Literature*, 4th edn. New York & London: W. W. Norton & Co.

Engels, Friedrich, 1884. *The Origin of the Family, Private Property, and the State*, New York: International Publishers, 1972.

Felski, Rita, 1990. *Beyond Feminist Aesthetics: Feminist Literature and Social Change*, Cambridge, MA: Harvard University Press.

Flax, Jane, 1981. 'Do Feminists Need Marxism?', in *Building Feminist Theory: Essays from 'Quest', A Feminist Quarterly*, New York: Longman, pp. 174–185.

Gilman, Charlotte Perkins, 1980. *The Charlotte Perkins Gilman Reader: The Yellow Wallpaper and Other Stories*, ed. Ann J. Lane. London: The Women's Press.

——, 1898. *Women and Economics: A Study of the Economic Relations Between Men and Women as a Factor in Social Evolution*, Mineola, NY: Dover Publications, 1998.

Goldman, Emma, 1970. *The Traffic in Women and Other Essays on Feminism*, Albion, CA: Times Change Press.

Hansen, Karen & Ilene J. Philipson, eds, 1990. *Women, Class and the Feminist Imagination: A Socialist-Feminist Reader*, Philadelphia: Temple University Press.

Hartsock, Nancy C. M., 1983. 'The Feminist Standpoint: Developing the Ground for a Specifically Feminist

Historical Materialism', rpt. in Nancy Tuana & Rosemarie Tong, eds, *Feminism and Philosophy: Essential Readings in Theory, Reinterpretation, and Application*, Boulder, CO: Westview Press, 1995, pp. 69–90.

Herndl, Diane Price, 1988. 'The Writing Cure: Charlotte Perkins Gilman, Anna O., and "Hysterical" Writing', *NWSA Journal*, vol. 1, no. 1 (Autumn), pp. 52–74.

Johnston, Georgia, 1992. 'Exploring Lack and Absence in the Body/Text: Charlotte Perkins Gilman Prewriting Irigaray', *Women's Studies*, vol. 21, no. 1, pp. 75–86.

Karpinski Joanne B., ed., 1992. *Critical Essays on Charlotte Perkins Gilman*, New York: G. K. Hall.

Kuhn, Annette & Ann Marie Wolpe, eds, 1978. *Feminism and Materialism: Women and Modes of Production*, Boston: Routledge & Kegan Paul.

Lane, Ann J., ed., 1980. *The Charlotte Perkins Gilman Reader: The Yellow Wallpaper and Other Stories*, London: The Women's Press.

Lanser, Susan S., 1989. 'Feminist Criticism, "The Yellow Wall Paper", and the Politics of Color in America', *Feminist Studies*, vol. 15, no. 3 (Fall), pp. 415–441.

Robinson, Lillian S., 1978. *Sex, Class and Culture*, Bloomington: Indiana University Press.

——, 1991. 'Killing Patriarchy: Charlotte Perkins Gilman, the Murder Mystery, and Post-Feminist Propaganda', *Tulsa Studies in Women's Literature*, vol. 10, no. 2 (Fall), pp. 273–285.

Showalter, Elaine, 1989. *Sister's Choice: Tradition and Change in American Women's Writing: The Clarendon Lectures*, Oxford: Oxford University Press, 1991, 'American Female Gothic'.

Shumaker, Conrad, 1985. '"Too Terribly Good to be Printed": Charlotte Perkins Gilman's "The Yellow Wallpaper"', *American Literature*, vol. 57, no. 4 (December), pp. 588–599.

Veeder, William, 1988. 'Who Is Jane? The Intricate Feminism of Charlotte Perkins Gilman', *Arizona Quarterly*, vol. 44, no. 3 (Autumn), pp. 40–79.

3

Gender and Consciousness: Psychoanalytic Feminism and Kate Chopin

This chapter begins with a survey of psychoanalytic feminist theorists, focusing upon Carol Gilligan's *In a Different Voice* (1982), Jane Flax's essay 'Political Philosophy and the Patriarchal Unconscious: A Psychoanalytic Perspective on Epistemology and Metaphysics' (1983) and Jane Gallop's essay 'The Father's Seduction' from *The Daughter's Seduction* (1982). Theoretical concepts explored here include: the Oedipus Complex; Imaginary and Symbolic Orders; patriarchal binary logic; language and the subconscious (écriture féminine). In the section that follows this theoretical survey, I turn to the psychoanalytic feminist analysis of Kate Chopin's *The Awakening*.

Survey of Psychoanalytic Feminist Theory

Summary of Psychoanalytic Feminist Principles

In *The Second Sex*, Simone de Beauvoir famously commented, 'One is not born a woman; one becomes one' – psychoanalytic feminists ask how this process of 'becoming' actually occurs. They ask how it is that a woman can come to identify with patriarchal interests, and set about answering this question by investigating the subconscious structure of gender identity. Feminist psychoanalytic theory builds upon the work of Sigmund Freud, especially his theory of the Oedipal stage of psychosexual development. The Oedipus Complex begins in the pre-Oedipal stage when the child experiences no distinction between itself and the world and is therefore pure ego. The Oedipal crisis comes about when

94

the boy discovers that he is different to his mother (he has a penis) but he is the same as his father. His mother is perceived as castrated through her lack of a penis and this symbolises the inferiority of the feminine, the child's love for which threatens to incite his father's anger and rejection. As a result, the boy shifts his allegiance and his love from the powerless mother to the authority of the father; in this way, the boy child differentiates himself from the surrounding world and in the process develops both a superego (social consciousness) and an id (instincts). The boy, then, emerges from the Oedipal stage in possession of a masculine gender identity.

The Oedipal stage is more complicated for girls who do not perceive any difference between themselves and their mothers. Freud argues that the girl will see her mother's lack of a penis as a sign that she has been castrated and this will give rise to 'penis envy'. The girl then shifts her love from mother to father, and develops a gender identity in response to the demands of the father's (patriarchal) culture. However, she never completely loses her pre-Oedipal identification with the mother. This places the girl in a position of ambivalence where she belongs completely to neither the mother nor the father but still she seeks to belong to the powerful masculine culture. According to theorists like Nancy Chodorow, as a consequence of this psychosexual development girls are less individuated than boys, with more fluid ego boundaries. So gender identity is much less secure for girls than for boys after the Oedipal stage. The Oedipus Complex produces 'the male-identified woman' who betrays her residual allegiance to her mother in order to promote and serve the interests of the father. In both cases, the passage through the Oedipal stage creates a gendered ego structure, which means that throughout life how we experience ourselves is inseparable from how we experience our sexuality: 'I' is then always a gendered term.

Feminists have reinterpreted and taken issue with Freudian theory, but even more than the writings of Freud himself they have engaged with the work of Jacques Lacan who offers a revision of Freudian psychoanalysis. Lacan renames the pre-Oedipal phase of development as the 'Imaginary Order', where there is no difference and no language to express the experience of difference between self and the outside world. But the Oedipal crisis brings about that perception of difference between self and Other, and a fundamental element of the entry into the post-Oedipal or 'Symbolic Order' is the acquisition of the father's language. Language offers a substitute for and a way of expressing the loss of a primal, maternal identification with the world. This experience of loss and the desire to recapture that sense of primal continuity are repressed and so create the unconscious. The unconscious does not remain entirely repressed but erupts into language, creating meaningless, contradictory expressions. All human society and culture is dominated by the Symbolic Order which itself represents a lack, the loss of the unity of the Imaginary Order. The Imaginary is gendered by its close association with the mother; the Symbolic is the realm of the father: the public, objective world of language and reason and social relations. To remain in the Imaginary would be to reject society in favour of a psychotic existence, though in reality we are never offered a choice. Gender identity is created by the entry into the Symbolic from the Imaginary; both boys and girls retain a desire to recapture the primary identity with the mother but girls retain a stronger allegiance to the Imaginary, the realm of the feminine, than do boys. The patriarchal Symbolic Order is associated with singularity, unicity, symmetry and sameness; the feminine Imaginary Order is associated with multiplicity, difference and asymmetry.

Mother and Father; pre-Oedipal and post-Oedipal stages; Imaginary and Symbolic Orders; primal and civilised identities; nature and culture; psychosis and rationality – these oppositions structure the processes whereby individuals are initiated into human society and acquire gender identities, language, social relationships, and the like. In other words, this is the process whereby we become subjects. But we become subjects in the terms offered by these binary categories, categories that are based on a fundamental distinction between man and woman, positive and negative, where woman always occupies the inferior, subordinate position. These binary oppositions are, then, arranged hierarchically and exist in an antagonistic relationship to each other.

The effort to subvert the binary oppositions upon which patriarchal gender identities depend is described by the French feminist Hélène Cixous as 'feminine writing' or 'écriture féminine'. This is a style of writing that seeks to recapture the pleasures of the Imaginary, which undermines the rationality of the Symbolic, fractures the closed state of binary oppositions, and seeks to construct an open-ended textuality. Feminine writing, then, rejects masculine reason and the logical use of language in favour of the fantastic, the grotesque, the insane use of language. Cixous makes an emphatic distinction between the sex of the writing and the biological sex of the author – men can write écriture féminine just as women can (James Joyce and Jean Genet are among examples she gives). Feminine writing then embraces the 'feminine' side of the binary divide and seeks to unsettle the entire binary system by upsetting the established hierarchy it expresses. But écriture féminine is a style of writing – it is not defined by subject matter – and so it is removed from the 'real' world of feminine oppression and discrimination. However, Cixous does make the point that entry into the masculine order of the Symbolic requires that a single, monolithic gender identity be adopted and this denies or represses the multiple nature of human personality. Cixous argues that men and women are essentially bisexual but monosexuality (heterosexuality) is demanded of us as part of the process of socialisation. The liberation of the self into an authentic multitude of personalities is akin to the liberation of language from the strictures of patriarchal categories into free imagistic association.

Arguments among feminists become especially fierce over the question of whether there is such a thing as 'femaleness' and what that 'gender essence' might be, where it might come from. The radical rejection of 'femaleness' and the associations with the bodily determination of sexuality that it carries has been severely criticised by cultural feminists who see the category of 'woman' as fundamental to the common recognition of shared oppression among all women. For psychoanalytic feminists, 'femaleness' is viewed as an oppressive concept that denies the plural nature of all human con-sciousness by forcing individuals into single identities. This coercion is masculine, so the aim of feminism must be to counter and abolish this oppression of both men and women. This interpretation of the concept of 'femaleness' is attacked by cultural feminists because the assault on the category of the feminine denies the basis for solidarity, for community action and struggle.

The opposition between psychoanalytic and cultural feminism is reflected in the distinct preferences of each in the kinds of literature read and promoted: psychoanalytic feminism prefers fantasy, avant-garde writing that represents the self as fractured and fragmented rather than realist texts with a clear sociological context. Psychoanalytic feminism prefers a literature of ideas and issues rather than characters and relationships. The concept of the fragmented self offers the opportunity to create a new self in the freedom of isolation. Psychoanalytic feminism sees division itself as potentially liberating; cultural feminist approaches see division as the instrument of oppression, as the personal is divorced from the political and gender oppression is rendered invisible. In psychoanalytic feminism the focus is on the individual female consciousness: the source of oppression is the symbolic power of the Father who defines 'woman' as an object of exchange, of definition, originating in childhood. Three prominent psychoanalytic feminist thinkers are Carol Gilligan, Jane Flax and Jane Gallop; in what follows I look more closely at the work of these women.

Carol Gilligan, In a Different Voice: Psychological Theory and Women's Development *(1982)*

Carol Gilligan's study begins with the perception that in existing psychological literature, there is a disparity between women's experience and the representation of human development. Rather than explain this disparity as a sign of women's problematical relationship to the model of human development, Gilligan suggests that the problem lies with the model itself and its representation of 'a limitation in the conception of human condition, an omission of certain truths about human life' (Gilligan, 1982, p. 2). Gilligan does not set out to define the truth or essence of women's experience; the 'different voice' of her title is linked with women through her observation, but rather than offer a theory of feminine development Gilligan is concerned to present two distinct 'voices' that articulate two distinct modes of thought which lie at the heart of the interpretative problem with which Gilligan begins. Women appear to comprise the group most frequently omitted from studies of 'human' development and it is this omission that Gilligan takes as the main focus of her efforts. As she remarks of previous studies: '[i]mplicitly adopting the male life as the norm, they have tried to fashion women out of a masculine cloth' (p. 6). She acknowledges that factors of culture, history, social class and power as well as biology affect the constitution of these 'voices', but she limits the scope of her study by claiming: 'My interest lies in the interaction of experience and thought, in different voices and the dialogues to which they give rise, in the way we listen to ourselves and to others, in the stories we tell about our lives' (p. 2). Three studies provide the basis for Gilligan's investigation: what she calls the 'college student study', the 'abortion decision study' and the 'rights and responsibilities study'. These separate studies each focus upon women's identity formation and moral development through adolescence and adulthood.

The masculine bias in psychological accounts of human development, Gilligan traces to Freud and his theory of the Oedipus complex, in terms of which female pre-Oedipal attachment to the mother is seen as the cause of women's developmental failure:

> Having tied the formation of the superego or conscience to castration anxiety, Freud considered women to be deprived by nature of the impetus for a clear-cut Oedipal resolution. Consequently, women's superego – the heir to the Oedipus complex – was compromised: it was never 'so inexorable, so impersonal, so independent of its emotional origins as we require it to be in men'. From this observation of difference, that 'for women the level of what is ethically

normal is different from what it is in men', Freud concluded that women 'show less justice than men, that they are less ready to submit to the great exigencies of life, that they are more often influenced in their judgements by feelings of affection or hostility' (Gilligan, 1982, p. 7).

This account provides a powerful example of the masculine bias to which Gilligan refers; Freud's theory of feminine development is fitted to his theory of human (masculine) development and is modified to make his theory of the Oedipus Complex coherent and consistent: 'a problem in theory became cast as a problem in women's development, and the problem in women's development was located in their experience of relationships' (p. 8). Women are assumed to have weaker ego-boundaries, to be more vulnerable to psychosis (being 'influenced in their judgements by feelings of affection or hostility'), because of the incomplete separation from the mother which is the incomplete resolution of the Oedipus Complex. Masculine development is closely tied to separation from the mother and individuation in gender terms (separation from the female opposite); femininity however is defined in terms of attachment to the mother and is threatened by separation. Gilligan goes on to explain how the 'quality of embeddedness in social interaction and personal relationships that characterises women's lives in contrast to men's, however, becomes not only a descriptive difference but also a developmental liability when the milestones of childhood and adolescent development in the psychological literature are markers of increasing separation. Women's failure to separate then becomes by definition a failure to develop' (pp. 8–9).

Gilligan highlights the expansion of Freud's theory of psychosexual development by Erik Erikson in the 1950s and 1960s. The developmental stage of adolescence is for boys characterised by the establishment of an autonomous, enterprising self, based upon the necessary industry and mastery of cultural technology necessary for a successful adulthood. Contrastingly, a girl, as Gilligan describes this stage of Erikson's scheme: '[s] holds her identity in abeyance as she prepares to attract the man by whose name she will be

Jane Flax, 'Political Philosophy and Patriarchal Unconscious: A Psychoanalytic Perspective on Epistemology and Metaphysics' (1983)

Where Carol Gilligan exposes the masculine bias in mainstream psychoanalysis, Jane Flax is concerned to reveal the same bias at work in the tradition of Western philosophy. Flax argues that Western philosophy represents the consequences of the denial by male philosophers of their own psychosexual experiences. This means that the masculine values of individuation and separation are given precedence over those feminine values of nurturance and connectedness. Flax argues: 'Both individual male development and patriarchy are partially rooted in a need to deny the power and autonomy of women. This need arises in part out of early infantile experience. The experience of maturing in a family in which only women mother insures that patriarchy will be reproduced' (Flax, 1983, p. 218). The distinction between male and female, and the subordination of the feminine, necessary to patriarchy, is perpetuated through the Oedipal crisis which is generated by the child's early identification with the mother. These early experiences of the pre-Oedipal and Oedipal crises must in course be denied and with them the process of shifting identification and allegiance from mother to father. Flax explains:

> Males under patriarchy must repress early infantile experience for several reasons: patriarchy by definition imputes political, moral and social *meanings* to sexual differentiation. Women are considered inferior in all these dimensions. The social world is thus both gender differentiated and stratified. ... Differentiation need not lead to stratification, but under patriarchy it does and must. Men want very much to attain membership in the community of men, in order to attain both individual identity and social privilege, even at great psychic pain. Patriarchal society depends upon the proper engendering of persons, since gender is one of the bases of social organization (p. 218).

The attainment of individual masculine identity in this way requires the rejection of the mother and all for which she stands. This is a deeply problematical process because the self is formed in relation with other people and, for the young child, especially with the mother who is the primary giver of care. According to Flax, the child is originally feminine, in psychic terms, and must actively become masculine. 'In order to do so he must become *not female*, since under patriarchy gender is an exclusionary category. He must repress part of himself – his identification with the mother and memories of his relation with her (which are now internalised) and identify with the father, who as an adult has repressed his female self' (p. 218). To aid this identification the son can devalue his mother and all that is associated with her, and so reduce the power of the feminine aspects of his own psyche. What the son finds is that this devaluation is mirrored and reinforced by the devaluation of the feminine in the social world. Under patriarchy, Flax notes, '[b]ecoming aware of gender means recognizing that men and women are not valued equally, that in fact, men are socially more esteemed than women. Being engendered, therefore, entails a coming to awareness of and to some extent internalizing asymmetries of power and esteem' (p. 222). Consequently, all that is associated with the infantile experience of the mother is repressed: nature, the body, feelings.

The repression of the feminine must be as complete as possible, in order to keep separate infantile memories from the conscious self; otherwise, Flax warns, 'it would threaten masculine identity and ego boundaries' (p. 218). But this repression can never be complete in this way. Instead, psychic experience is characterised by a profound ambivalence that has its origin in the twin desire for and fear of separation from the mother and the desire for and fear of fusion with the mother. This produces, both in the child and in the child within the adult, 'ambivalence about growing up and taking responsibility for its self and its actions in a world in which complete knowledge and control is not possible' (p. 219). In the attempt to deal with this ambivalence the child can transform the mother into a 'bad' object (or split her into 'good' and 'bad' objects) that is responsible for feelings of pain and confusion, and thus keep these experiences separate from the adult feelings of control over the external world. In Flax's view, this accounts for the binary division between mind and body, subject and object, knowledge and sense, that underpin patriarchal Western epistemology and metaphysics. And it is this binary thinking that is the target of necessary feminist revision. The subject matter of philosophy is 'the experience and actions of male human beings who were created in and through patriarchal social relations. ... This experience is seen not as typically male but constitutive of human experience itself' (p. 219). Thus, a feminist critique of the Western philosophical tradition reveals the inadequacy of philosophy to account for the experiences of women and children as well as revealing the misogynistic assumptions that underlie inherited concepts of knowledge (epistemology) and being (ontology).

Flax goes on to demonstrate a feminist psychoanalytic critique of Plato, Descartes, Hobbes and Rousseau, showing how '[f]eminist philosophy thus represents the return of the repressed, of the exposure of the particular social roots of all apparently abstract and universal knowledge' (p. 220). By bringing together the psychoanalytic concept of the unconscious and the feminist critique of patriarchal philosophy, Flax is able to expose the particularity of assumed universals and to reveal the extent of the conse-quences for both personal and social experience. As she observes, 'The repression of early infantile experience is reflected in and provides part of the grounding for our rela-tionship with nature and our political life, especially the separation of public and private, the obsession with power and domination and the consequent impoverishment of political life and theories of it. The repression of our passions and their transformation into something dangerous and shameful, the inability to achieve true reciprocity and cooperative relations with others, and the translation of difference into inferiority and superiority can also be traced in part to this individual and collective act of repression and denial' (p. 225).

The exposure of patriarchal bias within influential philo-sophical models of knowledge and being is only the starting point for the thorough revision of theories of human nature and politics for which Jane Flax calls. All bodies of knowledge, including those like Marxism and psychoanalysis that claim to be emancipatory, that have been developed under patriarchy, must be analysed for the absent feminine viewpoint; this feminine perspective alone is insufficient to provide the basis for theory but it must be incorporated into theory and its limitations transcended. Thus, a new feminist practice is required. 'Nothing less than a new stage of human development is required in which reciprocity can emerge for the first time as the basis of social relations' (p. 237).

Jane Gallop, The Daughter's Seduction: Feminism and Psychoanalysis *(1982)*

The essay 'The Father's Seduction', from Jane Gallop's book *The Daughter's Seduction*, engages with the influential psychoanalytic work of the French feminist Luce Irigaray and specifically Irigaray's essay 'Blind Spot in an Old Dream of Symmetry'. The essay takes on the logical structure of a series of Chinese boxes: in her essay, Irigaray uses Freud's analytic technique to analyse Freud's work; here, Gallop uses Irigaray's technique to analyse Irigaray. Gallop sets out to expose the extent to which feminist psychoanalytic thinking is enmeshed in a patriarchal language or system of representation. In this way, Gallop draws upon Lacan's idea of the patriarchal Symbolic Order as opposed to the feminine Imaginary Order to explore Irigaray's use of images of unicity/multiplicity, sameness/difference, symmetry/asymmetry. The symbolic economy of the same, of the One, is the rule of the phallus and Gallop seeks to expose the points at which Irigaray's feminist analysis becomes complicit with the rule of the Father by lapsing into phallocentric logic and language: 'It is the rule of the Phallus as standard for any sexuality which denigrates women, and makes any relation between the sexes impossible, any relation between two modalities of desire, between two desires unthinkable. The rule of the Phallus is the reign of the One, of Unicity' (Gallop, 1982, p. 496). Gallop, through her reading of Irigaray, discovers in Freud's writing the suggestion that both masculinity and femininity do not exist independently of the discourse of the phallus; but she observes that the 'difference ... between the phallic suppression of masculinity and the phallic suppression of femininity is that the phallic represents (even if inaccurately) the masculine and not the feminine' (p. 497). This representation is achieved by the dissociation of the idea of masculinity from the materiality of the masculine body. 'By giving up their bodies, men gain power – the power to theorize, to represent themselves, to exchange women, to reproduce themselves and mark their offspring with their name' (p. 497). The sacrifice of bodily pleasure is carried through Freud's theory of sexuality where sexuality is theorised in terms of the sexual (reproductive) function rather than in terms of sexual pleasure.

This model describes masculine psychosexual development, a model to which the feminine is assimilated or subjected – and is found wanting. Gallop highlights Freud's description of the female child in the phallic phase and his insistence that in this phase girls identify the clitoris as the primary sexual organ (analogous to the boy's identification of the penis). Freud reduces the girl's genitalia to her clitoris in order to sustain the coherence and consistency of his theory. Gallop comments, 'The girl is assimilated to a male model, male history and, "naturally," found lacking. The condition of that assimilation is the reduction of any possible complexity, plural sexuality, to the one, the simple, in this case to the phallomorphic clitoris' (p. 498). In her castrated state, the girl-woman represents a source of reassurance, a guarantee against the masculine castration anxiety: 'she can mirror him, provide him with a representation of himself which calms his fears and phobias about (his own potential) otherness and difference, about some "other view" which might not support his narcissistic overinvestment in his penis' (p. 499). Thus, the male castration anxiety is kept at bay so long as the perception of otherness, and specifically feminine otherness, is kept under control. This renders problematic the feminine experience of the Oedipal crisis. The girl's desire for her father, her expression of allegiance to the father rather than the mother, is the desire for personal value which can be derived only from the Father in a phallocratic culture. However, because to desire otherness, the feminine other sex, would awaken the castration anxiety, the father must refuse to be seduced by his daughter. This leaves open the opportunity for the daughter to express her desire to please by submitting to the phallocratic law of the Father: 'The daughter submits to the father's rule, which prohibits the father's desire, the father's penis, out of the desire to seduce the father by doing his bidding and thus pleasing him' (p. 499). Gallop describes Irigaray's perception that this vicious circle underpins feminine oppression; feminism must seek not only to 'change a woman's definition, identity, name as well as the foundations of her economic status' but must also undo the vicious circle 'by which the desire for the father's desire (for his penis) causes her to submit to the father's law, which denies his desire/penis ...' (p. 499). But this does not explain why women become complicit in this oppressive set of relations. In this connection, Gallop turns to Irigaray's phrase, 'the seductive function of the law itself', which describes the prohibition of sexual consummation between father and daughter as a mechanism by which the seduction of the daughter by the law of the father is prolonged indefinitely. In this way, the power of the law, and of the father, is sustained indefinitely. The prohibitive law also protects the father from his own attraction to the feminine otherness of the daughter and from his castration anxiety which is awakened by this otherness.

> The father gives his daughter his law and protects himself from her desire for his body, protects himself from his body. For it is only the law – and not the body – which constitutes his as patriarch. Paternity is corporeally uncertain, without evidence. But patriarchy compensates for that with the law which marks each child with the father's name as his exclusive property (p. 503).

Thus the law disguises the economy of sexual desire. This is the law of univocity or the One, the law of reason and rationality, precision and singular identity. Through operations of patriarchal law, the daughter is given an identity; even if, as Gallop notes, 'it is not her own, even if it blots out her feminine specificity' (p. 505). Also sacrificed is feminine desire, the multivocality and asymmetry and plurality that would challenge the law of the One that is the law of the Father.

Psychoanalytic Feminism in Praxis

In the following section, Kate Chopin's *The Awakening* is analysed in psychoanalytic feminist terms. The discussion of Kate Chopin's work focuses upon the themes of maternity versus paternity and the structuring of feminine identity. These themes are explored in terms of Edna's personal development; the opposition between maternity and creativity that is explored in the novel; and images of solitude, autonomy and death. In *The Awakening*, Edna Pontellier enacts the feminine Oedipal crisis; caught between Imaginary and Symbolic orders, she rejects her patriarchal gender identity but she is unable to embrace the feminine except in death. The narrative structure alternates between lyricism and realism as Chopin charts Edna's developing consciousness, and Chopin's use of symbolism of the sea; of shadows; of music; of animal sensuality; and of the rituals of eating, sleeping and gambling articulates the profound psychological drama that underlies and gives rise to the events of the narrative.

Kate Chopin, The Awakening

The significance of the title of *The Awakening* is apparently a simple matter: a young wife is awakened to her sexual needs that cannot be fulfilled within the confines of her conventional marriage. But more than this, Edna Pontellier is awakened to a yearning for freedom, a relation to and understanding of herself that she has not been aware of missing in the past. Edna's adolescent desires have been directed outward – we are told of the string of infatuations she had enjoyed before her marriage – but she has no corresponding desires for herself, no sense of personal integrity, to balance these relations with others. Edna has identified with the masculine interests of her father who, the narrator remarks, had managed or 'coerced' his wife into her early grave. This identification with her father's desires leads Edna to respect the conventions her father respects and to conform to the social pressures he perceives. She then marries a husband who is her father's equal in terms of observing and respecting social custom – and requiring the same of Edna. Thus, when Edna is awakened to the hidden potentialities she possesses, it is the yearning for freedom and the desire to overcome the limitations that are imposed on her from outside that determine her actions. This adds another dimension to the significance of the title, because Edna is awakened to the nature and extent of those social limitations that are placed upon her personal autonomy. It is from a very modest beginning that Edna develops her aspirations of freedom and autonomy. She had thought it impossible that she would even learn to swim and yet, that summer at the fashionable resort of Grand Isle, she finds that she can indeed swim:

> she was like the little tottering, stumbling, clutching child, who of a sudden realizes its powers, and walks for the first time alone, boldly and with over-confidence. She could have shouted for joy. She did shout for joy, as with a sweeping stroke or two she lifted her body to the surface of the water (Chopin, 1899, p. 36).

The sense of physical exhilaration that comes from the triumph of her will over her body introduces Edna to the possibility that other seemingly impossible things might be available to her. This dawning awareness transforms her attitude toward all aspects of her life; the family physician is the first to observe in detail the difference between the old, conventional Edna and the new: he 'noted a subtle change which had transformed her from the listless woman he had known into a being who, for the moment, seemed palpitant with the forces of life' (p. 92).

Chopin views her heroine ironically – her death is not a tragic loss; Edna is an ordinary and typical rather than gifted and unique woman. Her friend, Madame Ratignolle, tells her that '[I]n some way you seem like a child to me, Edna. You seem to act without a certain amount of reflection which is necessary in this life' (p. 127). It is true that Edna acts largely on impulse or caprice, but it is also true that she does not seek to analyse her own conscious and unconscious motivations. She has pretensions to being an artist but is warned by Mademoiselle Reisz, in words that return to her at the end of the narrative, that a true artist must not only possess innate gifts that cannot be learned but also must have 'the courageous soul': 'the soul that dares and defies' (p. 84). But Edna's struggle for sexual and personal emancipation is still very significant. Edna Pontellier frees herself from her social obligations in order to pursue her desire for individual autonomy but she herself is unable to develop a deep understanding of her situation. She is unable to explain to her husband, and Léonce understands no more clearly than she does, the changes that are taking place in her:

> It sometimes entered Mr. Pontellier's mind to wonder if his wife were not growing a little unbalanced mentally. He could see plainly that she was not herself. That is, he could not see that she was becoming herself and daily casting aside that fictitious self which we assume like a garment with which to appear before the world (p. 75).

Edna asks only that he leave her alone, that he refrain from questioning her behaviour, that he no longer demand that she display that conventional feminine submission that has been one of the foundations of their marriage. Her attempt to explain to the Doctor, like her earlier attempts to verbalise the changes she is experiencing, is largely inarticulate. She tries to explain: ' "I want to be let alone. Nobody has any right – except children, perhaps – and even then, it seems to me – or it did seem – " She felt that her speech was voicing the incoherency of her thoughts, and stopped abruptly' (p. 147).

In spite of her awakening and subsequent transformation of her life, Edna does not surrender her deepest, patriarchally inscribed, romantic fantasies; when she and Mademoiselle Reisz speculate about the reason for Robert Lebrun's return they do so within the paradigm of conventional romance. Edna is the object of Robert's affection who is 'not free to belong to him' (p. 106); Edna loves him for inexplicable, almost mystical reasons. Yet it is the right not to belong to any man, and especially not her husband, that Edna struggles to achieve. She does not realise her allegiance to the ideology of patriarchal romance, nor does Edna perceive the social dimension of her experiences; that is, the social network in which the gender roles that are imposed upon her are determined. Edna explains this in part as the consequence of the foreign Creole culture into which she has married and which she imperfectly understands. Even Madame Ratignolle is aware that Edna is different in this respect and she fears that Edna may not understand the conventions and social habits by which Creoles live. Edna rejects the constraints imposed upon her by her marriage, yet she imposes comparable constraints upon her lover; she wants to possess Robert in ways that she will not permit Léonce to possess her. Once she has Robert's declaration of love, 'She could picture at that moment no greater bliss on earth than possession of the beloved one' (p. 148). The narrator suggests that Edna's quest for self-determination takes the form of a rejection of civilisation; her awakening appears to the Doctor in terms of the image she evokes of 'a beautiful, sleek animal waking up in the sun' (p. 92) and the narrator observes that the attraction she feels, half-unwillingly, for Arobin appeals 'to the animalism that stirred impatiently within her' (p. 103).

Edna's awakening is directed not externally towards her society or towards the ideology of romance that is a part of her patriarchal culture; rather, her transformation acts upon her sense of herself as an individual:

> Every step which she took towards relieving herself from obligations added to her strength and expansion as an individual. She began to look with her own eyes; to see and to apprehend the deeper undercurrents of life. No longer was she content to 'feed upon the opinion' when her own soul had invited her (p. 124).

A psychoanalytical perspective enables us to see that Edna Pontellier is enacting the feminine Oedipal crisis – she is caught between the Imaginary and Symbolic Orders; she rejects her patriarchal gender identity, especially her relations with her father and his primary symbolic representative – her husband – yet is unable to embrace the feminine fully except in death, in her return to water – the feminine element. The family physician, Doctor Mandelet, when consulted by Léonce Pontellier about his wife's altered behaviour, comments on the relationship between women and psychologists: 'Woman, my dear friend, is a very peculiar and delicate organism – a sensitive and highly organized woman, such as I know Mrs. Pontellier to be, is especially peculiar. It would require an inspired psychologist to deal successfully with them' (p. 87). Self-reflexive comments such as this should not be interpreted as deterrents to a psychoanalytic approach to Edna's story. Indeed, the Doctor's comments reveal him to be a part of Edna's problem, a part of the world of the Father, of masculine authority and male-determined relationships, to which she is trying to find an alternative. Edna rejects her formative identification with the Father but she has to seek a feminine alternative within her patriarchal culture.

The narrative is structured according to the phases of Edna's psychosexual development. We are told that Edna was motherless as a child and this explains to some extent her reserve and self-containment. While she is attracted to Adèle Ratignolle, she holds herself aloof from the other women at Grand Isle. The narrator explains that '[e]ven as a child she had lived her own small life all within herself. At a very early period she had apprehended instinctively the dual life – that outward existence which conforms, the inward life which questions' (p. 18). This observation can be interpreted as an indication that Edna's Oedipal development was arrested by the death of her mother and the consequent absence of the mother figure during this formative period. She shifts her psychosexual allegiance from the absent mother to the authoritative father but she is left with no model of feminine gender construction. The identification with the father teaches Edna about the 'outward existence which conforms';

Edna is a dutiful daughter and, at first, she is also a dutiful wife and mother. When her father comes to visit, the narrator observes that '[s]he was not very warmly or deeply attached to him, but they had certain tastes in common, and when together they were companionable' (p. 89). Yet when Edna advises Mrs Highcamp and Alcée Arobin about race horses, drawing on her childhood familiarity with the horses of Kentucky, she unconsciously adopts the manner of her father: she 'did not perceive that she was talking like her father as the sleek geldings ambled in review before them' (p. 98). And at the end, as she is about to die and as 'the old terror' of isolation and solitude returns briefly to her, it is her father's voice that Edna recalls (p. 153). It is not, as in Freud's terms, penis envy that causes Edna to turn to her father and away from her mother; her mother's death removes from the developing child's purview the opportunity of returning to a residual pre-Oedipal identification with her mother. In place of the feminine gender model, Edna encounters death and the other half of the life of conformity which is life on the Father's terms: the feminine 'inward life which questions'. Edna has experienced the pre-Oedipal identification with the feminine which is the complete merger with the world through pure ego; she has moved through the Oedipal stage of separation from the feminine and the adoption of fixed ego-limits. This means that her dealings with the world and with others are regulated by social laws and conventions, conventions which include the regulation of gender relations and, especially, control of the feminine.

It is Madame Ratignolle who awakens Edna to a new awareness of her feminine sexuality; their relationship is erotic yet maternal. Edna is attracted to the 'excessive physical charm of the Creole' (p. 18) and her physical expressiveness. Adèle presides at Grand Isle over a little society of what the narrator calls 'mother-women' (p. 10), deliberately excluding Edna from that category. These women are intensely conservative in their identification with the feminine role prescribed for them: 'They were women who idolized their children, worshiped their husbands, and esteemed it a holy privilege to efface themselves as individuals and grow wings as ministering angels' (p. 10).

The society of Grand Isle is intensely feminine in this way, and Madame Ratignolle articulates the conservative feminine values of Creole culture. But it is in the company of Madame Ratignolle that she becomes 'Edna' rather than 'Mrs Pontellier'. In this intensely feminine environment, surrounded by so many quasi-Mother figures, Edna begins to shift her allegiance from the masculine world of patriarchal relations towards the unknown realm of the feminine.

She takes possession of herself, where before she had allowed herself to be one of her husband's possessions, like the silver, chinaware and other household possessions that he so proudly enjoys. Edna tries to discuss this issue of possession versus self-possession with Madame Ratignolle but to no avail; as the narrator remarks, 'the two women did not appear to understand each other or to be talking the same language' (p. 62). Madame Ratignolle cannot comprehend that there might be something more that a mother could sacrifice for her children beyond her life; Edna argues that while she would willingly give all her money or even die for her children, she would not surrender her self for their sake: she tries to explain, 'I wouldn't give myself. I can't make it more clear; it's only something which I am beginning to comprehend, which is revealing itself to me' (p. 62). It is only after she has decided to break with her husband, to move to a small house for which she herself can pay, with the income from her paintings and her win at the races, that Edna begins to consider the deeper motivation for this separation: 'she had resolved never again to belong to another than herself' (p. 106). And when she and Robert finally declare their love, Edna dismisses his concern that she is not available to him because she is the wife of another man:

> I am not one of Mr. Pontellier's possessions to dispose of or not. I give myself where I choose. If he were to say, 'Here, Robert, take her and be happy; she is yours', I should laugh at you both (p. 143).

But Robert is disconcerted by her response, by the idea that she would not be the possession of any man. It is only her romantic talk about how they will live, living only for each other that puts his mind at rest.

Where Madame Ratignolle offers Edna a nascent identification with the feminine, it is Mademoiselle Reisz who encourages her to discard the masculine social conventions and prejudices with which she has identified for so long. Mademoiselle Reisz is a renegade in Creole culture who violates all rules relating to conventional femininity and feminine consciousness; she awakens Edna's spirit and loosens the repressed passion Edna feels for Robert, but she also releases metaphysical longings that go beyond the sexual and perhaps symbolise for Edna a lost continuity with the unified world of the pre-Oedipal stage. Through Mademoiselle Reisz, and especially the music she plays, Edna rediscovers an additional dimension of her identification with the feminine which is the Imaginary Order, the pre-linguistic relation to the world. When Mademoiselle Reisz plays for her at Grand Isle, Edna expects that the music will conjure up vivid images of non-verbal experience: 'She waited in vain. She saw no pictures of solitude, of hope, of longing, or of despair. But the very passions themselves were aroused within her soul, swaying it, lashing it, as the waves daily beat upon her splendid body' (p. 34). It is the analogy between the music and the sea that reinforces the significance of this episode as Edna's re-experience of the pre-linguistic Order of the Imaginary. Here, her experience goes beyond the representational – the images that had before presented themselves to her through the music; now, the experience itself engulfs her in ways that cannot be verbalised. It is as a consequence of this new awareness of the Imaginary that Edna begins to reject, gradually at first, the trappings of her patriarchal identity. But of course there is no formal expression available in her world with which to articulate her experience of the Imaginary or, from that, an authentic feminine identity – outside the masculine order of the Symbolic, there is only madness and death.

It is the dawning awareness that this sense of personal authenticity is what she is missing that Edna struggles to articulate; she experiences this as a sense of loss, of being apart from the world with which she wants fully to engage but authentically as a woman: 'it seemed to her as if life were passing by, leaving its promise broken and unfulfilled' (p. 97). The promise of personal fulfilment is betrayed by the dominance of masculine society, of the Symbolic Order, which leaves only the world of tradition and convention. Edna finally recognises that she cannot discover an alternative. When Robert leaves her, she is forced to acknowledge that her illicit love for him is a symptom and not a cause of her awakening and transformation. He leaves her because it is not possible for them to remain together and still conform to the conventions of their society. Edna realises that her choice is whether to play the prescribed patriarchal role of dutiful wife and mother: 'The children appeared before her like antagonists who had overcome her; who had overpowered and sought to drag her into the soul's slavery for the rest of her days' (p. 151). The search for an authentic feminine identity is closely bound to the theme of maternity: motherhood is represented as being opposed to creativity or self-realisation: the musically gifted Mademoiselle Reisz is unmarried, Madame Ratignolle devotes herself exclusively to her children, and when Edna takes up painting her husband complains that the domestic routine of the household and the family is destroyed. In this way, the narrative represents an unreconcilable conflict between maternity and work, the feminine and the masculine. Edna rejects motherhood and marriage as the basis of her self-image: she turns the care of her children over to their nurse or to their paternal grandmother; she refuses to attend her sister's wedding, telling her husband that 'a wedding is one of the most lamentable spectacles on earth' (p. 87).

Masculinity and femininity are represented in the narrative in terms of the experience of, and attitudes towards, solitude, isolation and death. These experiences are also charged with meaning in terms of the Oedipal stage of psychological gender development. Solitude is represented in two distinct ways: as resignation which is hostile and masculine; and solitude as defiance which is welcoming and feminine. The sea is variously described as symbolising these two aspects of solitude. But solitude, even when it is sought in defiance and rebellion against patriarchal control of her as a woman, isolates Edna from the sources of feminine support that might save her and help her to reach a more mature analysis of her life. She becomes isolated as a consequence of her decision to accept a relationship with Robert in place of authentic self-determination, but her failure and the poverty of the choice that is available to her stand as evidence of Edna's entrapment between the Symbolic and the Imaginary, the patriarchal and the feminine. The isolation that becomes so much a part of her experience of the feminine once she has severed the patriarchal relations that have comprised her social network, is represented through the rich symbolic texture of the narrative. The sea provides the dominant source of imagery which carries a heavy gender inflection. Edna's experience of the sea at Grand Isle is confused with her growing unhappiness with her marriage. At the start of chapter six, the narrator connects Edna's 'shadowy anguish', described in chapter three, with the promise of an alternative world, a feminine order, that the sea appears to offer: 'The voice of the sea is seductive; never ceasing, whispering, clamoring, murmuring, inviting the soul to wander for a spell in abysses of solitude; to lose itself in mazes of inward contemplation. ... The voice of the sea speaks to the soul. The touch of the sea is sensuous, enfolding the body in its soft, close embrace' (p. 17). It is the sensuous embrace of an alternative mode of being that so many of the characters mistake for a new sensuality in Edna; even Edna herself mistakes this solitary embrace for physical sensuality. She confuses sexuality with gender and the cultural controls that are used by men to limit feminine sexuality through the imposition of feminine gender roles.

Edna experiences the sea as empowering, as an experience of freedom without limits such as she has not known since she was a young girl. She tells Adèle Ratignolle of her recollection of 'a meadow that seemed as big as the ocean to the very little girl walking through the grass' (p. 21) and this image returns to her at the end when she recalls 'the bluegrass meadow that she had traversed when a little child, believing that it had no beginning and no end' (p. 153) It is this immersion in and merger with a world that has no limits, that knows no boundaries and imposes no boundaries upon the ego that is characteristic of the Imaginary Order, the pre-Oedipal, feminine experience of the world. From the very beginning of the narrative then Edna has sought this connection with the feminine. She tells Madame Ratignolle that she is aware of being and feeling different, this summer at Grand Isle; the narrative betrays that it is her desire to sever her allegiance to the Father and to seek connection with the feminine that motivates Edna's disturbing sense of difference.

Edna's death by drowning represents a return to the feminine, to the pre-natal condition. The sea is represented symbolically as the feminine element, as Elaine Showalter observes: 'As the female body is prone to wetness, blood, milk, tears and amniotic fluid, so in drowning the woman is immersed in the feminine organic element. Drowning thus becomes the traditionally feminine literary death' (Showalter, 1994, p. 81). Water, the sea, symbolises Edna's development from initial fear, to a sense of control and achievement as she learns to swim, to her final sense of liberation: 'She felt like some new-born creature, opening its eyes in a familiar world that it had never known' (p. 152). But this image is counterbalanced by the juxtaposed image: 'A bird with a broken wing was beating the air above, reeling, fluttering, circling disabled down, down to the water' (p. 152). Edna rejects the patriarchal gender identity attributed to her by her male-dominated society, but this means that in terms of the world in which she must live she is crippled and maimed. She embraces the feminine as a return to a pre-Oedipal condition of unindividuated feminine existence, but this transformation is only possible in death. She tries to discover an alternative, feminine world in which to live, a world which is confused early in the narrative with the sea. The narrator comments that 'the beginning of things, of a world especially, is necessarily vague, tangled, chaotic and exceedingly disturbing. How few of us ever emerge from such a beginning! How many souls perish in its tumult!' (p. 17). Thus, Edna's awakening and her feminine 'beginning' is also her end, as in death she returns to the source of life.

References and Selected Further Reading

Brennan, Teresa, 1989. *Between Feminism and Psychoanalysis*, London: Routledge.

Brightwell, Gerri, 1995. 'Charting the Nebula: Gender, Language and Power in Kate Chopin's *The Awakening*', *Women and Language*, vol. 18, no. 2 (Fall), pp. 37–41.

Butler, Judith, 1990. *Gender Trouble: Feminism and the Subversion of Identity*, London & New York: Routledge.

Chesler, Phyllis, 1972. *Women and Madness*, New York: Doubleday.

Chopin, Kate, 1899. *The Awakening*, New York: Bantam, 1981.

Cixous, Hélène & Catherine Clement, 1986. *The Newly Born Woman*, trans. Betsy Wing. Minneapolis: University of Minnesota Press.

Dinnerstein, Dorothy, 1976. *The Mermaid and the Minotaur: Sexual Arrangements and Human Malaise*, New York: Harper & Row.

Feldstein, Richard & Judith Roof, eds, 1989. *Feminism and Psychoanalysis*, Ithaca, NY: Cornell University Press.

Flax, Jane, 1983. 'Political Philosophy and Patriarchal Unconscious: A Psychoanalytic Perspective on Epistemology and Metaphysics', in Nancy Tuana & Rosemarie Tong, eds, *Feminism and Philosophy: Essential Readings in Theory, Reinterpretation and Application*, Boulder, CO: Westview Press, 1995, pp. 217–246.

——, 1989. *Thinking Fragments: Psychoanalysis, Feminism and Postmodernism in the Contemporary West*, Berkeley: University of California Press.

Gallop, Jane, 1982. *The Daughter's Seduction: Feminism and Psychoanalysis*, London: Macmillan.

Gelfland, E. & V. Thorndike Hules, 1984. *French Feminist Criticism: Women, Language and Literature*, New York: Garland.

Carol Gilligan, 1982. *In a Different Voice: Psychological Theory and Women's Development*, Cambridge, MA: Harvard University Press.

Grosz, Elizabeth, 1989. *Sexual Subversions*, London: Allen & Unwin.

Hirsch, Marianna & Evelyn Fox Keller, eds, 1990. *Conflicts in Feminism*, New York: Routledge.

Kofman, Sarah, 1985. *The Enigma of Woman: Woman in Freud's Writings*, Ithaca, NY: Cornell University Press.

LeBlanc, Elizabeth, 1996. 'The Metaphorical Lesbian: Edna Pontellier in *The Awakening*', *Tulsa Studies in Women's Literature*, vol. 15, no. 2 (Fall), pp. 289–307.

Marks, Elaine & Isabelle de Courtivron, eds, 1980. *New French Feminisms*, Amherst, MA: University of Massachusetts Press.

Martin, Wendy, ed., 1988. *New Essays on The Awakening*, Cambridge: Cambridge University Press.

Miller, Jean Baker, 1986. *Toward a New Psychology of Women*, Boston: Beacon Press.

Juliet Mitchell, 1975. *Psychoanalysis and Feminism*, New York: Vintage.

——, 1984. *Women: The Longest Revolution. Essays in Feminism, Literature and Psychoanalysis*, London: Virago.

Mitchell, Juliet & Jacqueline Rose, eds, 1982. *Feminine Sexuality: Jacques Lacan and the Ecole Freudienne*, London: Macmillan.

Toril Moi, 1987. *French Feminist Thought*, Oxford: Blackwell.

——, ed., 1986. *The Julia Kristeva Reader*, Oxford: Basil Blackwell.

Nicholson, Linda J., ed., 1990. *Feminism / Postmodernism*, New York: Routledge.

Petry, Alice Hall, ed., 1996. *Critical Essays on Kate Chopin*, New York: Hall.

Rosaldo, Michelle Zimbalist & Louise Lamphere, eds, 1974. *Women, Culture and Society*, Stanford, CA: Stanford University Press.

Schweitzer, Ivy, 'Maternal Discourse and the Romance of Self-Possession' in Kate Chopin's *The Awakening*' in Silvestra Mariniello & Paul A. Bove, eds, *Gendered Agents: Women and Institutional Knowledge*. Durham, NC: Duke University Press, 1998, pp. 161–191.

Sellers, Susan, ed., 1988. *Writing Differences: Readings from the Seminar of Hélène Cixous*, Milton Keynes: Open University Press.

Shaw, Pat, 1994. 'Putting Audience in Its Place: Psychosexuality and Perspective Shifts in *The Awakening*' in Donald Keesey, ed., *Contexts for Criticism*. Mountain View, CA: Mayfield, pp. 179–185.

Elaine Showalter, 1994. *Sister's Choice: Tradition and Change in American Women's Writing*. Oxford & New York: Oxford University Press, ch.4 '*The Awakening*: Tradition and the American Female Talent', pp.65–84.

Stange, Margit, 1989. 'Personal Property: Exchange Value and the Female Self in *The Awakening*', *Genders*, vol. 5 (July), pp. 106–119.

Taylor, Walter & Jo Ann B. Fineman, 1996. 'Kate Chopin: Pre-Freudian Freudian', *Southern Literary Journal*, vol. 29, no. 1 (Fall), pp. 35–45.

Toth, Emily, 1991. 'Kate Chopin's *The Awakening* as Feminist Criticism', *Southern Studies*, vol. 2, no. 3 (Fall-Winter), pp. 4–41.

Walker, Nancy A., ed., 1993. *Kate Chopin: The Awakening; Complete, Authoritative Text with Biographical & Historical Contexts, Critical History, & Essays from Five Contemporary Critical Perspectives*, New York: St Martin's Press.

Wershoven, C. J., 1987. '*The Awakening* and *The House of Mirth*: Studies of Arrested Development', *American Literary Realism*, Spring, 19:3, pp. 27–41.

Wolff, Cynthia Griffin, 1996. 'Un Utterable Longing: The Discourse of Feminine Sexuality in *The Awakening*', *Studies in American Fiction*, vol. 24, no. 1 (Spring), pp. 3–22.

Wright, Elizabeth, 1998. *Psychoanalytic Criticism*, Cambridge: Polity Press.

4

Gender and Nature: Eco-feminism and Willa Cather

This chapter begins with a survey of eco-feminist theorists, focusing upon Carol Adams's *Neither Man Nor Beast* (1994), Carol Bigwood's *Earth Muse: Feminism, Nature, Art* (1993) and Carolyn Merchant's *Radical Ecology* (1992). The primary theoretical concepts explored here include: concepts of power and domination in relation to the feminisation of the powerless; the issue of hierarchy and the scale of value that organises and privileges all creation in terms recognised, and prescribed, by human culture; and gender identity which is viewed as predominantly cultural rather than sexual in that disempowered men are 'feminised' within the terms of Western patriarchal culture. In the section that follows, I turn to the ecofeminist analysis of Willa Cather's Plains Fiction – in particular *My Ántonia*, *O Pioneers!* and the short story 'Neighbour Rosicky'.

Survey of Eco-Feminist Theory

Summary of Eco-feminist Principles

The term ecofeminism or 'eco-feminisme' was coined by the French writer Françoise d'Eaubonne in 1974 as part of her call to women to save the planet (see d'Eaubonne, 1980). The concept was developed by Ynestra King, at the Institute for Social Ecology in Vermont, and the idea became a movement in 1980 with the Amherst conference 'Women and Life on Earth: Ecofeminism in the Eighties' (see Merchant, 1992, p. 184). Ecofeminism analyses the relationship between the patriarchal oppression of women and the human domination of non-human nature. In this respect, ecofeminism draws upon theoretical ideas developed by cultural feminists who use a mode of analysis based upon the identification of binary thought systems that is indebted to poststructuralist methodology. These systems privilege one side of the binaries they construct; for instance, writing over speech, mind over body, civilisation over nature, human over animal, masculine over feminine. Consequently, ecofeminism focuses upon all the practices of domination within culture: racism, sexism, class oppression, and the exploitation of nature. In her 1989 essay, 'Healing the Wounds: Feminism, Ecology, and Nature/Culture Dualism', Ynestra King argues:

> The ecological crisis is related to the systems of hatred of all that is natural and female by the white, male western formulators of philosophy, technology, and death inventions. I contend that the systematic denigration of working-class people and people of color, women, and animals are all connected to the basic dualism that lies at the root of western civilization. But this mindset of hierarchy originates within human society, its material roots in the domination of human by human, particularly women by men. Although I cannot speak for the liberation struggles of people of color, I believe that the goals of feminism, ecology, and movements against racism and for the survival of indigenous peoples are internally related; they must be understood and pursued together in a worldwide, genuinely prolife, movement' (King, 1989, p. 353).

The main structure of power in Western culture is identified by King as a hierarchical system of relationships of domination and subordination which structures relationships between people and groups within society. And so, she continues, the 'task of an ecological feminism is the ongoing forging of a genuinely antidualistic, or dialectical, theory and praxis' (King, 1989, p. 365). The relationship between men and women is the paradigm for oppressive hierarchical relationships: that which is dominant is gendered as masculine, that which is subordinate is feminised. The process of feminisation, which is cultural and political rather than biological, is the process whereby powerless individuals learn to play the role of the subordinate. The basic duality in Western patriarchal society is that between masculine and feminine: culture and nature, civilisation and primitivism, mind and body, reason and emotion, rationality and irrationality, control and uncontrollability, power and weakness, human and less-than-human (psychoanalytic feminism adds a distinction between consciousness and the subconscious, or the post-Oedipal and pre-Oedipal stages of psychosexual development). Those who are not on the masculine side of the divide are thus deprived of their humanity and the rights and privileges that accompany full humanity.

Gender roles therefore enable the continued domination of disempowered groups: women, men of colour, children, the disabled, animals, nature. Within a centralised, hierarchical society, groups are divided into 'masculine' and 'not-masculine'. Power is centralised and focused in the masculine ruling class, with the 'not-masculine' requiring protection, control, guidance – in short, the paternalistic 'wisdom of the father' to compensate for the lack of power that is the defining characteristic of the 'not-masculine' (see Ferguson, 1983). In return for this protection, the feminine serves the interests of the male: nature sacrifices 'herself' to culture. Wilderness submits to the civilising pressure of organised agriculture (and other forms of engineering), animals sacrifice their flesh to human appetites and their bodies to human research (vivisection and medical experimentation).

The assumption that human interests are superior to non-human interests encourages a habit of thought that presumes a scale of value among all aspects of creation: the human is more valuable than the animal or the natural, men are more valuable than women, the rich are more valuable than the poor, whites are more valuable than blacks, the First World is more valuable than the Third World, and so on. According to the ecofeminist worldview, rather than address only the inequity of gender relations, feminism has to eradicate this whole habit of mind and embrace the ideal of egalitarianism. In patriarchal terms, 'more valuable' means not simply more powerful but intrinsically more worthwhile, deserving of the power and privilege that are attributed to them: it is this assumption that ecofeminism sets out to dismantle. Some ecofeminists, such as Carol Bigwood, discussed below, contest this dualistic worldview by identifying its profound roots in the Western philosophical tradition; others act to expose the reality of the class-, race- and gender-specificity of this oppression. To take one limited example, ecofeminism acts by exposing the location of toxic waste dumps in areas of the US populated largely by poor and coloured people, or by exposing the recruitment of poor women of colour in Third World countries to work in factories with toxic chemicals.

Ecofeminism does urgently put into question the relation of women and nature; on the one hand contesting the identification that makes women as passive and powerless as the exploited natural world, but on the other hand, promoting a positive identification of nature with the reproductive capacity of women who share a material commitment to the survival of the planet through the children they bear. Ynestra King describes ecofeminism as a woman-identified movement; she claims that in defying patriarchy 'we are loyal to future generations and to life and this planet itself. We have a deep and particular understanding of this both through our natures and our experience as women' (King, 1983, p. 10). Recent developments in biotechnology, genetic modification, reproductive technologies, and the like, focus ecofeminist concern upon the masculine bias of Western science and technology. The desire to control and to appropriate nature – both the human female reproductive capacity and the reproductive power of non-human nature – through technology is a powerful instance of the connection between the oppression of women and of nature. Spiritual ecofeminists look to a global feminine principle that is immanent within the material world as a principle of connectivity and unity. Allied to the New Age movement in the West, this spiritual mode of ecofeminist thought links the power of the feminine principle inherent in nature with the sexual energy or life force possessed by women and which connects women with the world and promotes the feminine concern with survival and continuance.

Ecofeminist theory does remind us that gender oppression is not always necessarily biological but is also cultural –

biological males are *just as* susceptible to domination as women, but the process by which they are oppressed involves first relegating them to the class of the 'less worthy', the powerless: the feminine. Ecofeminist activism involves, then, a campaign to challenge this classification of the 'less worthwhile': campaigns on behalf of laboratory animals, veal calves, dam construction, road building, etc. There is a grey area separating ecofeminism from radical feminist activism: ecofeminism identifies the cause of oppression as the hierarchical organisation of social and economic relations and claims that society can be restructured to ensure equality for all; radical feminism identifies the cause of oppression as heterosexual masculinity itself, which is expressed in such traits as competitiveness, exploitation, greed, violence, and so radical feminists argue that the only way to abolish these motives from social life is to install feminine values in place of masculine ones. Ecofeminists do not seek a gender-based quality of 'femininity' to replace 'masculinity' which would only invert the patriarchal values upon which exploitative hierarchies are based; instead, ecofeminism seeks a feminine organising principle that would transform consciousness as well as relations of production and reproduction within the global community. Three prominent ecofeminist thinkers are Carol Bigwood, Carolyn Merchant and Carol Adams; in what follows I look more closely at the work of these women.

Carol Bigwood, Earth Muse: Feminism, Nature, Art *(1993)*

The kind of ecofeminism practised by Carol Bigwood could be described as 'philosophical eco-feminism'; her book *Earth Muse* represents an ecofeminist appraisal of key thinkers in the Western philosophical tradition: Socrates, Aristotle, Plato, Heidegger, Nietzsche, Merleau-Ponty, Derrida and Foucault. Bigwood locates the project of the book in her critique of Western phallocentrism; that is, the privilege and power accorded the phallus in Western philosophy, as a mark of presence, what she describes as 'the morphological marks of the male body in some of our most important concepts' (Bigwood, 1993, p. 2). These concepts include self-identity, unity, teleology, and important cultural ideals like selfhood and reason. But her explorations go beyond the idea that Western philosophy might be gender-biased in its vocabulary and methods; Bigwood considers the possibility that 'Being' itself might be a gendered metaphysics and a gendered experience. In Bigwood's terms, Being is a relational rather than absolute concept. It is not synonymous with God or presence but is 'the living web within which all relations emerge' (p. 3). And these relations have been masculinised according to the structure of sexual difference. So gender is an ontological concept, inherent in the way Being is conceptualised and experienced in the West. It is within this context that Bigwood offers her re-conceptualisation of ideas like culture and nature, her re-visioning of those concepts, and her account of how those concepts came to be so powerfully associated with the masculine and the feminine. She explains:

> As I see it, an analysis of the exile of the 'feminine' in metaphysics (and the related exploitation of the earth and oppression of non-Western peoples) involves a postmodern attempt to disrupt the phallocentric unity, stability, and fullness of pure presence of western Being with a view to restoring the ruptures and irregularities, the movement, flux, and play of existence (p. 4).

The method of Bigwood's book, then, draws upon poststructuralist analysis by decentering the structure of gender difference that informs the Western idea of Being; she uses existential-phenomenology to critique transcendental notions of Being that refuse to be grounded in lived or local experience or consciousness; she follows Luce Irigaray and Hélène Cixous in exposing patriarchal discourse to contradiction and in modelling alternative forms of subjectivity that are grounded in the experience of the body.

She responds to the current trend towards 'denaturalising' nature and the body, as she calls it (p. 8), which furthers our alienation from nature and perpetuates the exploitation and repression of nature by culture. The dualism between nature and culture, and woman's inextricable relation to this dualism, is revealed in Bigwood's analysis of Aristotle's account of the primacy of the masculine *techne* (art) over the feminine *phusis* (nature) as 'a central dichotomy that underlies many modes of western existence and our white conception of being in the world' (p. 9). The primacy of art over nature, the domination of nature by human art, establishes within Western philosophical tradition the singular importance of art or culture and the necessary disempowerment of nature. The concluding chapters of *Earth Muse* set out Bigwood's re-visioning of the relation between the feminine and the body and the earth that allows the free play of difference both through feminine experience and subjectivity and through experience of the other in the form of racial difference, cultural difference, and the difference between human and non-human nature.

This free play is an alternative mode of thinking through difference that refuses the dualistic thought that opposes art to nature, masculine to feminine, mind to body, subject to object, and so on. What is important to avoid, however, is the danger of disregarding the feminine as one moves from gender dualism to a conception of the multiple subject. In other words, we can move from a view of the feminine as associated with lack and absence direct to an androgynous vision of the subject without considering the concept of a positive femininity. In the same way, Bigwood points to a tendency in poststructuralist feminist thought to reject the essentialist (or a fixed and falsely universalised) notion of 'woman' or 'the feminine' as oppressive in favour of a concept of the self as the product of cultural forces, and in this way to perpetuate the historical privileging of culture over nature. This tendency would represent a kind of assimilation to rather than transformation of patriarchal values. What Bigwood pursues is a new connection between biological difference and cultural representations of the sexual body. It is the body as culturally and historically 'embodied', as a living body, that makes this new philosophical connection possible. Recent developments in communications, transportation and information systems, she observes, have contributed to the Western experience of the world as a 'global village', with an increase in localisation and the experience of the 'nearness' of diverse cultures to Western consumers. And yet, Bigwood observes, this development has not given rise to what she calls 'neighborhoods of nearness':

> On the contrary, the expansion of the West and the resultant 'small world' is still, as in colonial days, primarily a movement of domination. It depends on the exploitation of the labor and lives of the majority of the earth's peoples. Because the oppression of the earth, of women, and of those who do not belong to 'the abstract dominant non-group' called whites (Minh-ha 1989, 54) are intimately related and reinforce one another, caring for women and for the earth cannot be separated from caring for diverse human communities (p. 264).

In this way, Bigwood links the philosophical legitimisation of masculine dominance over the feminine with the economic and cultural exploitation of the natural world and those categories of being associated with nature: non-white peoples, women and non-human entities.

Carolyn Merchant, Radical Ecology *(1992)*

It is with this perception of the interconnected character of oppression that Carolyn Merchant begins her book. She describes radical ecology as a response to a growing sense of crisis in the industrialised world: 'It acts on a new perception that the domination of nature entails the domination of human beings along the lines of race, class, and gender' (Merchant, 1992, 1). This will to domination, according to Merchant, is promoted by the mechanistic worldview that arose in the seventeenth century alongside and in support of early capitalism, and which supplanted the earlier Renaissance model of nature as a living organism. 'It entailed an ethic of the control and domination of nature and supplanted the organic world's I-thou ethic of reciprocity between humans and nature. Mechanism and its ethic of domination legitimates the use of nature as commodity, a central tenet of industrial capitalism' (p. 11). The return to an ethic of reciprocity, an 'eco-centric' ethic where all parts of the ecosystem are equally valued, is central to the ecology movement despite the diverse emphases identified by deep ecologists, spiritual ecologists, social ecologists, radical environmentalists and ecofeminists. The latter she identifies in terms of concern about the environmental impact upon women's bodies in biological reproduction and women's role in social reproduction. It is the transformation of modes of production, reproduction and consciousness that radical ecology seeks to achieve, and this transformative goal is shared by those within the ecological movement whose commitment is to changing the conditions of women's lives by altering the ecological paradigm or worldview within which we live. Merchant is concerned to emphasise the fact that the ecological movement is not singular and monolithic but is very diverse and this diversity promotes awareness that, while the global ecological crisis involves all levels of society, impacts are experienced differently by the First, Second and Third World peoples and by individuals according to race, class and gender. There is, however, a significant difference between the 'deep' ecology movement and reformist environmentalism. Where the latter seeks to establish legal controls or limits on pollution and emissions and the like, deep ecology is concerned with fundamental changes in the relations between humans and non-human nature. As Merchant explains, deep ecology 'offers a new science of nature, a new spiritual paradigm, and a new ecological ethic ... It is thus socially produced and socially constructed. It focuses, however, on transformation at the level of consciousness and worldview, rather than the transformation of production and reproduction' (p. 86).

Ecofeminism shares the transformative goals of deep ecology but is as diverse as the ecological movement itself. Carolyn Merchant points to several approaches to ecofeminism: liberal ecofeminism which shares the reformist concern of mainstream environmentalism and seeks change through legislative and regulatory means; cultural ecofeminism approaches environmental issues within the context of the critique of patriarchy; socialist ecofeminism identifies the connection between the patriarchal domination of women by men and the capitalist domination of nature by men by pointing to the commodification of both women and nature under the system of patriarchal capitalism. Ecofeminists must confront the different modes of domination experienced by women according to their class, age and race, and position in the First, Second or Third Worlds. However, ecofeminists do have in common the advocacy of what Merchant describes as 'some form of an environmental ethic that deals with the twin oppressions of the domination of women and the domination of nature through an ethic of care and nurture that arises out of women's culturally constructed experiences' (p. 185). In response to the accusation of essentialism, implicit in this idea that a feminine ethic must necessarily be based upon nurture, some ecofeminists prefer a 'partnership ethic' that treats all humans as equal partners in all relations, and non-human nature as equal with, rather than sub-servient to, humans. The advantage of this ethical stance, Merchant points out, is that it 'avoids gendering nature as a nurturing mother or a goddess and avoids the ecocentric dilemma that humans are only one of many equal parts of an ecological web and therefore morally equal to a bacterium or a mosquito' (p. 188). The critique of domination is then linked to the critique of economic, social and cultural hierar-chies that situate men above women and both above non-human nature.

Carol Adams, Neither Man Nor Beast: Feminism and the Defense of Animals *(1994)*

The title of Adams's book neatly sums up her perception of the position of women under patriarchy. Femininity, defined in opposition to masculinity on the one hand and the non-human on the other, is positioned in Western culture in between man and beast. Working from the insights of those like Carol Bigwood who have exposed the patriarchal bias of Western philosophy, Adams accepts that in the Western philosophic tradition women have been aligned with animals and the animalistic reproductive function, in opposition to men. 'Historically, ... women were positioned in between man and other animals, so that women, and especially women of color, were traditionally viewed in Western culture as neither man nor beast' (Adams, 1994, p. 11). The feminist response to this positioning, a response to which Adams objects strongly, has been to assert the shared humanity of men and women, in opposition to animals. This response has, of course, left untouched the assumed opposition between humans and other animals; only women have been moved from one side of the opposition to the other. The structure of prejudice remains unchallenged. 'An alternative feminist position asserts that we are not man, since man is not and never can be generic, and we are not beasts, since beast exists largely as metaphor for human behavior, as self-judgment. Rather than resituating any of the players from one side to the other, this position calls the human/animal dualism into question' (p. 12). What Adams proposes then is the destabilisation of the entire notion of the subject, both human and animal, through the rejection of dualistic thinking. The concept of 'beast' belongs to human nomenclature, not to animals, and so the feminist defence of animals is based upon the challenge to reject the identification of animals as beasts. This challenge works hand in hand with the challenge to dispense with the identification of masculinity with the category of 'man': 'not only because being a man is tied into identities about what "real men" do and don't do ... but because "man" (read: white man) can exist as a concept and a sexual identity only through negation ("not woman, not beast, not colored," i.e., "not the other")' (p. 12). What Adams is arguing is the perception that attitudes towards animals cannot change radically without a radical shift in the ways in which humans view themselves. The categories of 'man', 'woman', 'beast' are structured in an ontological hierarchy that presupposes the superiority of men over women and humans over animals. Animals are available to be exploited by humans just as women are available for exploitation by men. To deconstruct this hierarchy requires the destabilisation of the constituent categories of being. Adams claims, '[a]s the destabilized human subject opens up the space to acknowledge animal subjects, our notions of humanity could also be shorn of gender, race, and species preoccupations' (pp. 12–13).

The link between the exploitation of women and of animals is explored by Adams in a number of different contexts, from pornography to militarism, but the fundamental connection between them is an interconnecting pattern of violence: sexual violence, racist violence, violence against animals. This pattern suggests that violence serves the interests of a cultural ideology, an ideology that attributes to animals, women and persons of colour an ontology that renders them usable, and that violence is a strategy by which privilege is sustained and relationships of power and domination are preserved. Adams's strategy for exposing this ideology and its operations is the analysis of the human-animal dualism as it functions within a racist patriarchy. She sets out clearly the assumptions that underlie her analysis and it is worth quoting these at some length:

- First, oppression is a reality. Privilege is the state of being for those who benefit from oppression. Race- and sex-hate crimes are ways that oppression is maintained and perpetuated.
- Second, just as gender and race are constructs, so too is species. They are categories of social construction that have been postulated as essentially natural.
- Third, environmental exploitation takes place through social domination of the bodies of some people by other people. The legacy of colonialism is that elite Euro-Americans have institutionalized oppressive systems that control non-dominant white people and people of color as well as exploiting the natural resources of the land upon which they live. Owners and decision-makers maintain high profits for the few by passing on the costs to the many in the form of low wages, high prices, bad working conditions, and toxic side effects. Many of us are seeking new structures that do not uphold the exploitation of people or the earth and its other creatures.

- Last, feminism does not solely address relationships between women and men, but is an analytic tool that helps expose the social construction of reality. For instance, feminism identifies how gender becomes a marker of the oppression of animals too, as when rodeos feature a competition that involves putting lace underpants on a calf (p. 14).

Thus, Adams's ecofeminist effort is directed at the deconstruction or destabilisation of those ontological categories that legitimise and authorise the exploitation not only of women and animals but also the earth and its resources, people of colour and the victims of neo-colonialism and economic imperialism. It is the status of these ontological categories as 'natural' rather than social constructions that Adams sets out to contradict. In part, she does this by challenging the terms in which debate is cast; she challenges the tendency to identify with the scientific 'knower' rather than the animal that is 'known' in debates over vivisection; or the identification with the (human) consumer rather than the (animal) consumed in debates over vegetarianism. This 'natural' identification with the human who is situated as agent in these debates is disrupted by Adams's restoration of what she calls 'the absent referent'. The human language of food substitutes meat for the living animal and thus removes the individual animal in its material being from the act of consumption: '[a]nimals in name and body are made absent as animals in order that flesh can exist. If animals are alive they cannot be meat' (p. 16). But by restoring the materiality of this 'absent referent' Adams exposes what is done to individual creatures that are categorised as 'animals' in order that they can be transformed into meat, and she also exposes 'the interlocking system of oppression that defines them as such and places them there' (p. 17). It is the interlinked nature of the system of oppression that feminism seeks to challenge and to transform; but where some feminist approaches narrowly define the scope of oppression, Adams recognises that women live lives that are embedded in a network of social relations that involve all sentient beings, human and non-human.

Ecofeminism in Praxis

In the following section, Willa Cather's Plains Fiction is analysed in ecofeminist terms. This discussion of Cather's work focuses upon two primary areas: first, Cather and the notion of a 'pioneer spirit' that is represented in her work, especially *My Ántonia* (1918) and *O, Pioneers* (1913) which, through their heroines, celebrate the women who struggled heroically on the frontier. These heroines symbolise the fusion of wilderness and civilisation that is nature tamed and rendered powerless, or feminine. Second, I discuss the issue of Cather's use of imagery, in the story 'Neighbour Rosicky' (1932), to represent the gendering of nature and human-nature relationships. Gendering of the primary narrative figures to represent feminine nature versus masculine society is used in thematic terms to represent the conflict that Cather perceives between the reality of the socially-produced, gendered exploitation of nature and a nostalgic, idealistic yearning for harmony with nature. Her primary thematic interests, then, are tied to these two issues: the opposition between city and country or competition and nurturance; community and individuality, or the prescriptive effect of the social as opposed to the natural environment on personal identity; and the universal versus the particular, where Cather dwells upon the significance of small, seemingly trivial things, especially the natural objects that are rendered invisible in Western patriarchal culture.

Willa Cather's Plains Fiction

The image of a 'pioneer spirit' is represented in Cather's fiction of the Nebraska plains, especially *My Ántonia* (1918) and *O Pioneers!* (1913). These novels, through their heroines, celebrate the immigrant women who struggled heroically on the frontier: both Ántonia Shimerda and Alexandra Bergson immigrate as young girls, bringing with them to the Nebraska frontier vague memories of the European birthplace their parents have left behind. Thus, these heroines symbolise the fusion of the Old World and the New that is the pioneer spirit, at the same time that they represent the confrontation of wilderness and civilisation that results in nature tamed and rendered powerless, or 'feminised'.

My Ántonia is characterised by a nostalgic, elegiac tone; in important respects this loss for which the narrative mourns is the loss of the original wilderness of the frontier as it is brought under the control of the plough. But the nostalgia is firstly that of the narrator, Jim Burden, as he attempts to recover some lost sense of innocence, grace and hope: what he calls 'an original relation to the world'. This relation, a sense of being at home in the world, is symbolised by Ántonia who appears to him as a spiritual pioneer, as her parents were literal pioneers. Ántonia is placed in a symbolic relation by several of the characters in the narrative. She does not tell her own story; rather, she is described and discussed by others for whom her significance is more than that of a simple individual. Consequently, she can become symbolically whatever the other characters wish to make of her; in the case of Jim Burden, she symbolises the feminine, or feminised, harmony with nature that he seeks, and which stands in contrast to the masculine exploitation of nature, symbolised by her surly brother Ambrosch. The exploitation of nature brings about the destruction of the prairie wilderness through organised agriculture and the civilisation that it supports. In contrast, Jim recalls his own experience of communion with nature: as a young boy, lying on the earth, he recalls 'I was something that lay under the sun and felt it, like the pumpkins, and I did not want to be anything more' (Cather, 1918, p. 18). This awareness is encouraged by his grandmother who warns him of snakes and the badger she protects by forbidding any of the men to kill it, explaining 'In a new country a body feels friendly to the animals' (p. 17). The proximity of women like his grandmother and Ántonia promotes in Jim an almost feminine closeness with the earth and with nature.

The narrative explores two kinds of pioneer experience: the literal experience of settling the untamed prairie by families like the Shimerdas, and Jim's grandparents, and the experience of Jim's life which unfolds the symbolic dimension of pioneer achievement. At the end of the novel,

Jim describes his life as having taken the form of a quest which culminates in 'the sense of coming home to myself' (p. 371). This sense of peace and reconciliation with himself Jim discovers through the recollection of his shared childhood with Ántonia. It is her relationship with the land, and the quasi-sacred power Jim perceives in the land, that enables his complex realisation of harmony. Early in the narrative, he tells of an incident when Ántonia resuscitated a dying insect by making a nest for it in her hair; her sympathy with the tiny creature, her instinctive understanding of how to preserve it, is generalised in Jim's recollection so that the whole afternoon becomes 'magical' and the prairie, as he surveys it, appears 'like a bush that burned with fire and was not consumed' (p. 40). This biblical allusion, to the burning bush through which God spoke to Moses, suggests not only that the wilderness of the prairie is infused with a sacred power but that the wilderness is able to communicate information of the utmost importance if only one can understand its language. Ántonia is possessed of this understanding and so is Jim, though his is not such a sustained relationship with the land; indeed, his relationship with the prairie is mediated by Ántonia's intuitive, feminine understanding of the wilderness and its potential. Jim's first reaction to the prairie as he rides over it at night, travelling from the train to his grandfather's farm, is a feeling of being 'erased, blotted out' (p. 8) by the immensity of the untamed natural world that surrounds him: 'I had the feeling that the world was left behind, that we had got over the edge of it, and were outside man's jurisdiction' (p. 7). He recalls this incident at the end of the novel, and relives the feeling of mystical union with the land and the 'obliterating strangeness' that he had experienced. At both moments, Ántonia is a crucial part of his experience:

> This was the road over which Ántonia and I came on that night when we got off the train at Black Hawk and were bedded down in the straw, wondering children, being taken we knew not whither. I had only to close my eyes to hear the rumbling of the wagons in the dark, and to be again overcome by that obliterating strangeness (p. 371).

The narrative develops from this childhood sense of a mystical belonging in the world, which for the young Jim compensates in some way for the death of his parents. The narrative moves away from this sense of harmony with the natural world as Jim enters adolescence and moves into the masculine adult world of the town and then the city; but the narrative culminates in his final rediscovery of the significance of his childhood experience which is symbolised by the figure of Ántonia.

In Jim's recollection of the Shimerda family, Ántonia alone among her family is cheerful, eager to learn and full of life. Her mother is a mean and grasping woman who has focused all of her hope for the future upon her ill-tempered son Ambrosch; Ántonia's father, in contrast, is a cultured, sensitive and gentle man who remains so closely identified with the Old World he has left behind that he is defeated by the hardships of life on the prairie and commits suicide. Ántonia combines her father's spiritual and emotional sensitivity with her mother's fierce determination to succeed in their new lives. But where her mother is male-identified, living through her visions of Ambrosch's future, Ántonia identifies with feminised nature and for Jim she becomes symbolic of the power of life itself. This power is revealed in a negative aspect in that part of the narrative which deals with the lives Jim and Ántonia lead in the town of Black Hawk. In the town, masculine society and class distinctions dominate in ways that are irrelevant on the prairie. This masculine domination is exemplified by the character of Mr Harling who Jim describes as 'autocratic and imperial in his ways. He walked, talked, put on his gloves, shook hands, like a man who felt that he had power' (p. 157). It is Mr Harling who enforces social conventions most explicitly in the narrative. These conventions primarily concern the need to control relations between local boys and the immigrant 'hired girls', who the boys find so attractive and lively, and the 'American girls' who are their intended wives. The hired girls are perceived to be a threat to the social order of the town, and the space offered by the dancing pavilion for the free association of all classes of people is especially dangerous. When Ántonia refuses to give up the dancing that she loves so much, and when a string of admirers cluster around her, it is Mr Harling who insists she is dismissed from his home. The significance of the gender difference that separates Jim and Ántonia becomes very apparent in this part of the narrative. Jim belongs in the respectable, male-dominated houses from which Ántonia has been exiled; Jim shares the perception of all the boys that the hired girls and the dancing they enjoy represent the exuberance of life that is missing from the staid, respectable gatherings of his social equals. In this way, Jim reveals his complicity in the civilising process that is destroying the 'feminine' nature with which he seeks union: the same process that is promoting and expanding the 'masculine' civilisation of town and country.

Jim's complicity is revealed more subtly by his gradual shift eastward in the course of the narrative. First he moves to Black Hawk, then to Lincoln, and finally to Boston. This movement away from the frontier is matched by a growing disillusionment with the direction of his life. The conclusion of the narrative takes up the relationship between Jim and Ántonia after a lapse of twenty years, during which time he has avoided the idea of seeing Ántonia again because he fears that his image of her will be shattered, as so many of his illusions have been. But when finally he does visit her, he discovers that all he had thought lost has in fact been preserved. Ántonia has 'not lost the fire of life' (p. 336); she has been 'battered but not diminished' by life (p. 332), and thus Ántonia still presents the same image Jim has accurately preserved in his memory:

> She lent herself to immemorial human attitudes which we recognize by instinct as universal and true. I had not been mistaken. She was a battered woman now, not a lovely girl; but she still had that something which fires the imagination, could stop one's breath for a moment by a look or gesture that somehow revealed the meaning in common things.(p. 353).

In her ability to give herself completely to living, Ántonia not only fulfils her individual nature but she transcends it. She represents both Ántonia and a universal attitude. She embodies in her daily life the surrender of the self that Jim experienced so powerfully as a boy – that sense of dissolution into something that is complete. Because Ántonia's life is imbued with imagination and the sensitivity of the spirit, she is able to make present for others this spiritual dimension of life. But this spiritual acuity arises from her proximity to nature.

Ántonia regrets her time spent in the town, the depression that would capture her when she was away from the farm for too long; she recognises that she belongs on the prairie, that it is from nature that her powers derive. Alexandra Bergson develops the same self-awareness; she moves beyond a sense of deep appreciation of nature to a personal, mystical relation with the natural world:

> It fortified her to reflect upon the great operations of nature, and when she thought of the law that lay behind them, she felt a sense of personal security. That night she had a new consciousness of the country, felt almost a new relation to it. ... She had felt as if her heart were hiding down there, somewhere, with the quail and the plover and all the little wild things that crooned or buzzed in the sun. Under the long shaggy ridges, she felt the future stirring (Cather, 1913, p. 28).

Late in the narrative the prosperous Alexandra is characterised by her preference for the open space of the prairie rather than the closed domestic space of her homestead; it is outside rather than inside that she belongs. Early in the narrative, Alexandra is not associated with the future, with progress, and the forces of civilisation. Nor does the land itself appear to offer a future for the pioneers who settle it. Rather, the prairie asserts its own autonomous being. The narrator remarks upon the seeming absence of signs of human life, noting that the land has resisted human efforts to tame it: 'It was still a wild thing that had its ugly moods; and no one knew when they were likely to come, or why' (p. 7). In the early part of the narrative in particular Alexandra is represented as sharing emotional sympathy and spiritual understanding with the untamed prairie, qualities such as those that characterise Ántonia and make her special.

To emphasise this special understanding, Alexandra is closely associated with the character of Crazy Ivar who of all the characters enjoys the most intimate relation with the natural world. Where most of the characters – those who seek only profit from the land – fail to understand its 'ugly moods', Ivar lives in a clay bank on the prairie 'without defiling the face of nature any more than the coyote that had lived there before him had done' (p. 14). He is able to understand and communicate with animals and birds, to heal them when they are ill, to ensure that they grow and that the herds flourish. This ability renders Ivar 'crazy' in the eyes of his neighbours who, like Alexandra's brothers, believe that he 'would never be able to prove up on his land because he worked it so little' (p. 18). Ivar does lose his land and he is taken in by Alexandra, who becomes prosperous partly by heeding his advice. Ivar is the single most powerless character in the narrative. He loses his land, he has no personal pos-sessions, he relies upon Alexandra's protection to prevent his neighbours committing him to the public insane asylum. Yet he is also the character most closely united to the untamed land with a spiritual bond that only Alexandra recognises and shares. Ivar has rejected the masculine culture of compe-tition and financial advancement; rather, he participates in the feminine culture of nurturance, healing and communion with nature.

The purity of Alexandra's relation with the land is placed in question early in the narrative when her business acuity is contrasted with her brothers' lack of commercial sense. Her dying father perceives from his sickbed: 'It was Alexandra who could always tell about what it had cost to fatten each steer, and who could guess the weight of a hog before it went on the scales closer than John Bergson himself' (p. 9). Thus, Alexandra is involved in the taming of non-human nature, the development of organised agriculture, and the promotion of commercial values in the appraisal of the land. She becomes more deeply complicit in the process of civilisation through her devotion to her young brother Emil. Alexandra measures her success as a farmer according to her ability to send Emil to college and so to fulfil her father's ambition for at least one of his children. She does not see what the narrator perceives in her rich, carefully worked land: 'something frank and joyous and young in the open face of the country. It gives itself ungrudgingly to the moods of the season, holding nothing back' (p. 29), the narrator continues. This is not the untamed, non-human nature with which Ivar communes; this is nature made over in human terms and transformed into a willing sacrifice to the human desire for advancement.

Alexandra's complicity, or compromising of her feminine powers in the interests of masculine values and the priority she accords two men (her father and her brother Emil), leads to disaster. While Alexandra is not thought of as a woman by any of the characters except her childhood friend Carl and her neighbour Marie, she also neglects the gender relationships into which her friends and family enter. So habitually she sends Emil to assist her pretty young neighbour without thought for the consequences that might, and do, follow. Alexandra compromises her femininity, as Ivar's masculinity is compromised by his adoption of feminine values. And so she remains oblivious to the sexual attraction that develops between Emil and the unhappily married Marie, until Marie's jealous husband murders them both. The narrative begins and ends with death – first the death of Alexandra's father, later the death of her brother. The deaths of these two men, the men whose interests Alexandra is unable to resist, underline the ambiguous attitude revealed by the narrative towards the death of the wilderness that it portrays. The destruction of the wild prairie, the reduction of wilderness to human terms, the triumph of civilisation over nature, is the domination of masculine over feminine values. The struggle to dominate nature is represented in heroic terms by Cather, but at the same time the loss of the original purity and innocence of the prairie is a cause for lament. Alexandra struggles to bring commercial prosperity to the farm her father established, and to give her brother a future that is free of that very struggle, but in the process she has participated fatally in the destruction of the very landscape with which she identifies.

The way in which Cather attributes gender characteristics to the landscapes her characters inhabit depends heavily upon her use of imagery. The style of imagery Cather uses in 'Neighbour Rosicky'(1932) is distinctive for the way in which she achieves the gendering of the primary narrative figures. The main figures of the narrative are gendered according to a pattern that privileges feminine nature over masculine society. Nature, like a good wife, feeds, nurtures and provides; society is the place for ambition, competitiveness, and the greedy acquisition of goods. The fundamental complication of this story is that to the male protagonist are attributed feminine characteristics. In this way, Cather indicates Rosicky's departure from the attitudes and values of the other, richer farmers. As the narrative begins, Rosicky is placed in a position of inferiority in relation to the Doctor; his ill health means that he cannot do manual, masculine, labour any more; he is told to help his wife; he is rendered a spectator rather than an actor. 'He sometimes complained that though he was getting to be an old man, he wasn't an old woman yet' (Cather, 1932, p. 1011).

Rosicky shares significant similarities with the nurturing figure of his wife: 'to feed creatures was the natural expression of affection' (p. 1007); this view is shared by her husband who also shops and mends, does the dishes for his daughter-in-law in disregard of conventional distinctions between women's work and men's work. Mrs Rosicky considers that in contrast to her husband, 'She was rough, and he was gentle – city-bred, as she always said. ... They agreed, without discussion, as to what was most important and what was secondary. ... They had been at one accord not to hurry through life, not to be always skimping and saving' (p. 1001). But Rosicky is also like his daughter-in-law: she perceives in him 'a special gift for loving people' and he sees in her what he calls 'sweetness of heart'. Above all, the conventional feminine qualities of generosity, love and nurturance binds Rosicky to the soil, to nature.

The feminised hero, Rosicky, represents conflict between the reality of the socially-produced, cultural, and so gendered exploitation of nature – the domination of nature that is represented by organised agriculture – and a nostalgic, idealistic yearning for harmony with nature, such as Jim Burden seeks in *My Ántonia*. Nature takes her revenge on those farmers who seek only financial profit, and in this narrative nature is not represented romantically as an ideal realm that mirrors human hopes and ideals. However, a sense of harmony is represented by images like the description of graveyard and farmyard united by a blanket of snow that 'seemed to draw things together' (p. 1009) into a unity which Rosicky is able to perceive. But harmony is represented only nostalgically and in the context of death. At the end of the narrative, Dr Burleigh stops by the graveyard and reflects upon the significance of the scene and the significance of Rosicky's life and death: 'Nothing could be more undeathlike than this place; nothing could be more right for a man who had helped to do the work of great cities and had always longed for the open country and had got to it at last. Rosicky's life seemed to him complete and beautiful' (p. 1025). The bringing together of life and death, human and non-human life, is only possible in the context of loss. Though Rosicky may feel a special bond with nature, a bond emphasised for us in the narrative by his feminine qualities, still he is a man who has participated in the conquest of nature by bringing civilisation and social life to the once untamed prairie. So Rosicky is an agent of destruction as well as an agent of creation, and as a result it is impossible to disentangle nature itself from the investment of hope that humans like Rosicky have made in it. In other words, it is a humanised nature with which Rosicky feels in harmony, not non-human nature or nature on its own terms. And the conflicting ways in which his character is gendered within the imagistic structure of the narrative reflects this ambiguity.

The thematic texture of the narrative is based upon a conflict between feminine and masculine codes of value. For example, the conflict between the pursuit of financial wealth versus its cost in terms of poverty of spirit embodies the Doctor's view of the Rosicky family as opposed to Marshalls where he finds 'a great deal of expensive farm machinery of the newest model, and no comfort whatever' (p. 1006). 'Maybe, Doctor Burleigh reflected, people as generous and warm-hearted and affectionate as the Rosickys never got ahead much; maybe you couldn't enjoy your life and put it into the bank, too' (p. 1008). But the failure to strive, to engage in competition, to work his way up through the social hierarchy, is Rosicky's most dramatic rejection of masculine cultural values. He seeks the wealth of spirit that he finds in life amid nature.

The opposition between competition and nurturance is represented in part as an opposition between the city and the countryside. In Rosicky's recollection, New York City offers a good but very limited life. Rosicky's remembered image of the city is poisoned by his memories of his time living in the city of London – the grinding poverty, self-interest and degradation he experienced there. Where the countryside represents freedom and fulfilment, the city represents emptiness:

> So much stone and asphalt with nothing going on, so many empty windows. The emptiness was intense, like the stillness in a great factory when the machinery stops and the belts and bands cease running. It was too great a change, it took all the strength out of one. ... this was the trouble with big cities; they built you in from the earth itself, cemented you away from contact with the ground (p. 1013).

It is the countryside or nature which, despite the hardships of the farming life, offers fulfilment for Rosicky who is identified with nature: 'He was like a tree that has not many roots, but one tap-root that goes down deep' (p. 1013), and his daughter-in-law Polly identifies a characteristic of his hands: 'something nimble and lively and sure, in the way that animals are' (p. 1024).

The city harbours the worst elements of humanity and encourages the worst elements of human nature. No hardship, no natural disaster or betrayal by nature faced as a farmer compares with Rosicky's experience of life in the city:

> ... in the city, all the foulness and misery and brutality of your neighbours was part of your life. The worst things he had come upon in his journey through the world were

human, – depraved and poisonous specimens of man. ...
There were mean people everywhere, to be sure, even in
their own country town here. But they weren't tempered,
hardened, sharpened, like the treacherous people in cities
who live by grinding or cheating or poisoning their fellow-
men (p. 1021).

He concludes that town is the place for 'mean boys' but those
who are good and honest, who know nothing of cruelty,
belong in the country.

Cather presents a powerful image of the prescriptive effect
of the social environment on personal identity: Rosicky tells
Polly, 'Dem big cities is all right fur de rich, but dey is terrible
hard fur de poor' (p. 1015). The main transformation of the
story comes about in the relationship between Rosicky and
his daughter-in-law; he convinces her of the value of a life
lived on the land: 'To be a landless man was to be a wage-
earner, a slave, all your life; to have nothing, to be nothing'
(p. 1016). Nature, and the open space of the Nebraska prairie,
offer the opportunity for a kind of freedom that is not
possible in cramped and squalid urban conditions. Rosicky
recalls how hunger and deprivation led him to betray the
trust of Mrs Lifschnitz by eating the goose she has scrimped
and saved to buy for Christmas dinner, and how his guilt and
shame led him to consider suicide, at first, and then led him
to beg for the first time in his life. The brutal conditions of
the big city turn Rosicky into a beggar; these conditions
reduce him until he is no longer recognisable even to
himself. The hardships suffered as a result of crop failure are
insignificant compared to the destruction of dignity and self-
worth that wage-slavery can cause. As a farmer, Rosicky
reflects, '[y]ou didn't have to do with dishonest and cruel
people. They were the only things in his experience he had
found terrifying and horrible: the look in the eyes of a
dishonest and crafty man, of a scheming and rapacious
woman' (p. 1021). Both city and countryside produce
particular types of human personalities: the city produces
those possessed of the worst masculine qualities of aggression
and self-interest; the countryside produces individuals who
are motivated by feminine qualities of care and nurturing.

But the countryfolk will never be rich and powerful, just as the cityfolk will never live in harmony with each other and their environment.

In this narrative, as in *My Ántonia* and *O Pioneers!* small things (especially natural things) are endowed with a significance that elevates them to universal importance. For example, the image of the small country graveyard that occurs early in the narrative and recurs at the end after Rosicky's death represents a union of the human with nature. The open sky and the seemingly endless fields possess an almost mystical quality: the Doctor finds that everything 'seemed strangely moving and significant, though signifying what, he did not know' (p. 1024). The infusion of the human and non-human, the land and the spirit, in a vision of mystical communion, is represented by the mundane and ordinary which is still lifted up by the memory of Rosicky and his life.

The emphasis placed by eco-feminist analysis upon structures of power and domination allows us to see levels of complexity that otherwise are difficult to discern in such simple stories as Willa Cather's Plains Fiction. The notion of 'feminisation', the attribution of feminine qualities to the powerless, allows us to appreciate Cather's ambivalence about the civilising of American nature. At once she values the sacrifices and sufferings of those, especially the immigrant families, who tamed the prairie but at the same time she laments the bringing of civilisation, with all of its human ills, to the pristine state of nature. The loss of innocence can be seen to be matched by the benefits of society but nature is not 'completed' by this process of civilisation and in fact is belittled by it. The possibility of heroism still exists but these stories end ambivalently – 'Neighbour Rosicky' tells of the death of its hero, *My Ántonia* ends with the image of Ántonia as a survivor, but *O Pioneers!* ends with Alexandra dealing with the consequences of the murder of her brother and her friend. Consequently, we must see Cather's representation of heroism as inseparable from the context of loss and nostalgic recollection for a past that perhaps never existed.

References and Selected Further Reading

Adams, Carol, 1990. *The Sexual Politics of Meat: A Feminist-Vegetarian Critical Theory*, New York: Crossroads/Continuum.

——, 1994. *Neither Man Nor Beast: Feminism and the Defense of Animals*, New York: Crossroads/Continuum.

Allen, Paula Gunn, 1986. *The Sacred Hoop: Recovering the Feminine in American Indian Tradition*, Boston: Beacon.

Bailey, Jennifer, 1982. 'The Dangers of Femininity in Willa Cather's Fiction', *Journal of American Studies*, vol. 16, no. 3 (December), pp. 391–406.

Biehl, Janet, 1991. *Finding Our Way: Rethinking Ecofeminist Politics*, New York: Black Rose Books.

Bigwood, Carol, 1993. *Earth Muse: Feminism, Nature, Art*, Philadelphia: Temple University Press.

Bloom, Harold, ed., 1991. *Ántonia*, New York: Chelsea House.

——, 1987. Willa Cather's *My Ántonia*, New York: Chelsea House.

——, 1985. *Willa Cather*. New York: Chelsea House.

Caldecott, Leonie & Stephanie Leland, eds, 1983. *Reclaim the Earth: Women Speak Out for Life on Earth*, London: The Women's Press.

Cather, Willa, 1918. *My Ántonia*, Boston: Houghton Mifflin, 1954.

——, 1913. *O Pioneers!*, New York: Dover Publications, 1993.

——, 1932. 'Neighbour Rosicky', in Nina Baym, et al., eds, *The Norton Anthology of American Literature*. 4th ed. New York & London: W. W. Norton & Co., 1994, vol. 2, pp. 1005–1025.

Collard, Andree, with Joyce Contucci, 1988. *Rape of the Wild: Man's Violence Against Animals and the Earth*, London: The Women's Press.

Diamond, Irene & Gloria Feman Orenstein, 1989. *Reweaving the World: The Emergence of Ecofeminism*, San Francisco: Sierra Club Books.

D'Eaubonne, Françoise, 1980. 'Feminism or Death', in Elaine Marks & Isabelle de Courtivron, eds, *New French Feminisms: An Anthology*, Amherst: University of Massachusetts Press. Originally published as *Le Féminisme ou la mort*, Paris: Pierre Horay, 1974.

Ferguson, Kathy E., 1983. 'Bureaucracy and Public Life: The Feminization of the Polity', *Administration and Society*, 15, 3 (November), rpt. in Nancy Tuana & Rosemarie Tong, eds, *Feminism and Philosophy: Essential Readings in Theory, Reinterpretation and Application.* Boulder, CO: Westview Press, 1995, pp. 374–390.

Fetterly, Judith, 1986. '*My Ántonia*, Jim Burden, and the Dilemma of the Lesbian Writer' in Judith Spector, ed. *Gender Studies: New Directions in Feminist Criticism.* Bowling Green, OH: Popular Press, pp. 43–59.

Gaard, Greta, ed., 1993. *Ecofeminism: Women, Animals, Nature*, Philadelphia: Temple University Press.

Gregory, Robert, 1985. 'Cather in the Canon', *Modern Language Studies*, vol. 15, no. 4 (Fall), pp. 95–101.

Horwitz, Howard, 1988. '*O Pioneers!* and the Paradox of Property: Cather's Aesthetics of Divestment', *Prospects*, vol. 13, pp. 61–93.

Howarth, William, 1998. 'Ego or Eco Criticism? Looking for Common Ground' in Michael P. Branch, Rochelle Johnson, Daniel Patterson & Scott Slovic, eds, *Reading the Earth: New Directions in the Study of Literature and Environment*, Moscow, ID: University of Idaho Press, pp. 3–8.

Hypatia, 1991. Special issue on ecological feminism, vol. 6, no.1 (Spring).

Irving, Katrina, 1990. 'Displacing Homosexuality: The Use of Ethnicity in Willa Cather's *My Ántonia*', *Modern Fiction Studies*, vol. 36, no. 1 (Spring), pp. 91–102.

King, Ynestra, 1982. 'Toward an Ecological Feminism and a Feminist Ecology', in Joan Rothschild, ed., *Machina Ex Dea*, New York: Pergamon.

——, 1983. 'The Eco-Feminist Perspective', in Leonie Caldecott & Stephanie Leland, eds, *Reclaim the Earth: Women Speak Out for Life on Earth.* London: The Women's Press.

——, 1989. 'Healing the Wounds: Feminism, Ecology and Nature/Culture Dualism', in Alison M. Jaggar & Susan R. Bordo, eds, *Gender/Body/Knowledge: Feminist Reconstructions of Being and Knowing*, New Brunswick: Rutgers University Press, reprinted in Nancy Tuana & Rosemarie Tong, eds, *Feminism and Philosophy: Essential Readings in Theory, Rein-*

terpretation and Application. Boulder, CO: Westview Press, 1995, pp. 353–373.

Kvasnicka, Mellanee, 1991. 'Anything a Woman Can Be: Women's Roles in *My Ántonia'*, *Nebraska English Journal*, vol. 37, no. 1 (Fall), pp. 110–117.

Laird, David, 1992. 'Willa Cather's Women: Gender, Place, and Narrativity in *O Pioneers!* and *My Ántonia'*, *Great Plains Quarterly*, vol. 12, no. 4 (Fall), pp. 242–253.

Merchant, Carolyn, 1979. *The Death of Nature: Woman, Ecology and the Scientific Revolution*, New York: Harper & Row.

——, 1992. *Radical Ecology: The Search for a Liveable World*, New York: Routledge.

Mies, Maria, 1988. *Women: The Last Colony*, London & Atlantic Highlands, NJ: Zed Books.

Mies, Maria & Vandana Shiva, eds, 1993. *Ecofeminism*, London & Atlantic Highlands, NJ: Zed Books.

Minh-ha, Trinh T., 1989. *Woman Native Other*, Indianapolis: Indiana University Press.

Murphy, John J., ed., 1984. *Critical Essays on Willa Cather*, Boston: Hall.

Norwood, Vera, 1993. *Made From this Earth: American Women and Nature*, Chapel Hill: University of North Carolina Press.

O'Brien, Sharon, 1984. ' "The Thing Not Named": Willa Cather as a Lesbian Writer', *Signs*, vol. 9, no. 4 (Summer), pp. 576–599.

Paniccia Carden, Mary, 1999. 'Creative Fertility and the National Romance in Willa Cather's *O Pioneers!* and *My Ántonia'*, *Modern Fiction Studies*, vol. 45, no. 2 (Summer), pp. 275–302.

Plant, Judith, ed., 1989. *Healing the Wounds: The Promise of Ecofeminism*, Santa Cruz: New Society Publishers.

Plumwood, Val, 1991. 'Nature, Self and Gender: Feminism, Environmental Philosophy and the Critique of Rationalism', *Hypatia*, vol. 6, no. 1 (Spring), pp.3–27.

Radford Ruether, Rosemary, 1975. *New Woman/New Earth: Sexist Ideologies and Human Liberation*, New York: Seabury.

Romines, Ann, 1997. 'The Little House and the Big Rock: Wilder, Cather, and the Problem of Frontier Girls', *Willa Cather Pioneer Memorial Newsletter*, vol.41, no. 2 (Summer-

Fall), pp. 25–32.

Rosowski, Susan J., 1981. 'Willa Cather's Women', *Studies in American Fiction*, vol. 9, no. 2 (Autumn), pp. 261–275.

——, ed., 1989. *Approaches to Teaching Cather's My Ántonia*, New York: MLA.

——, 1995. 'Willa Cather's Ecology of Place', *Western American Literature*, vol. 30, no. 1 (Spring), pp. 37–51.

Saposnik Noire, Shelley, 1990. 'The Silent Protagonist: The Unifying Presence of Landscape in Willa Cather's *My Ántonia*', *Midwest Quarterly*, vol. 31, no. 2 (Winter), pp. 171–179.

Shiva, Vandana, 1988. *Staying Alive: Women, Ecology and Development*, London: Zed Books.

Schubnell, Matthias, 1991. 'The Farmer as Cultural Model: Neighbor Rosicky's American Dream', *Nebraska English Journal*, vol. 37, no. 1 (Fall), pp. 41–50.

Warren, Karen J., ed., 1997. *Ecofeminism: Women, Culture, Nature*. Bloomington: Indiana University Press.

Warren, Karen J. & Duane L. Cady, eds, 1996. *Bringing Peace Home: Feminism, Violence, and Nature*, Bloomington: Indiana University Press.

Zamora, Lois Parkinson, 1990. 'The Usable Past: The Idea of History in Modern US and Latin American Fiction' in Gustavo Pérez Firmat, ed., *Do the Americas Have a Common Literature?* Durham: Duke University Press, pp. 7–41.

5

Gender and Sexuality: Radical Feminism and Adrienne Rich

This chapter begins with a survey of radical feminist theorists, focusing upon Shulamith Firestone's *The Dialectic of Sex* (1970), Andrea Dworkin's *Right-Wing Women: The Politics of Domesticated Females* (1978), Mary Daly's *Gyn/Ecology: The Metaethics of Radical Feminism* (1978) and Audre Lorde's *Sister Outsider* (1984). The primary theoretical concepts explored here include: the idea of a 'sex class', which in Shulamith Firestone's work describes the condition of women as the most fundamentally oppressed class within a misogynistic Western patriarchal culture; the view of gender as a system that operates to ensure continued male domination; the lesbian feminist representation of the control of feminine sexuality by males through 'compulsory heterosexuality'; and the understanding of the diversity of male sexual violence against women as an institution within the power structure of patriarchy. In the section that follows this theoretical survey, I turn to the radical feminist analysis of the poetry of Adrienne Rich, a writer who is herself a notable radical lesbian feminist theorist and scholar.

Survey of Radical Feminist Theory

Summary of Radical Feminist Principles

Radical feminist theory begins with the assumption that women form a 'sex class'. The condition of women not just as a class but as the fundamentally oppressed class is the starting point for radical feminist analysis. Radical feminism analyses the relationship between social inequality and sexual difference; the domination of women by men is seen to provide the foundation of social inequality, and the sexual oppression of women is seen to underlie the economic, cultural and social subordination of women. For example, a powerful expression of the radical feminist project, 'The New York Radical Feminist Manifesto', claims:

> Radical feminism recognizes the oppression of women as a fundamental political oppression wherein women are categorized as an inferior class based on their sex. It is the aim of radical feminism to organize politically to destroy this sex-class system. As radical feminists we recognize that we are engaged in a power struggle with men, and that the agent of our oppression is man in so far as he identifies with and carries out the supremacy privileges of the male role (quoted by Mitchell, 1971, p. 51).

Examples of misogynistic practices are represented by such texts as Alice Walker's novel *Possessing the Secret of Joy*, which exposes the reality of sexual mutilation and the imprisonment of women in their bodies (women who are unable to walk or run and are constantly in pain). The same representation of gender violence is found in Maxine Hong Kingston's description of Chinese foot-binding in *China Men*; cosmetic surgery and, earlier, corsetry in Western society represent the same kind of gender violence (again, women are rendered unable to move freely, breathing is difficult, they become prone to fainting); the threat posed by rape and violent assault keeps women confined in terms of where they can go and when; pornographic images of sexual torture and violence represent the values of gender violence. Intimidation, terrorism, fear – these strategies keep women in a subordinate position where they are dominated by men.

By viewing gender in this way, radical feminism is able to treat gender as a system. The systemic nature of gender ensures continued male domination through the masculine control of feminine sexuality. In radical feminist terms, gender oppression is the most fundamental form of oppression and precedes the economic structure of patriarchal societies. 'The New York Radical Feminist Manifesto' sets out clearly the independence of patriarchy and sexual oppression from particular economic and political systems:

> We believe that the purpose of male chauvinism is primarily to obtain psychological ego satisfaction, and that only secondarily does this manifest itself in economic relationships. ... For this reason we do not believe that capitalism, or any other economic system, is the cause of female oppression, nor do we believe that female oppression will disappear as a result of a purely economic revolution. The political oppression of women has its own class dynamic. And that dynamic must be understood in terms previously called 'non-political' – namely the politics of the ego. ... Man establishes his 'manhood' in direct proportion to his ability to have his ego override hers, and derives his strength and self-esteem through this process (quoted by Mitchell, 1971, pp. 63–64).

The sexualised hierarchy prescribes that all meanings within society are determined in sexual terms; that is, in terms of the sexuality of the dominant group – men. Catherine MacKinnon asks, 'Is whatever defines women as "different" the same as whatever defines women as "inferior" the same as whatever defines women's "sexuality"?' (MacKinnon, 1990, p. 137). Following this logic, domination is masculine and therefore erotic in men; passivity is feminine and therefore erotic in women. 'Sexuality' is not a neutral term; it refers to male sexuality of which feminine sexuality is seen as a variant (or deviant). Adrienne Rich begins her essay, 'Compulsory Heterosexuality and Lesbian Existence' (1980) by observing the 'bias of compulsory heterosexuality, through which lesbian experience is perceived on a scale ranging from deviant to abhorrent or simply rendered invisible' (Rich, 1993, p. 205). Sexuality is prescribed as heterosexuality, of which masculine heterosexuality is the norm and feminine heterosexuality is somehow the complement. Sex not only expresses but also determines how power is experienced in personal relationships and social behaviour. Consequently, the reform of discriminatory laws is insufficient to end the oppression of women because this kind of reform leaves untouched the oppressive control of women's sexuality by men. Radical feminism is most radical when viewed in contrast with liberal feminist reformist ideas; it is this liberal feminism to which Mary Daly refers as a 'pseudo-feminism [which] has been actively promoted by the patriarchs' (Daly, 1978, p. li). Daly goes on to describe the feminist reform movement as 'male-designed, male-orchestrated, male-legitimated, male-assimilated' (p. lii).

The control of feminine sexuality is achieved through strategies such as the ideology of 'compulsory heterosexuality', restrictions upon the right to contraception and abortion, control of reproductive technologies including sterilisation, and male sexual violence; all of which ensure masculine control of feminine sexuality. Other powerful strategies include the objectification of women – the creation of cultural artefacts from women's bodies; and the representation of dominance or male authority as sexually arousing. The 'erotic' is defined in terms of masculine power, as is the concept of sexuality that every woman is taught. In 'Uses of the Erotic: The Erotic as Power' (1978) Audre Lorde notes that '[o]n the one hand, the superficially erotic has been encouraged as a sign of female inferiority; on the other hand, women have been made to suffer and to feel both contemptible and suspect by virtue of its existence' (Lorde, 1984, p. 106). Because of this indoctrination in patriarchal ways of experiencing sexuality, radical lesbian feminists have been led to assert that heterosexuality itself is reactionary and that heterosexual women are collaborators in the patriarchal oppression of all women. The early lesbian feminist group, the New York Radicalesbians, published in 1970 the groundbreaking essay 'The Woman Identified Woman', the title of which provided a concept that freed lesbianism from the constraints of sexual preference and a set of sexual practices and instead described lesbianism as a set of ideological and political preferences opposed to male supremacy.

In this way, lesbian feminists promoted the idea that heterosexuality rather than economic discrimination forms the basis of male dominance. It is the shared understanding that women are oppressed through their sexuality, whether straight or gay, that connects lesbian feminist theory with radical feminism. The difference resides, however, in the claim by lesbian theorists that the marginal status of lesbians – both as women and as gay women – lends a critical viewpoint that heterosexual women cannot achieve because they are blinded by the privileges accorded to heterosexuality. Lesbian feminism claims the awareness of the outsider to patriarchal institutions, such as the nuclear family, that enables a clear understanding of how all institutions of domination and oppression operate. As well as a more incisive critique of patriarchy, lesbian feminism also claims a powerful identification among all women, based upon the common sexual oppression that all women suffer in a misogynistic culture. Thus, radical lesbian theorists like Mary Daly, Charlotte Bunch, Adrienne Rich and Audre Lorde propose the feminist revaluation of lesbian sensibility and sexuality, the reversal of anti-female masculine myths, and the reconstruction of language and belief systems that have been corrupted by patriarchy, substituting for these misogynistic institutions alternative discourses derived from women's history and culture. Four prominent radical feminist thinkers are Shulamith Firestone, Mary Daly, Andrea Dworkin and Audre Lorde; in what follows I look more closely at the work of these women.

Shulamith Firestone, The Dialectic of Sex *(1970)*

Shulamith Firestone was one of the founders of the early radical feminist group, the New York Redstockings, and with Anne Koedt she wrote the group's first liberation manifesto. Her influential work, *The Dialectic of Sex*, begins with the statement: 'Sex class is so deep as to be invisible' (Firestone, 1970, p. 1); she goes on, '[i]t is everywhere. The division Yin and Yang pervades all culture, history, economics, nature itself; modern Western versions of sex discrimination are only the most recent layer' (p. 2). Firestone presents a number of theoretical perspectives – Marx, Engels, Freud – adapting them to the requirements of a radical feminist analysis of the sex class. She begins with the Marxist analysis of class but shifts the emphasis away from economic to sexual determinants. Engels's observation that the original division of labour was between man and woman in the relation of biological reproduction; so man is the owner, woman the means of production and children the labour. But where Engels then focuses his interest in the economic oppression of the class divisions to which this original division gives rise, Firestone concentrates on the implications of his observation of biological determination. She asks whether biology, and specifically biological reproduction, may not be at the origin of the division between men and women: '[t]he immediate assumption of the layman that the unequal division of the sexes is "natural" may be well-founded. We need not immediately look beyond this. Unlike economic class, sex class sprang directly from a biological reality: men and women were created different, and not equally privileged' (p. 8). So Firestone suggests that the reproductive difference between the sexes led to the first division of labour and subsequently to all further division into economic and cultural classes. This does not mean, however, that she wants to argue that female biology dictates women's destiny. On the contrary, Firestone is quick to point out that the maintenance of a discriminatory sex class on the basis of 'natural origins' cannot be justified. She argues, 'though man is increasingly capable of freeing himself from the biological conditions that created his tyranny over women and children, he has little reason to want to give this tyranny up' (pp. 10–11). And indeed, transformation of the biological basis of oppression (through advanced reproductive technologies, in Firestone's argument) does not guarantee that the oppression of women originally created by this biology will disappear. The sex class identified by Firestone has become independent of the conditions that created it; indeed it has become the model for a range of exploitative cultural relations. The aim of the radical feminist movement, therefore, is not simply the end of male privilege; it is the destruction of the sex class, of the cultural distinction between the sexes, that radical feminism seeks.

The sexual class to which individual women are assigned by reason of their gender generates, then, an entire system of discriminatory relationships and castes, or classes. But sexual oppression is the fundamental and foundational form of oppression in patriarchal society. Firestone uses Freudian theory, reoriented towards the emphasis upon the sex class that is grounded in the biological family, and builds upon Freud's perception that sexuality is the key to understanding the structure of social and cultural relations: Freudian theory is 'examined in power, i.e., political, terms; the antidote of feminism cancels the sex bias that produced the initial distortion' (p. 58). Firestone is dismissive of the therapeutic value of psychoanalysis; however, as a starting point for the analysis of the power dynamic within the biological family and the perpetuation of this power structure, Freudian theory offers a very useful paradigm. Firestone uses Freud, as she says, 'to show how the power hierarchies in the biological family, and the sexual repressions necessary to maintain it – especially intense in the patriarchal nuclear family – are destructive and costly to the individual psyche' (p. 81). She also shows how women and children are educated to accept their place in a lower class, a rigidly segregated class modelled upon the sexual class that is 'woman', through the twin mythologies of femininity and childhood. Physical and economic dependence, upon men, upon parents, link women and children in a common class experience, and consequently the liberation of children must be part of the radical feminist project: Firestone proclaims, 'our final step must be the elimination of the very conditions of femininity and childhood themselves that are now conducive to this alliance of the oppressed, clearing the way for a fully "human" condition' (p. 118). Firestone shows how racism, similarly, depends upon a gendered hierarchy of power relations modelled upon the patriarchal family and originating in the creation of a sexual class of the oppressed. Race relations are described as akin to the hierarchical relations within the nuclear family:

> [t]he white man is father, the white woman wife-and-mother, her status dependent on his; the blacks, like children, are his property, their physical differentiation branding them the subservient class, in the same way that

children form so easily distinguishable a servile class vis-à-vis adults. This power hierarchy creates the psychology of racism, just as, in the nuclear family, it creates the psychology of sexism (pp. 122–123).

Firestone uses her feminist reinterpretation of the Oedipus and Electra Complexes to analyse the class relations that underlie racial oppression. She uses the same analysis of the psychosexual dynamic to answer the question she poses herself about the mythology of love and romance in patriarchal culture: 'How does the sex class system based on the unequal power distribution of the biological family affect love between the sexes?' (p. 146). She concludes that love and romance are very different for men and for women; the difference is determined by the early relationship with the mother: men idealise, mystify and glorify the individual women with whom they fall in love in order to obscure her inferior class status; women, in contrast, pursue the male love and approval that will raise her up from her subordinate class position and validate her existence. In this way, love becomes a political force, a force for unequal power relations.

The separation of women into a sexually-defined class gives rise, in Firestone's analysis, to the gendered divisions of culture as well. Women are excluded from the realms of art and science, aesthetics and technology, as an extension of the basic sexual division. And yet it is through technological advance that Firestone is able to envision a revolution in the structure and operations of society by freeing humanity from the tyranny of biology. She focuses upon two areas of technological advance: first, the transformation of family relations through fertility control and artificial reproduction, and secondly cybernation or the use of machines to transform the human relation to work and economic relations. This is the best remedy for the oppression Firestone locates in the sexual slave class that is 'woman': subject to the tyranny of biology, '[w]omen were the slave class that maintained the species in order to free the other half for the business of the world' (p. 232). Only by overcoming the tyranny of nature, by destroying comprehensively the biological basis of the sex class, and sexual classification or discrimination itself, can women be truly liberated.

Andrea Dworkin, Right-Wing Women: The Politics of Domesticated Females *(1978)*

In chapters entitled 'The Coming Gynocide' and 'Antifeminism' Andrea Dworkin sets out her understanding of the implications of reproductive technologies for the liberation of women. While Dworkin shares Firestone's perception that the oppression of women arises from causes that are fundamentally biological, that women are oppressed through their sexuality, she sees in medical and technological advances only more sophisticated patriarchal strategies for controlling women's sexuality and keeping women imprisoned in their biology.

In the preface to the British edition of her book, Andrea Dworkin makes clear what she means by the label, 'right-wing women': these are 'women who claim to be acting in the interests of women as a group [who] act effectively in behalf of male authority over women, in behalf of a hierarchy in which women are subservient to men, in behalf of women as the rightful property of men, in behalf of religion as an expression of transcendent male supremacy' (Dworkin, 1983, p. xii). Dworkin deals with the case of radically male-identified women, women who struggle *against* the women's movement, in order to highlight the ways in which patriarchy forces conformity and assimilation to its value structure. There are numerous patriarchal strategies that Dworkin explores. She begins with the stereotype of women as conservative, home-bound and nurturing:

Noxious male philosophers from all disciplines have, for centuries, maintained that women follow a biological imperative derived directly from their reproductive capacities that translates necessarily into narrow lives, small minds, and a rather meanspirited puritanism (p. 13).

While Dworkin obviously does not agree with this biological explanation for women's condition, she describes this condition as one in which women are obliged to give their assent and conform in their social behaviour to this paradigm. To rebel against this prescription for female behaviour is to risk incurring the wrath of the men around her: 'a woman acquiesces to male authority in order to gain some protection from male violence' (p. 14). This is the bottom line, in Dworkin's view: women are kept passive and subordinate by the ever-present threat of male violence. Women internalise patriarchal values to perfect their obedience; they conform to the stereotypes, they display unwavering loyalty, they do not betray any sign of dissatisfaction or resistance to male control – all in order to avoid violence against their persons. And this threat of male violence is present all around each individual woman in patriarchal culture: 'rape, wife beating, forced childbearing, medical butchering, sex-motivated murder, sadistic psychological abuse' (p. 20) – these are some of the punishments Dworkin catalogues, in addition to destitution, ostracism, confinement in a mental institution or gaol, or death, that await the rebellious woman. Conformity means survival in a misogynistic patriarchal culture; this is despite the fact that the list of violent acts which men inflict upon women demonstrates that this conformity does not work, conformity does not defuse the male hatred of women that is constitutive of patriarchy. But there seems to be no alternative. Dworkin observes that women hang on, tenaciously,

> to the very persons, institutions, and values that demean her, degrade her, glorify her powerlessness, insist upon constraining and paralyzing the most honest expressions of her will and being. She becomes a lackey, serving those who ruthlessly and effectively aggress [sic] against her and her kind. This singularly self-hating loyalty to those committed to her own destruction is the very essence of womanhood as men of all ideological persuasions define it (p. 17).

In this paragraph, Dworkin sets out the fundamental terms of her radical feminism. First, both men and women occupy sexual classes; differences in socio-economic class status are insignificant compared to the common experience of oppression of women by men. Women constitute the oppressed class in patriarchal society and men constitute the class of oppressors. Men 'of all ideological persuasions' define women and femininity in the same patriarchal terms, and all women are subject to this definition. This sexual oppression through the gender relation is the most basic relation of social and cultural oppression, and the one from which all other oppressive relations derive. Secondly, the relation is maintained by means of unceasing physical violence and psychological aggression against women. Thirdly, the operations of gender class and sexual coercion work within the context of patriarchy as a system that operates through 'persons, institutions, and values'. Gender oppression is systematic under patriarchy and not a matter of isolated violent and discriminatory incidents. But the systemic nature of patriarchy is obscured, except when subjected to feminist questioning and analysis. As Dworkin points out, the stories of female suffering, of the brutal violence that women experience, do not get told: '[t]he tellers and the stories are ignored or ridiculed, threatened back into silence or destroyed, and the experience of female suffering is buried in cultural invisibility and contempt' (p. 20). Without a male witness to validate these stories they are meaningless in patriarchal terms; the experience of someone who is regarded as an object or even as an absence, 'someone who by definition has no legitimate claim to dignity or freedom' (p. 21), is no experience at all.

What the contemporary political Right in the United States offers women is a response to the fears created by the violence of patriarchal society; Dworkin lists the components of this political promise as: a fixed worldview, protection for the home and women's place in it, personal safety, a fixed set of behavioural rules for both men and women, and love both personal and religious that is based on order and stability. This promise of safety and security answers to, but also perpetuates, the fear of women and their perception that survival is only possible on male terms. This means, Dworkin argues, that the anger women feel for their male abusers and oppressors must be displaced elsewhere, on to 'those far away, foreign, or different' (p. 34), so these women become extreme nationalists, racists, anti-Semites, homophobes and bigots; they hate religious or political groups other than their own, people on welfare or unemployed, the destitute, pregnant teenagers and single mothers, and so on. 'Having good reason to hate, but not the courage to rebel, women require symbols of danger that justify their fear. The Right provides these symbols of danger by designating clearly defined groups of outsiders as sources of danger' (p. 34). Dworkin points to the ironic situation of these right-wing women who believe they are protecting their own survival when in fact they are committing moral and spiritual suicide. The role of radical feminism is to offer an accurate analysis of the condition of these women and all women, to offer a means by which female rage can be properly directed against those who do terrorise women, and to point to a struggle for both 'individual and collective survival that is not based on self-loathing, fear, and humiliation, but instead on self-determination, dignity, and authentic identity' (p. 35).

Mary Daly, Gyn/Ecology: The Metaethics of Radical Feminism *(1978)*

The retrieval of feminine authenticity motivates Mary Daly's work. The subject of *Gyn/Ecology* is patriarchy: specifically, the universal patriarchal religion and not just Christianity, which was the subject of Daly's 1973 book, *Beyond God the Father: Toward a Philosophy of Women's Liberation*. Daly seeks out and exposes the phallocratic myths and symbols that are direct sources of Christian myth which promotes a male-centred view of the world to the exclusion of female experience. Daly is concerned not only to expose the lies that have been told in order to obscure the truth about women's experience and history; she is engaged in the rediscovery of women's meanings (myths and symbols) that have been hidden, buried, their significance reversed by the historical operations of patriarchy. Patriarchy exerts an intellectual or cerebral violence which fragments reality by dividing meanings into sexual classes, repressing feminine meanings and perceptions with the consequence that women experience the world in artificially segmented fragments. Consequently, Daly is concerned to recover the connections among these fragments and to weave together the 'threads of connectedness' (as she calls them) that will restore a gyno-centric reality. It is in this relation that one of Daly's controlling metaphors gains its multiple significances; she refers to her writing as an activity, the activity of spinning – spinning as in joining threads to be woven, 'the whirling movement of creation' (p. 3), spinning as a non-linear movement towards and away from a centre that remains implied, in what Daly calls 'the metapatriarchal journey of exorcism and ecstasy'. 'Radical feminist consciousness spirals in all directions, dis-covering the past, creating/dis-closing the present/future' (p. 1). The term 'metapatriarchal' Daly coins to describe the nature of the journey upon which she is embarked; a journey that is in some respects post-patriarchal, that locates patriarchy in the past, a journey that delves behind patriarchal constructions of reality, into what Daly calls the 'background' of unified feminine experience and which is fragmented by the lies and delusions that comprise the patriarchal 'foreground' in which women are forced to live if they would live 'normal' lives.

There are four primary patriarchal strategies used to keep women mystified about their true condition. First, there is 'erasure' which means the removal of women from the historical record: Daly cites the execution of witches that does not appear in patriarchal scholarship. Secondly, there is 'reversal', such that women are placed in subordinate and passive roles: Daly cites the example of Adam giving birth to Eve. Thirdly, there is 'false polarization', for example, male-defined feminism set up in opposition to male-defined sexism. Fourthly, there is 'divide and conquer' which Daly illustrates with the example of '[t]oken women [who] are trained to kill off feminists in patriarchal professions'. The exposure of these strategies as patterns that are part of women's education in patriarchal culture is an important part of the process of stripping away the layers of oppressive 'mindbindings' that is the process of Daly's 'metapatriarchal' journey. The term 'metapatriarchal' is also used to signify transcendence of patriarchy, by which she does not mean the reform of patriarchy but instead the entire transformation of the female subject that has been created by patriarchy.

This new feminine subject and unified female worldview cannot be articulated or described in the language of patriarchal oppression. A new woman-centred language is needed and Daly invents just such a language in order to resist and move beyond 'patriarchal mind manipulation'. In the preface to *Gyn/Ecology* Daly explains that three words in particular, from her earlier work, have now become unusable: God, androgyny, and homosexuality. She explains:

There is no way to remove male/masculine imagery from *God*. Thus, when writing/speaking 'anthropomorphically' of ultimate reality, of the divine spark of be-ing, I now choose to write/speak gynomorphically. I do so because *God* represents the necrophilia of patriarchy, whereas *Goddess* affirms the life-loving be-ing of women and nature. The second semantic abomination, *androgyny*, is a confusing term which I sometimes used in attempting to describe integrity of be-ing. The word is misbegotten – conveying something like 'John Travolta and Farrah Fawcett-Majors scotch-taped together' – as I have reiterated in public recantations. The third treacherous term, *homosexuality*, reductionistically 'includes', that is, excludes, gynocentric be-ing/Lesbianism (Daly, 1978, p. xlviii).

Daly's intention is not simply to substitute alternative words for these same concepts, but entirely to supplant the patriarchal language that embodies and communicates a male-centred worldview. She does this with an alternative vocabulary that belongs to a woman-identified experience of the world; a gynocentric or lesbian 'be-ing', in Daly's terms.

This language is distinguished by its power to expose the values of male supremacy and female selflessness or invisibility that pervade everyday life under patriarchy. The normalisation of violence and the naturalisation of atrocities against women are achieved through patriarchal norms and values. Violence against women is a normal part of life in a patriarchal society; the assumption that evil has a feminine character is a patriarchal value: Daly uses the then topical example of the movie *The Exorcist* to point to the fact that in our culture it is considered appropriate for a movie to represent a Jesuit who exorcises a girl who is possessed. 'Why is there no book or film about a woman who exorcises a Jesuit?' (p. 2) Daly asks. Revealingly, it is her question that seems outrageous, not the association our culture makes between women and metaphysical evil – an association that is then used to victimise women. The bulk of Daly's study is concerned with the modes of patriarchal violence and atrocities committed against women: Daly catalogues Goddess-murdering atrocities; mutilation, sexual abuse, pornography, battering and incest, prostitution, the new reproductive technologies, the torture of animals under vivisection, global pollution and the environmental destruction of what she calls 'Sister Earth'. While Daly makes clear that she is concerned with 'the mind/spirit/body pollution inflicted through patriarchal myth and language at all levels, she clarifies the relation between her concern and the material realities of global destruction: '[p]hallic myth and language generate, legitimate, and mask the material pollution that threaten to terminate all sentient life on this planet' (p. 9). Her term for this pervasive violence that is constitutive of patriarchy is the Sado-Ritual Syndrome, and in a series of chapters she explores the patriarchal practices or customs of widow-burning (suttee) in India, Chinese footbinding, the genital mutilation or 'circumcision' of young girls in Africa, the massacre of women as witches in Renaissance Europe, and the 'gynocide' that goes by the names of gynaecology and psychotherapy in America.

The exposure of these practices and the profound hatred of women that underlies patriarchy are directed by Daly at women who find that their anger has been displaced and focused against other women rather than against the woman-hating culture of patriarchy. This displacement is revealed in symptoms like self-hatred and what Daly calls, in the 'New Intergalactic Introduction' to the second edition of *Gyn/Ecology*, the 'horizontal violence' that is shared among the community of women (Daly, 1978, p. xxxiii). Daly seeks then the focusing of this rage, in order that women might survive, physically and spiritually, by reconnecting with their own female selves and with other women in sisterhood.

Audre Lorde, Sister Outsider *(1984)*

One of the best-known responses to Mary Daly's achievement in *Gyn/Ecology* is Audre Lorde's 'An Open Letter to Mary Daly' (1979) which is reprinted among the essays, speeches and journals that comprise *Sister Outsider*. Lorde refers to the common condition of 'outsider' that she shares with Daly, as radical lesbian feminists. It is this perspective of the outsider that offers a privileged insight into the operations of patriarchal discourses and institutions from which the lesbian is excluded in ways that the heterosexual woman is not. Lorde highlights the concern she and Daly share about the violence done to feminine traditions, myths and 'herstory' (or history) by the power of white patriarchy. But she points to the different experiences of oppression by white and black women: she remarks that the 'white women with hoods on in Ohio handing out KKK literature on the street may not like what you have to say, but they will shoot me on sight' (pp. 122–123). Lorde's point is that while the oppression of women does not respect the differences between women, these differences mean that women experience the oppressive power of patriarchy differently. Lorde is very aware of the danger that these differences may be internalised by the women's movement, which ghettoises poor women, women of colour and lesbians, and used against women and against positive change.

In 'The Master's Tools Will Never Dismantle the Master's House' (1979) Lorde asks, 'What does it mean when the tools of a racist patriarchy are used to examine the fruits of that same patriarchy?' And she offers the answer, 'It means that only the most narrow perimeters of change are possible and allowable' (p. 158). Though Lorde and Daly are both radical lesbian feminists, the fact that Daly is white and Lorde is black is a difference that potentially separates them but is also potentially an empowering dynamic between them.

Different tools of oppression are experienced by women in different circumstances, but they remain the tools of patriarchal oppression. Lorde's criticism of Daly's colour-blindness is based on her reading of *Gyn/Ecology* where white, European, Judeo-Christian goddesses are cited as examples of the female tradition that has been obscured by the long historical influence of patriarchy, but the experience of non-European women is used to illustrate the position of women as what Lorde calls 'victims and preyers-upon each other' (p. 120), as in Daly's account of African genital mutilation. In her letter, Lorde writes,

> Mary, I ask that you be aware of how this serves the destructive forces of racism and separation between women – the assumption that the herstory and myth of white women is the legitimate and sole herstory and myth of all women to call upon for power and background, and that nonwhite women and our herstories are noteworthy only as decorations, or examples of female victimization (p. 122).

Lorde expresses here her anxiety that the patriarchal destruction of feminine power is being repeated by the absence of black women's words from the vocabulary of white radical feminism: she observes that 'so little material on non-white female power and symbol exists in white women's words from a radical feminist perspective' and so, for Daly also to omit this material, 'is to deny the fountain of non-european [sic] female strength and power that nurtures each of our visions' (p. 121).

The denial of feminine power is also explored in the influential essay, 'Uses of the Erotic: The Erotic as Power' (1978), where Audre Lorde explores the relationship between the power of the erotic, as opposed to the degrading, influences of pornography or sadomasochism. Pornography is defined as the opposite of the erotic; pornography is sensation divorced from feeling and hence from knowledge. Power, and the power of the erotic, in Lorde's terms is the power of creativity, of what she calls 'nonrational knowledge', of dialogue between women of diverse races and sexualities:

'The erotic is a resource within each of us that lies in a deeply female and spiritual plane, firmly rooted in the power of our unexpressed or unrecognized feeling' (p. 106). The erotic becomes a source of creative power – a life-giving force in Lorde's argument – capable of bridging differences among women, and a part of everyday experience rather than an experience apart from the rest of life. Lorde describes the experience of the power of the erotic as the sharing of joy with others, which 'forms a bridge between the sharers which can be the basis for understanding much of what is not shared between them, and lessens the threat of their difference' (p. 109). The power of the erotic is also a bridge between the mind and the body, bringing them into a powerful conjunction. Because of this transformative power, the erotic must be suppressed if patriarchal oppression is to perpetuate itself.

Lorde identifies the erotic only as a feminine power; to experience the erotic is to 'do that which is female and self-affirming in the face of a racist, patriarchal, and anti-erotic society' (p. 112). The erotic empowers, but difference becomes paralysis when silence, separation and lack of dialogue reign among women. This kind of paralysis is promoted in a patriarchal society by practices that teach us to mistrust and to suppress the power of the erotic in our own lives; Lorde refers to 'the false belief that only by the suppression of the erotic within our lives and consciousness can women be truly strong. But that strength is illusory, for it is fashioned within the context of male models of power' (p. 106). In place of this suppression, Lorde describes the empowerment through the erotic that she sees taking place around her as women act upon the power of *eros*, of love in all its aspects: 'an assertion of the lifeforce of women; of that creative energy empowered, the knowledge and use of which we are now reclaiming in our language, our history, our dancing, our loving, our work, our lives' (p. 108). In significant ways, this concept of the erotic describes the achievement of Audre Lorde's friend and colleague, Adrienne Rich. Rich's poetry and also her radical lesbian feminist theory realise this reclamation of feminine language, history, loving, work and lives.

Radical Feminism in Praxis

In the following section, some of the major poem sequences written by Adrienne Rich – 'Snapshots of a Daughter-in-Law', 'Diving into the Wreck', and 'Twenty-One Love Poems' – are analysed in radical feminist terms. The discussion of Adrienne Rich's work focuses upon themes of male violence and aggression against women; the disempowerment of women especially by patriarchal language; the history of demeaning and destructive patriarchal images of women; the connection between the personal and the political; and the importance of acknowledging and celebrating the strong female figures that have been hidden from history. The reconstruction of gender, ethics, morality, history, sexuality is tied to the necessary resistance to oppression and self-discovery that is available to all women through the women's culture that has been hidden and denied by the patriarchy. These themes are brought into relation with Rich's practice of lesbian feminist poetics and her innovative poetic techniques of free association; free verse forms; the strategic deployment of a fragmentary style; collage; use of juxtaposition; her use of imagery taken from the devalued domestic and feminine realms in order to subvert the oppressor's language by reclaiming images, symbols, myths that have been used for misogynistic purposes but properly belong to a vibrant and rich women's culture.

Adrienne Rich's influential essay 'Compulsory Heterosexuality and Lesbian Existence' (1980) begins by questioning how and why this vibrant women's culture should be so fragmentary and divided, and invisible to so many women. Her answer is revealed by uncovering the connection between the enforcement of heterosexuality and the erasure of lesbian existence in patriarchal society. Thus, in Rich's view, the most fundamental form of oppression experienced by women is heterosexuality and specifically this enforced, compulsory heterosexuality. She sets out two major areas of exploration:

first, how and why women's choice of women as passionate comrades, life partners, co-workers, lovers, community has been crushed, invalidated, forced into hiding and disguise; and second, the virtual or total neglect of lesbian existence in a wide range of writings, including feminist scholarship. Obviously there is a connection here (Rich in Gelpi & Gelpi, 1993, p. 205–206).

Rich begins with the question why women should surrender the original mother-daughter bond, so crucial to female gender identity, in favour of heterosexual relationships. Contrary to the patriarchal assumption that all women are 'naturally' predisposed to a sexual attraction towards men, Rich points out that the original love object for both the male and the female child is the mother. She points to the confusion between reproduction and love, and suggests that if we are to discover the mechanisms by which women are forced to abandon woman-identified values in favour of the values of patriarchy then we must ask two fundamental questions: 'why species survival, the means of impregnation, and emotional/erotic relationships should ever have become so rigidly identified with each other; and why such violent strictures should be found necessary to enforce women's total emotional, erotic loyalty and subservience to men' (p. 206). Because of these strictures, the feminist strategy proposed by theorists such as Nancy Chodorow and Carol Gilligan, that men should become active agents in childcare and the nurturing of infants, will not achieve its feminist objectives, according to Rich. Men can 'mother' but the exercise of male power in a male-dominated, male-identified society will ensure that the power imbalance between men and women remains unchanged. Strategies of male power range from the physical control of women's bodies, such as the chastity belt or arranged marriage, to the control of feminine conscious-ness, such as 'the erasure of lesbian existence' or the 'idealization of heterosexual romance and marriage'. Women are trained by the cultural images that surround them to romanticise their resulting subservience. Among the most pernicious of these images are the pornographic images which teach 'that women are natural sexual prey to men and love it, that sexuality and violence are congruent' (p. 209). But Rich points out that the influence of pornography goes beyond even this:

> Pornography does not simply create a climate in which sex and violence are interchangeable; *it widens the range of behavior considered acceptable from men in heterosexual intercourse* – behavior which reiteratively strips women of their autonomy, dignity, and sexual potential, including the potential of loving and being loved by women in mutuality and integrity' (Rich's emphasis, pp. 209–210).

Other strategies of male power that ensure male sexual access to women include: 'prostitution, marital rape, father-daughter and brother-sister incest, wife beating, ... bride price, the selling of daughters, purdah, and genital mutilation' (p. 212). From the perspective of male domination and female subservience, these strategies of terrorism and sexual abuse appear natural and inevitable, if they are not rendered invisible.

Rich not only suggests that all women are originally female-identified and that the process of becoming a woman in patriarchal societies is also the process of becoming heterosexual, or male-identified. She also suggests that women's experience, values and culture are quite distinct from those of patriarchal heterosexual culture. This female culture is rendered invisible and marginal, if not taboo in the manner of lesbianism, by the imposition of heterosexuality and the insistence upon lesbianism as abnormal and perverse, 'written out of history and catalogued under disease' (p. 216). Rich thus proposes a kind of feminist separatism that is based upon the perception that all women participate in the woman-identified experience that she calls a 'lesbian continuum', which is constituent of every woman's emotional being; Rich invokes Audre Lorde's understanding of the erotic as a sharing of joy among women. The lesbian continuum suggests 'both the fact of the historical presence of lesbians and our continuing creation of the meaning of that existence' (p. 217). She distinguishes this cultural and historical continuum from the additional physical sexual experience of lesbianism, which she terms 'lesbian experience'. Lesbian existence challenges not only the strategies of male power through compulsory heterosexuality but also the underlying assertion of the male right of sexual, emotional and economic access to women.

Adrienne Rich's Poetry

The strategies of male power and the resources for feminist resistance form Rich's primary poetic subject. Adrienne Rich's career divides clearly into two phases which are marked by her dramatic shift away from Modernist formalism (her work in the 1950s was praised by W. H. Auden and her first volume, *A Change of World* [1951], was chosen by him for the Yale Younger Poets Award) to openly political engagement. In the 1960s Rich was active in the Civil Rights and anti-war movements, in 1970 she joined the Women's Movement, and her poetry from the 1960s reflects her growing radical feminist commitment. Rich sees poetry as embodying experience; it should contribute to knowledge, that deep non-rational knowledge to which Audre Lorde refers, and to the emotional life while reflecting and assimilating life. Poetry should be a learning experience as well as being about experience. This is how it should, in turn, affect the reader. So Rich's poetry is grounded in the physical present; she resists the transcendence of symbolism; she exposes the political and gender biases of poetic formalism as she attempts to discover a form that expresses experience but does not falsify that experience within an artificial form – form is a process of discovery. The difference between her early and later poetry lies in a refusal to be silenced or to censor her thoughts, emotions and awareness. The rejection of convention and propriety represents a difference in consciousness, which is a radical lesbian feminist consciousness.

Adrienne Rich's poetic subject matter coincides with her radical feminist commitment. Consequently, she writes of: male violence and aggression against women; the disempowerment of women especially by patriarchal language; demeaning and destructive patriarchal images of women. The connection between the personal and the political, a major motivation of her poetry, is explored in relation to the confessional poetic voice. She tells of the important but suppressed female figures in history and their achievements; she writes of the reconstruction of gender, ethics, morality, history, and sexuality from a lesbian feminist basis; and the motivation both to resist oppression and to seek self-knowledge that is to be found in women's culture.

These radical ideas require that the poet transcend poetic convention to discover a voice that will articulate a genuine radical feminist vision. Rich rejects the use of formal rhyme schemes; regular rhythmic patterns; formal stanzaic structure; conventional generic forms and conventionally 'poetic' image structures, in favour of free expression that matches her subject matter. She makes use of free association; free verse forms; a fragmentary style; collage; juxtaposition; imagery taken from the domestic and feminine realms; she subverts the oppressor's language by reclaiming images, symbols, myths that have been used for misogynistic purposes. In these ways, both in subject and in form, she rejects the conventional, the traditional and the public forms of articulation in favour of a politicised feminist voice.

The poem sequence 'Snapshots of a Daughter-in-Law' (1958–60) marks the beginning of Rich's awareness of the personal character of sexual politics: the oppression of women, by means of their (hetero-)sexuality, by society and individual men. In the first of the ten numbered stanzas, the wife's mind is 'moldering like wedding cake' (l. 7, p. 9) – an image that links the patriarchal institution of marriage with the dissolution of individual feminine identity. In the second stanza madness approaches in the form of violence turned inward, in the self-harm she inflicts in casual, domestic ways, and in the form of the angelic voices that voice her desires, desires that are quite illegitimate in patriarchal terms. *'Have no patience'*, they say; and, *'Be insatiable'*; and *'Save yourself; the others you cannot save'* (ll. 17, 18, 19, Rich's emphases, p. 9). Stanza three introduces the idea of female monsters, 'A thinking woman sleeps with monsters' (l. 26, p. 9) and of monstrous feminine desires – as these erotic impulses are defined by the male cultural tradition. Feminine dissatisfaction is related to the position of women under patriarchy: domesticity which is constitutive of the social image of femininity; and misogyny which generates the marginality, silence, and invisibility of women. In this and many poems throughout her career, Rich writes of the forgotten lives of women who have defied patriarchal definitions: Emily Dickinson in the poem, '*I Am in Danger-Sir-*' (1964), the astronomer Caroline Herschel who was forgotten whilst her brother is remembered in 'Orion' (1965), Marie Curie in 'Power' (1974), 'For Ethel Rosenberg' (1980). In the stanzas that follow in 'Snapshots of a Daughter-in-Law', Rich introduces historical women who were derided and rejected for their attempts to live independent lives: Emily Dickinson, 'writing, My Life had stood – a Loaded Gun – / in that Amherst pantry while the jellies boil and scum' (ll. 45–46, p. 10), and Mary Wollstonecraft:

> a woman, partly brave and partly good,
> who fought with what she partly understood.
> Few men about her would or could do more,
> hence she was labelled harpy, shrew and whore
> (ll.73–76, p. 11).

And Rich cites the kind of dismissive remarks published by intellectual men such as Diderot and Dr Johnson to silence and belittle these women, and all women, who are defined by patriarchy in terms of their usefulness and availability to men.

The poem juxtaposes images of women who have defied patriarchal convention with images of women who conform: she who 'shaves her legs until they gleam / like petrified mammoth-tusk' (ll. 51–52) and Corinna, of Thomas Campion's poem, who makes music but can claim neither the words nor the music as her own. At the end of the poem the ideal woman is seen in Rich's feminist terms as one who defines herself as an autonomous woman, 'who must be / more merciless to herself than history' (ll. 109–110, p.12). The poem focuses upon culturally defined images of women to expose the unnaturalness of oppression, but this is twinned with an awareness of the strategies of male power that keep women passive and servile. For those who conform, 'mediocrities [are] over-praised, / indolence read as abnegation, / slattern thought styled intuition, / every lapse forgiven' (ll. 99–102, p. 12). But for those who resist patriarchal domination the punishment is violent and extreme:

'solitary confinement, / tear gas, attrition shelling' (ll. 105–106, p. 12). Rich exposes the fact that gender roles are created and sustained by a pattern of cultural behaviours, though gender difference is constructed and manipulated primarily through language and cultural imagery. Consequently, Rich needs to define an alternative to the language constructed by a male-identified patriarchal society. She seeks a style of art that resists social prejudice but still uses the language of her society in order to transform it from within. The link she forges between art and politics was controversial, even dangerous, during the Cold War era but such a link is necessary if the will to change, to reform consciousness and society, is to be fostered through language.

The urgency of change is emphasised in poems where feminine oppression is linked with the Indo-Chinese War and violence against women is identified with military aggression. One such poem is 'The Burning of Paper Instead of Children' (1968), the title of which, Rich explains in a prefatory paragraph, comes from a neighbour's complaint about the burning of some textbooks by her son and his. She quotes him as saying, *'there are few things that upset me so much as the idea of burning a book'* (Rich's emphasis, p. 40). This poem is devoted to the exposure of the many things that should be more upsetting: the language of the oppressor that is contained in the carefully preserved books written by men is juxtaposed with the image of a hungry child, and a mother too poor to feed her children, and no language with which to articulate the horror of this suffering. Throughout the poem, this exploration of language and specifically the language of the oppressor that is preserved in books, is juxtaposed with imagery of heterosexual lovemaking. Rich draws together the significance of the written signs and the language of heterosexual intercourse by referring to both as 'knowledge of the oppressor'. To enter a temple, to enter a heterosexual relationship, to enter the world of a book, is to enter the world of the oppressor and to adopt his prescribed language. Imagery of burning is used to bring together the various significances of patriarchal violence: the napalm of military violence, the lynchings and burnings of racial violence, the violence of sexual jealousy, and the burning of anger, righteous feminist anger. She concludes the poem, 'The burning of a book arouses no sensation in me. I know it hurts to burn. There are flames of napalm in Catonsville, Maryland. I know it hurts to burn. The typewriter is overheated, my mouth is burning. I cannot touch you and this is the oppressor's language' (pp. 42–43). In these terms, relationships between men and women within the context of male-domination and male-identification can only be mutually self-destructive. Importantly, Rich questions how anger should be expressed, how anger *can* be expressed in language other than the oppressor's. In 'The Phenomenology of Anger' she identifies the difficulty of locating an alternative vocabulary for anger in the very difficulty she experiences of locating the oppressor: 'at once the most destructive / and the most elusive being / gunning down the babies at My Lai / vanishing in the face of confrontation' (ll. 46–49, p. 57). The killing of Vietnamese civilians by the US military offers a powerful image of patriarchal violence that is obvious in its deeds but impossible to identify positively in individuals. Only by the acts committed in its name can patriarchy be known by its victims.

The first step of the journey described in 'Diving into the Wreck' (1972) is to identify the strategies of patriarchal oppression; specifically, the oppressive nature of language, images and myths – we need to see clearly in order to discover the origin of the patriarchal cultural structures that oppress women. Images of knives (needed to re-form experience) and the camera (needed to re-vision women's experience) are cited in the first and last stanzas. Only with this clarity of vision, a vision informed by a radical feminine awareness, can one refocus and redefine the nature of feminine experience. The 'wreck' that Rich metaphorically explores is the wreck of women as an historically oppressed sexual class:

> I came to explore the wreck.
> The words are purposes.
> The words are maps.
> I came to see the damage that was done
> and the treasures that prevail
>   (ll.52–56, p. 54).

Only through the awakening or 'raising' of personal consciousness can each woman begin to penetrate the depths of patriarchal oppression, and to realise for herself the violence and destruction wreaked upon women as a class throughout history. And this experiencing of feminine oppression as an historical reality and a reality in her own life is what Rich seeks in this poem: 'the thing I came for: / the wreck and not the story of the wreck / the thing itself and not the myth' (ll.61–63, p. 54). The myth is the masculine explanation for feminine failure and the invisibility of women from the historical record, 'a book of myths / in which / our names do not appear' (ll.92–94, p. 55); Rich seeks her own experience of that failure as a political experience. Rich's poetry is motivated by her activism: her critique of masculine poetic and linguistic forms, and the patriarchal definitions of women and female sexuality they express.

'Twenty-One Love Poems' (1974–76) is devoted to the promotion of a genuine, autonomous feminine identity free from patriarchal constraints and prescriptions. This is expressed through a lesbian sexuality in 'The Floating Poem, Unnumbered'. Only in separation from men can women voluntarily develop a genuine woman-identified sexuality, independent of patriarchal coercion and those definitions that serve the interests of male sexuality and masculine domination. In this poem, Rich formulates a poetic vocabulary to describe sexual love between women: a circumstance not accounted for by conventional poetic diction. This exemplifies the radical feminist view that heterosexuality under patriarchy is regarded as 'natural', as the only 'real' form of sexuality; all other forms of sexual desire are deviant and abnormal – if not non-existent – and so are not appropriate as subject matter for poetry. Images such as:

> your lovemaking, like the half-furled frond
> of the fiddlehead fern in forests
> just washed by sun...
> the live, insatiate dance of your nipples in my mouth
> (ll.3–5, 8, p. 83)

attempt to create just that set of images to describe experiences which until now poetry has been unable to describe. The domination of feminine sexuality by the patriarchal heterosexual imperative is explored in the poems in this sequence, together with Rich's own imperative that women must exert themselves and their moral imaginations to envision some alternative way of experiencing our lives.

In the first poem of the series, Rich moves through three stages of reasoning (in a mock sonnet form) – first, she reasons that the violent sexual images of masculine domination and feminine submission have consequences for the acts of sexual violence that poison our social lives; secondly, we need to be aware of this destructive environment in which we live and not be destroyed by it; thirdly, we need to imagine ourselves, autonomously and independently of these destructive pressures. The juxtaposition of natural images with images of industrial pollution, 'sycamores blazing through the sulfuric air', expresses this difficult relationship between personal autonomy and cultural oppression. The environmental pollution that is toxic to the trees symbolises the pollution of feminine sexuality by patriarchal domination and control. In the seventh poem of the series, Rich writes of 'the worst thing of all': 'the failure to want our freedom passionately enough / so that blighted elms, sick rivers, massacres would seem / mere emblems of that desecration of ourselves' (ll.11–13, p. 80). Male power is the pollutant that destroys women's lives, and our cultural lives.

But the possibility of a woman-centred, woman-identified alternative culture is explored through the motif of the lesbian lovers who are charged with the moral responsibility to use their 'outsider' status to imagine an alternative way of living; in the fifth poem she remarks, 'we still have to stare into the absence / of men who would not, women who could not, speak / to our life – this still unexcavated hole / called civilization, this act of translation, this half-world' (ll. 17–20, p. 79). In Rich's poetry gender conflict, the domination of feminine sexuality by a misogynistic patriarchal culture is the foundation of all relationships of domination and submission including militarism, colonialism, environmental abuse, racism, and so on. The insight to perceive these relationships and the common ground they share in patriarchal domination come from the privileged perspective offered by Rich's lesbian existence. Rich writes of her personal rage in the politicised terms of radical lesbian feminism, which reach out to the community of women and other victims of patriarchal violence.

References and Selected Further Reading

Altieri, Charles, 1984. *Self and Sensibility in Contemporary American Poetry*, Cambridge: Cambridge University Press.

Annas, Pamela, 1982. 'A Poetry of Survival: Unnaming and Renaming in the Poetry of Audre Lorde, Pat Parker, Sylvia Plath, and Adrienne Rich', *Colby Library Quarterly*, vol. 18, no. 1 (March), pp. 9–25.

Barry, Kathleen, 1979. *Female Sexual Slavery*, Englewood Cliffs, NJ: Prentice-Hall.

Carruthers, Mary J., 1983. 'The Re-Vision of the Muse: Adrienne Rich, Audre Lorde, Judy Grahn, Olga Broumas', *The Hudson Review*, vol. 36, no. 2 (Summer), pp. 293–322.

Cooper, Jane Roberta, ed., 1984. *Reading Adrienne Rich: Reviews and Re-Visions, 1951–81*, Ann Arbor: University of Michigan Press.

Daly, Mary, 1978. *Gyn/Ecology: The Metaethics of Radical Feminism*, 2nd ed., London: The Women's Press, 1991.

——, 1984. *Pure Lust: Elemental Feminist Philosophy*, Boston: Beacon Press.

Dennis, Helen M., 1991. 'Adrienne Rich: Consciousness Raising as Poetic Method' in Antony Easthope & John O. Thompson, eds, *Contemporary Poetry Meets Modern Theory*, Toronto: University of Toronto Press, pp. 177–194.

Dworkin, Andrea, 1974. *Woman Hating: A Radical Look at Sexuality*, New York: E.P. Dutton.

——, 1978. *Right-Wing Women: The Politics of Domesticated Females*, London: The Women's Press, 1983.

——, 1981. *Our Blood: Prophecies and Discourses on Sexual Politics*, New York: G.P. Putnam.

——, 1981. *Pornography: Men Possessing Women*, New York: Perigee Books.

Ehrenreich, Barbara, Elizabeth Hess & Gloria Jacobs, 1986. *Re-Making Love: The Feminization of Sex*, New York: Anchor Press.

Farwell, Marilyn R., 1995. 'The Lesbian Narrative: "The Pursuit of the Inedible by the Unspeakable"', in George E. Haggerty & Bonnie Zimmerman, eds, *Professions of Desire: Lesbian and Gay Studies in Literature*, New York: MLA, pp. 156–168.

Farwell, Marilyn R. 1993. 'Toward a Definition of the Lesbian Literary Imagination', in Susan J. Wolfe & Julia Penelope, eds, *Sexual Practice, Textual Theory: Lesbian Cultural Criticism*, Cambridge, MA: Blackwell, pp. 66–84.

Firestone, Shulamith, 1970. *The Dialectic of Sex: The Case for Feminist Revolution*, London: Jonathan Cape.

Flowers, Betty S., 1995. 'Wrestling with the Mother and the Father: "His" and "Her" in Adrienne Rich', in Nancy Owen Nelson, ed., *Private Voices, Public Lives: Women Speak on the Literary Life*, Denton: University of North Texas Press, pp. 54–63.

Foster, Thomas, 1990. '"The Very House of Difference": Gender as "Embattled" Standpoint', *Genders*, vol. 8 (July), pp. 17–37.

Frye, Marilyn, 1983. *The Politics of Reality: Essays in Feminist Theory*, Trunamsburg, NY: Crossing Press.

Gelpi, Barbara Charlesworth & Albert Gelpi, eds, 1993. *Adrienne Rich's Poetry and Prose*, rev. ed., New York & London: W. W. Norton & Co.

Hedley, Jane, 1992. 'Surviving to Speak New Language: Mary Daly and Adrienne Rich', *Hypatia*, vol. 7, no. 2 (Spring), pp.40–62.

Hirsh, Elizabeth, 1994. 'Another Look at Genre: Diving into the Wreck of Ethics with Rich and Irigaray', in Lynn Keller & Cristanne Miller, eds, *Feminist Measures: Soundings in Poetry and Theory*, Ann Arbor: University of Michigan Press, pp. 117–138.

Hoagland, Sarah, 1988. *Lesbian Ethics: Toward New Values*, Palo Alto: Institute of Lesbian Studies.

hooks, bell, 1995. ' "This is the Oppressor's Language/Yet I Need It to Talk to You": Language, a Place of Struggle', in Anuradha Dingwaney & Carol Maier, eds, *Between*

Languages and Cultures: Translation and Cross-Cultural Texts, Pittsburgh: University of Pittsburgh Press, pp. 295–301.

Hull, Gloria T., 1989. 'Living on the Line: Audre Lorde and Our Dead Behind Us' in Cheryl A. Wall, ed., *Changing Our Own Words: Essays on Criticism, Theory, and Writing by Black Women*. New Brunswick, NJ: Rutgers University Press, pp. 150–172.

Jaggar, Alison M., 1983. *Feminist Politics and Human Nature*. Totowa, NJ: Rowman & Allanheld.

Jay, Karla, Joanne Glasgow & Catharine R. Stimpson, eds, 1990. *Lesbian Texts and Contexts: Radical Revisions*, New York: New York University Press.

Lorde, Audre, 1984. *Sister Outsider*, rpt. in *The Audre Lorde Compendium: Essays, Speeches and Journals*, London: Pandora, 1996.

MacKinnon, Catharine A., 1977. *Feminism Unmodified: Discourses on Life and the Law*, Cambridge, MA: Harvard University Press.

——, 1990. 'Sexuality, Pornography, and Method: "Pleasure Under Patriarchy"', rpt. in Nancy Tuana & Rosemarie Tong, eds, *Feminism and Philosophy: Essential Readings in Theory, Reinterpretation, and Application*, Boulder, CO: Westview Press, 1995, pp. 134–161.

Martin, Wendy, 1984. *An American Triptych: Anne Bradstreet, Emily Dickinson, Adrienne Rich*, Chapel Hill: University of North Carolina Press.

McGuirk, Kevin, 1993. 'Philoctetes Radicalized: "Twenty-One Love Poems" and the Lyric Career of Adrienne Rich', *Contemporary Literature*, vol. 34, no. 1 (Spring), pp. 61–87.

Millett, Kate, 1970. *Sexual Politics*, London: Abacus.

Mitchell, Juliet, 1971. *Woman's Estate*, New York: Pantheon Books.

Munt, Sally, ed., 1992. *New Lesbian Criticism: Literary and Cultural Readings*, New York: Columbia University Press.

Raymond, Janice, 1986. *A Passion for Friends*, Boston: Beacon Press.

Rich, Adrienne, 1976. *Of Woman Born: Motherhood as Experience and Institution*, New York: W. W. Norton & Co.

——, 1993. *Adrienne Rich's Poetry and Prose*, ed. Barbara Charlesworth Gelpi & Albert Gelpi. Rev. ed. New York & London: W. W. Norton & Co.

Rof, Judith, 1995. 'How to Satisfy a Woman "Every Time"...', in Diane Elam & Robyn Wiegman, eds, *Feminism Beside Itself*, New York: Routledge, pp. 55–69.

Runzo, Sandra, 1993. 'Intimacy, Complicity, and the Imagination: Adrienne Rich's *Twenty-One Love Poems*', *Genders*, vol. 16 (Spring), pp. 61–79.

Smith, Barbara, 1997. 'The Truth That Never Hurts: Black Lesbians in Fiction in the 1980s', in Robyn R. Warhol & Diane Price Herndl, eds, *Feminisms: An Anthology of Literary Theory and Criticism*. New Brunswick, NJ: Rutgers University Press, pp. 784–806.

Stimpson, Catharine, 1985. 'Adrienne Rich and Lesbian/Feminist Poetry', *Parnassus*, vol. 12–13, no. 2–1 (Spring-Winter), pp. 249–268.

Templeton, Alice, 1994. *The Dream and the Dialogue: Adrienne Rich's Feminist Poetics*, Knoxville: University of Tennessee Press.

Tong, Rosemarie, 1989. *Feminist Thought: A Comprehensive Introduction*, Boulder, CO: Westview Press.

Tuana, Nancy & Rosemarie Tong, eds, 1995. *Feminism and Philosophy: Essential Readings in Theory, Reinterpretation, and Application*, Boulder, CO: Westview Press.

6

Gender and Class: Socialist Feminism and Ann Beattie

This chapter begins with a survey of socialist feminist theorists, focusing upon Juliet Mitchell's *Woman's Estate* (1971), Sheila Rowbotham's *Woman's Consciousness, Man's World* (1973) and Zillah Eisenstein's essays in *Capitalist Patriarchy and the Case for Socialist Feminism* (1979). The primary theoretical concepts explored here include: the nature of power relationships; the concept of 'woman' as a political category; the collectivity of oppression; and the theoretical model of 'the resisting reader'. In the section that follows this theoretical survey, I turn to the socialist feminist analysis of a selection of Ann Beattie's short stories from her 1978 volume *Secrets and Surprises*.

Survey of Socialist Feminist Theory

Summary of Socialist Feminist Principles

Socialist feminism focuses upon power relationships, especially the intersection of capitalism, racism and patriarchy, and the production of a politicised personal (subjective) life. Socialist feminism is concerned with the roles allocated to women that are independent of class status (mother, sister, housewife, mistress, consumer and re-producer). Feminism within a socialist framework offers the analysis of the ideological construction of femininity under patriarchal white supremacist capitalism. Violence, pornography, working conditions, but above all the political dimension of private life – the family, reproduction and sexuality – these are the issues that concern socialist feminists. The power relationships between men and women within the family reproduce the power relationships that exist in society; so women find job opportunities primarily in the caring professions – like teaching and nursing – and the clerical posts that require the same kinds of organisational skills that a woman needs to run a household. Consequently, 'socialist feminists claim that the labor of women in the domestic realm serves not only the interests of specific families but also the interests of capitalism in that the family reproduces the attitudes and capabilities needed to enter into the wage labor force' (Tuana & Tong, 1995, p. 262). So the family is a powerful instrument of socialisation, where we learn to adopt particular postures in relation to the patriarchal power structure; that is, where we learn positions of subordination and domination.

Socialist feminism treats the concept of 'woman' not as a matter of individual gender consciousness but as a political category. 'Femaleness' is a cultural construction created to counter oppressive male images of women; this concept functions as the basis for the social, economic and political betterment of women. Socialist feminists attack the psychoanalytic preference for a fragmented female subject which is seen as free to reconstitute itself in new and liberated forms. Controversy between socialist and psychoanalytic feminism is related to their distinct literary preferences in terms of the kinds of literature read and promoted: psychoanalytic feminism prefers fantasy and avant-garde writing that represents the self as fractured and fragmented rather than the realist texts with a clear sociological context preferred by socialists. Where psychoanalytic feminists tend to write about the fiction of ideas and issues, socialist feminists address texts that stress characters and relationships. Fragmentation is interpreted by socialists as neither liberating nor exciting: division is what must be overcome – the division of the personal from the political, sex from society – so that the processes of gender socialisation become visible.

Collectivity of oppression is a fundamental assumption of socialist feminism. The social class structure is seen to be inseparable from gender divisions: just as the rich oppress the poor, so men oppress women and this is not something that can easily be blamed on individual men who oppress individual women. This collective oppression of all women by men is the effect of culture or the social relations which define our existence as gendered individuals. Consequently, a change in society is needed before any significant change in gender relations can be brought about. As Nancy Hartsock explains, 'since we do not act to produce and reproduce our lives in a vacuum, changed consciousness and changed definitions of the self can only occur in conjunction with a restructuring of the social (both societal and personal) relations in which each of us is involved' (Hartsock, 1979, p. 61). How is this change to be brought about? By convincing individual women to change their lives; by producing structural alterations in the economy that change men's lives; by producing a generation of 'resisting' readers who are sceptical of all the cultural messages that are offered to them; most of all by transcending subjectivism (the debilitating emphasis on the individual that keeps women blaming their own individual inadequacies for what are social problems) and formulating an effective concept of collective oppression. Socialist feminism represents not only female oppression but also the entire oppressive patriarchal power structure by exposing (as unnatural) relationships of male domination, especially in their relation to capitalist modes of production.

The term 'resisting reader' was made famous by Judith Fetterley in her 1978 book of that name. The 'resisting reader' is diametrically opposed to the 'male-identified woman' who identifies against her own gender interests and with the interests of patriarchal authority. The resisting reader refuses to adopt the perspective of male interest because the resisting reader asks, 'Whose interests are served by this way of seeing the world?' What the reader resists is the pressure placed upon us by culture to view all issues and all situations from the point of view of male interests. Fetterley invites us to cast a discriminating eye over the power relationships that inform all issues and situations, and especially the way we have been taught to view these. Fetterley rereads classic texts like *The Great Gatsby*, but from Daisy Buchanan's point of view (not Nick Carraway's male viewpoint), and the stories of Hemingway's doomed heroines like *For Whom the Bell Tolls* and asks why in these canonical texts the primary female characters must always die. Fetterley finds that repeatedly the personal fulfilment of literary heroes depends upon the ⚹ suffering and death of literary heroines; men mature and develop but at the expense of the women around them and this is seen as a normal pattern of behaviour. It is natural, within the terms of reference of these texts, for women to sacrifice themselves so that their men may benefit. The resisting reader refuses to give unconscious assent to this view of 'the natural' and 'the normal' and resists such conventional gender roles. The concept of the resisting reader enables us to translate the socialist feminist analysis of power into literary terms and to perceive how literature functions within the context of patriarchal power relationships. Three prominent socialist feminist thinkers are Juliet Mitchell, Sheila Rowbotham and Zillah Eisenstein; in what follows I look more closely at the work of these women.

Juliet Mitchell, Woman's Estate *(1971)*

In this study of the Women's Movement, Mitchell engages the relationship between second wave feminism and Marxist-socialist thought in order to discover a revolutionary strategy for women's liberation. She begins by locating the Women's Movement within the context of the radicalism of the 1960s – the Civil Rights movement, Black Power, the student movement, the peace movement, draft resistance, hippies, and the anti-imperialist struggle in the Third World. As Mitchell points out, women share economic poverty with Blacks and an intellectually and emotionally impoverished lifestyle with students and youth, with this impoverishment ironically situated within one of the most affluent countries of the world. A growing consciousness of the conflict between context and circumstance, Mitchell argues, gave rise to the radicalism of the 1960s in America. Oppression alone is insufficient to motivate protest; it is critical consciousness that gives rise to radical action. This critical consciousness is realised in the perception that women form an oppressed class within capitalist society. Mitchell describes the growing awareness motivating the Women's Liberation Movement as the perception that: 'women's oppression manifests itself in economic and cultural deprivation, that oppressed women are found in all exploited minorities, in all social classes, in all radical movements' (Mitchell, 1971, p. 39). The oppression of women as a class is more obvious under capitalism than under the feudal and pre-capitalist economies because capitalism offers what Mitchell calls 'a mystifying emancipation and ... ideology of equality' (p. 41), where earlier economies were more openly dominating and discriminative. For this reason, Mitchell identifies the process of consciousness-raising as one of the most important activities of the Women's Movement. It is through the raising of political consciousness to an acute perception of the area of politics that is experienced as personal that women acquire the ability to see that their individual situations are in fact part of a social condition and for that reason are political rather than 'only' personal. She writes,

> The process of transforming the hidden, individual fears of women into a shared awareness of the meaning of them as social problems, the release of anger, anxiety, the struggle of proclaiming the painful and transforming it into the political – this process is *consciousness-raising*' (Mitchell's emphasis, p. 61).

This intersection of the political and the personal within the context of social relations is at the centre of socialist feminist thought and activism.

The socialist class-theory of society and analysis of societal relations, together with the socialist revolutionary imperative, is the starting point for new socialist feminist analyses of women's oppression. Mitchell observes that most socialist analyses of women's oppression begin with the assumption of women's physical weakness in contrast to male physical strength. Mitchell points out, however, that in many societies women are required to perform much more exhausting physical labour than are men; social coercion rather than biological necessity has forced women into a gendered division of labour: '[w]omen have been *forced* to do "women's work"', Mitchell observes (p. 103). She goes on to explain that 'coercion implies a different relationship from coercer to coerced than does exploitation. It is political rather than economic. ... far from women's *physical* weakness removing her from productive work, her *social* weakness has ... made her the major slave of it' (p. 104). In contemporary patriarchal society the power of this social coercion is mediated to women through the operations of ideology which is shared by both men and women.

A key element of this patriarchal ideology is maternity. Mitchell points to the absence of any extensive consideration of the material reality of maternity in Marxist analysis. Rather, women's role in reproduction has been subsumed under the issue of the family and family relations. But as Mitchell points out, the assumption that maternity is a universal, ahistorical fact leads inexorably to women's social subordination: the 'causal chain then goes: maternity, family, absence from production and public life, sexual inequality' (p. 107). The idealisation within patriarchal ideology of reproduction and the feminine role of socialisation of children within the family not only reinforces women's oppression but obscures the true nature of the patriarchal family; rather than provide an enclave of intimacy and security apart from the chaotic world, the internal family relationships 'reproduce in their own terms the external relationships which dominate the society. The family as refuge from society in fact becomes a reflection of it' (pp. 146–147). In this way, the family becomes a powerful force of socialisation for both men and women. The family produces individuals who have internalised society's hierarchical relations by defining themselves, and being defined, according to the structure of patriarchal capitalist relations. So the role of the family is ideological as well as economic, under capitalism. And it is the false unity of the family, and the oppressive power it exerts, that is the focus of socialist feminist analysis.

Sheila Rowbotham, Woman's Consciousness, Man's World
(1973)

The role of the family in maintaining capitalism as well as the nature of women's work within the family are key aspects of Rowbotham's analysis of relations between Marxism and feminism. Rowbotham points out that feminism in the early suffrage era was liberal and focused upon the achievement of equal rights; this feminist movement assumed that 'there could be changes in woman's position in capitalism without either transforming the outer world of production or the inner world of the family and sexuality' (Rowbotham, 1973, p. xiv). Not only suffragist feminism but also early second wave feminism, like Betty Friedan's, failed to challenge the socio-economic context of women's experience. Of *The Feminine Mystique*, Rowbotham comments that it: 'excludes working-class women from the terms of reference and never penetrates the manifestations of women's oppression through the material structure of society' (pp. 5–6), though Rowbotham readily acknowledges Friedan's pioneering effort to strip the confusion away from the 'mystique'. Likewise, the Marxist tradition of the mid-twentieth century was concerned to emphasise improvements in women's position at work and reform of legal relations. Neither movement focused in an effective way upon the relations between the family unit and what Rowbotham calls 'the culture and consciousness of capitalist society'. She goes on to explain that 'Capitalism does not only exploit the wage-earner at work, it takes from men and women the capacity to develop their potential fully in every area of life' (p. xv). And it is in this respect, according to Rowbotham, that the revolutionary potential of women resides. The sexual division of labour has traditionally placed women in the feminine realm of the home and only incompletely granted women a place in the public world of paid work, or commodity production. The contradiction between these private and public realms, between 'family and industry, ... personal and impersonal, is the fissure in women's consciousness through which revolt erupts' (p. xv).

This revolutionary consciousness is difficult to achieve; Rowbotham uses the image of mirrors to describe the way in which any oppressed group must 'shatter the self-reflecting world which encircles it', because in order to discover an authentic identity 'distinct from that of the oppressor it has to become visible to itself' (p. 27). The status quo, however, promotes what Rowbotham calls 'a paralysis of consciousness' that prevents being made the kinds of connections that would forge a group or class consciousness. This is the feminine condition that Rowbotham describes; women divided 'inside and against ourselves and one another' (p. 34). The maintenance of capitalism depends upon this divisiveness: 'The organization of production within capitalism creates a separate and segmented vision of life which continually restricts consciousness of alternatives. People perceive themselves in opposition to one another' (p. 57). The isolation of the family unit under capitalism is especially powerful in maintaining this atomised form of socialisation.

The relations between the personal and political dimensions of experience set feminism apart from Marxism; Rowbotham very pertinently observes that where the objective of Marxism is the abolition of the capitalist, this objective does not translate into feminist terms: '[w]e cannot imagine our world in which no men exist' (p. 35). And she quotes Simone de Beauvoir to this effect: 'The division between the sexes is a biological fact and not an event in human history ... she is the other in a totality of which the two components are necessary to one another (*The Second Sex*, quoted by Rowbotham, p. 35). But there are important respects in which Marxism and feminism do share common concerns. Rowbotham cites the example of women's lack of control over their own bodies as comparable with the workers' lack of control over production, or the way in which women and members of the working class must fit themselves into the categories made available to them by a middle-class male-dominated society. Men and women share the same experiences of alienation and exploitation in commodity production, but women take primary responsibility for maintaining and reproducing commodity producers within the home. This limits the amount of female labour that can be available for the production of commodities. Women's role in the patriarchal family then 'acts both to maintain and to restrict the exploitation of labour power by capital' (p. 59). Men and women are placed in different relations to production, according to the sexual division of labour.

But more than this, the difference in the structure of these relations shape differently the consciousness of men and women. As Rowbotham observes, '[i]n the relation of husband and wife there is an exchange of services which resembles the bond between man and man in feudalism. The woman essentially serves the man in exchange for care and protection' (p. 62). In some respects, therefore, the relations between men and women within the family unit resemble precapitalist modes of relation. Rowbotham explains that this is the case because women do not sell their labour to men, and so the relation between them is independent of the cash-nexus and is instead a service relation or property relation which was common in the early stages of capitalism. This is akin to Marx's description of the relation between master and serf: 'an essential relation of appropriation [which] is the relationship of domination' (*Pre-Capitalist Economic Formations*, quoted by Rowbotham, p. 64). The end of feudalism and serfdom did not bring about the end of male domination of women, however. 'Both his wife's capacity to labour and her capacity to bear his children were still part of his stock in the world. Moreover, the notion that this was part of the order of things was firmly embedded in all political, religious and educational institutions' (pp. 118–119).

Rowbotham argues that capitalism and patriarchy share no necessary relationship and, indeed, that capitalism has weakened patriarchy in key ways by bringing women into the work force, by holding out at least the promise of individual autonomy and freedom, by making available work that can be done equally by men and women, and by making sexual liberation possible through the development of contraceptive technology. But still, capitalism maintains the subordinate position of women: firstly through the unequal structure of the wage system and the assumption that a woman's wage is to supplement a man's, and then through the sexual division of labour in industry that reflects the division of labour within the family. Rowbotham does not discuss ideology, in connection with either patriarchy or capitalism. She does, however, indicate the subordination and domination of women by men that pervades every aspect of 'economic, legal, social and sexual life' (p. 122).

Zillah Eisenstein, Capitalist Patriarchy and the Case for Socialist Feminism *(1979)*

This edited collection represents an early coming together of socialist feminist theory and practice; like Sheila Rowbotham in *Woman's Consciousness, Man's World*, Eisenstein points out in her introduction that socialist feminism proposes a synthesis between Marxist social theory and radical feminist theory, both of which are still in a process of continual redefinition, and so socialist feminism itself cannot be other than in a process of formulation. Eisenstein contributes the two essays that open the volume, 'Developing a Theory of Capitalist Patriarchy and Socialist Feminism' and 'Some Notes on the Relations of Capitalist Patriarchy', which are my focus here. As these titles indicate, the points at which Marxist theory and radical feminist theory meet in socialist feminist analysis are the relations of patriarchy and capitalism, and the ways in which these relations are mediated through material life in the relations between the personal and political realms. Eisenstein defines the term 'capitalist patriarchy' as descriptive of the 'mutually reinforcing dialectical relationship between capitalist class structure and hierarchical sexual structuring'. She continues:

> Although patriarchy (as male supremacy) existed before capitalism, and continues in postcapitalist societies, it is their present relationship that must be understood if the structure of oppression is to be changed. In this sense socialist feminism moves beyond singular Marxist analysis and isolated radical feminist theory (Eisenstein, 1979, p. 5).

Power is experienced differently according to the individual's class and gender position. The distinction between men and women, bourgeoisie and proletariat, production and reproduction, is viewed as a network of interconnected relations rather than a set of dichotomies in socialist feminist theory. It is the system of power that derives from these relations that socialist feminism seeks to analyse, understand and transform. These two sets of relations are not simply analogous or parallel but fuse in the sexual division of labour. The Marxist analysis of class and class conflict provides an historical and dialectical method for the study of patriarchal relations and gender-based conflict through the analysis of power relations.

Marx's theory of alienation is of particular relevance to the analysis of women's condition under capitalist patriarchy. In his analysis of class struggle, Marx uses a theory of exploitation which Eisenstein includes in her study of alienation but she does not reduce her analysis to that; rather, she extends the analysis to include the revolutionary potential of women. Alienation is what prevents workers from being simply exploited and makes them potentially revolutionary; it is the creative capacity to overcome one's alienation that is a revolutionary potential. But this potential is experienced differently according to one's place within the class structure: 'the bourgeoisie and the proletariat are positions of power deriving from a relation to the economic means of production' (Eisenstein, 1979, p. 13). It is class existence that is alienating and exploitative; but it is in the dialectic between class existence and individual creative essence that the potential for revolutionary consciousness exists. In socialist feminist terms this view can be extended to include women who are additionally defined in terms of their sex, where it is patriarchy that defines feminine consciousness. The alienated forms of social experience that are allowed under capitalism are further constrained for women by patriarchy which places further restrictions upon the realisation of individual essence or creative possibilities. Thus, the dismantling of the class system is insufficient to liberate women into the free experience of their own creative potentiality. As Eisenstein explains:

Marx did not understand that the sexual division of labor in society organizes noncreative and isolating work particularly for women. The destruction of capitalism and capitalist exploitation by itself does not insure species existence, i.e., creative work, social community, and critical consciousness for women (p. 11).

Marxist theory situates gender relations as a reflection of economic class relations within the structure of the family unit, the man is to the bourgeoisie as the woman is to the proletariat. It is then no surprise that Marx should envision the end of gender conflict as accompanying the end of class struggle.

Eisenstein uses a distinction between exploitation and oppression to represent the departure of socialist feminist thought from Marxist analysis. In Eisenstein's use of the terms, oppression encompasses the economic experience of exploitation within capitalist class relations but also takes account of those experiences that arise from woman's place within the patriarchal sexual hierarchy; as she notes, '[o]ppression reflects the hierarchical relations of the sexual and racial division of labor and society' (p. 23). These relations, which are power relations, exist in both material form, as sex roles, and as ideological constructions, as the stereotypes, myths and ideas that support the sex roles. The task of socialist feminism, therefore, in Eisenstein's estimation is the reappraisal of class relations in a feminine context. But she warns: '[w]e must not just reexamine the way women have been fit into class categories. We must redefine the categories themselves. We need to define classes in terms of woman's complex reality and her consciousness of that reality' (p. 31). A powerful example cited by Eisenstein is the unpaid housewife who is defined as middle-class because her husband belongs to the middle-class; but, Eisenstein asks, does this woman have the same freedoms, security and autonomy as her wage-earning husband? How does her situation differ from a low-paid single woman? Through this kind of questioning, Eisenstein suggests the need for a new 'vocabulary and conceptual tools which deal with the question of differential power among women in terms of their relation to men and the class structure, production and reproduction, domestic and wage labor, private and public realms, etc'. (p. 33). The socialist feminist project outlined by Eisenstein then promotes greater understanding both of the differences that separate and the commonalties that potentially unite all women.

This is Eisenstein's starting point in the essay, 'Some Notes on the Relations of Capitalist Patriarchy'. In this essay she suggests how a Marxist analysis might be refocused by the socialist feminist perception that power relations exist as a mutually supportive web of relations within capitalist society; as she says, this is the perception 'that society's ideas and people's consciousness are part of the objective social reality and that they operate out of the relations of sex, class, and race' (Eisenstein, 1979, p. 42). These oppressive relations are motivated by the power structures existing in patriarchal society, which cause oppression to be experienced differently according to class and race. Social relations are reflected in social ideology, embodied in individual women and engaged by women's activities. Eisenstein takes the example of the act of giving birth to illustrate the ways in which an objective act is invested with the values of capitalist patriarchy: birth is an act of motherhood when associated with marriage and family; but the same act can be valued as adultery or as illegitimacy when an 'unwed mother' alters the set of relations in which the act is enmeshed. The actions of women in society at particular historical moments, moments that are shaped by relations of power and defined by ideology, are the objects of socialist feminist analysis: not the concept of woman in the abstract but the activities of individual women in their historical and social lives. Eisenstein concludes, '[s]ince life activity in this society is always in process, in process through power relations, we must try to understand the process rather than isolated moments. To understand the process is to understand the way the process may be changed' (p. 52).

Socialist Feminism in Praxis

In the following section, Ann Beattie's short fiction is analysed in socialist feminist terms. The discussion of Ann

Beattie's work focuses upon her style, which is characterised by minimalism and is based on understatement. Her characterisation is unsentimental, even iconographical. Her themes, of alienation, isolation, and entrapment experienced by the white upper-middle classes are well suited to her spare and economical style and yet her exploration of such further themes as the representation of 'woman', the intersection of public and private worlds, and the reading of the social text all open these narratives to a socialist feminist analysis.

Ann Beattie, Secrets and Surprises *(1978)*

Ann Beattie's much commented upon literary style is based on understatement – there is no obvious meaning to any of her narratives, explanation gives way to description, she tends to show how rather than why things are as they are for her characters. The narrator does not interpret on behalf of the characters, and the characters refuse to explain to each other and themselves. 'Never mind', says one of the characters in the story 'Colorado', 'Never mind bothering to converse' (Beattie, 1978, p. 153). These characters are alienated, from each other and themselves, and the narrator similarly perceives no meaning in the events that are described. The narrative focus lingers on one consciousness and all social relationships are mediated by that single consciousness: in the story 'Weekend' this consciousness is the character of Lenore; in 'A Reasonable Man' it is the unnamed wife; in 'Friends' it is the character of Perry. This narrative focus lends the stories a unity they would not otherwise possess, dealing as they do with snapshots in the lives of individuals who constantly move about, both geographically and emotionally, with little apparent motive and no explanation. Many of the characters in the stories that comprise this volume die – like Starley in the story of that name, or the brother of the narrator of 'A Clever-Kid's Story', or the father of the narrator of 'La Petite Danseuse' – or they are maimed, physically like the narrator of 'The Lawn Party', emotionally like the narrator of 'A Reasonable Man'. The emphasis upon death and disfigurement underlines the conflict upon which so many of the stories are based, a conflict that reveals complex power relationships that are based in class and gender differences.

Larry and Natalie, the main characters of the story 'Shifting', are separated by class and gender differences. Early in the narrative we are told that Larry's parents are afraid that he will marry Natalie, but once he has started graduate school he does so. Relations of power and control are represented in this story through the motif of cars. Larry's parents force him to attend graduation by giving him a car on graduation day. Natalie thinks, 'If they had given it to him when he was still in college, it would have made things much easier' (p. 55) – especially for her who must take the train to see him at weekends. Natalie's inferior class position is revealed obliquely in the narrative through the extensive set of expectations that are brought to bear upon her by Larry and his family, once they are married. She is expected to clean, to efface herself so that her presence does not interfere with his studying, and to fit in with his daily schedule. The most important of these schedules relates to the use of their car. She is allowed access to the car in order to shop on Tuesdays and Wednesdays only, which are days of relative freedom for her; so when her uncle unexpectedly dies and leaves his old car to her, Natalie is presented with an opportunity to grasp at a more permanent kind of freedom. That Larry also perceives this as the primary significance of the uncle's bequest is revealed by his enthusiasm to sell the car. When Natalie successful evades all potential buyers, Larry refuses to teach her how to drive the car which has a manual gearbox:

> 'it's not an automatic shift', he said. 'You don't know how to drive it'. She told him that she could learn. 'It will cost money to insure it', he said, it's old and probably not even dependable'. She wanted to keep the car. 'I know', he said, 'but it doesn't make sense. When we have more money, you can have a car. You can have a newer, better car' (p. 59).

What these characters are unable to articulate is the true reason for their disagreement. The discussion they have consists of his presenting minor obstacles or objections to her keeping the car and her stubborn refrain that she wants to keep it. They cannot expose to conscious consideration the shift in power relations that ownership of her own car will bring about in their relationship. In this way the title of the story takes on multiple meanings – referring to the 'shifting' that takes place in their relationship as well as the gear-shifting that initially prevents Natalie from driving this car. Larry wants to maintain her dependence upon him; when he is sufficiently successful then he will buy her a 'newer, better car'. But it is precisely to obtain some independence from him and all that he and his parents represent that imbues the car with value for Natalie. The gender aspect of this power struggle becomes apparent when Natalie arranges that the young man who runs errands for her elderly neighbour will teach her how to drive the car. Old Mrs Larsen warns her that she will have to pay Michael. 'Of course, everything has its price' (p. 59) she warns. Natalie assumes that she means only the amount of money Natalie will have to pay for lessons but, in the episode that follows in the narrative, Natalie takes an inventory of the objects that fill their apartment, as Larry has asked her to do. This creates the impression that Natalie is adding up the cost of the life for which she pays with her labour, and her dependence upon Larry; and this impression is emphasised when Michael insists that Natalie can decide what the lessons were worth once she has learned.

The influence upon Natalie of these lessons is subtle but pervasive. She begins to avoid Larry's questions about the events of her days; she doesn't tell him that she has started smoking; she refuses his suggestion that his disabled friend come to stay with them, saying that Larry can take him along to work with him but she is not going to look after him all day. The lessons increase her assertiveness and her sense of herself as an agent in the external world freed from the confines of the domestic world, but she also realises how different she and Larry are. This realisation is crystallised for her when Larry asks whether she will vote Republican or Democrat in the forthcoming election. After she has answered, Natalie wonders: 'How could he not have known that? She knew then that they were farther apart than she had thought. She hoped that on Election Day she could drive herself to the polls – not go with him and not walk' (p. 65). Here, the car represents the conjunction of her realisation of their fundamental class difference together with her subordination as a woman; she not only wants to travel to the polls by herself but she wants not to walk – she wants to drive and to experience in that way her new-found power and independence. Class, gender and empowerment are brought together by Beattie through her use of the mundane image of driving. But this is an image that conveys the concepts of freedom versus entrapment, within a context determined by class and gender distinctions.

The image of the car also dominates in the story 'A Vintage Thunderbird' but to different effect. In this story physical objects, of which the car is the most expensive and sophisticated, represent the manner in which gender images are constructed in patriarchal society. It is Nick's consciousness that controls our access to information in this narrative. He admires and is perhaps in love with Karen. What he admires most about her, however, are the objects with which she surrounds herself:

> The car they drove was hers – a white Thunderbird convertible. Every time he drove the car, he admired it more. She owned many things he admired ... He loved to go to her apartment and look at her things. He was excited by them, the way he had been spellbound, as a child, exploring the playrooms of schoolmates (p. 3).

From this, he constructs an entire image of Karen, of the sort of individual she must be. He acknowledges that this image is not only based on gender but also on class differences: 'Part of the problem was that she had money and he didn't. She had had money since she was twenty-one, when she got control of a fifty-thousand-dollar trust fund her grandfather had left her' (p. 7). The story tells of his growing disillusionment, as he comes to recognise the extent to which the image he has constructed departs from the reality of her. This recognition coincides with the gradual withdrawal of her objects from his use: she forbids him to wrap up in her squirrel coat, she no longer invites him to drive her car, and eventually she sells the car. In the heat of his anger, he likens Karen's possession of that car to the money he possessed and for which he was mugged: 'He had had an impulse to get up and hit her. He remembered the scene in New Haven outside the bar, and he understood now that it was as simple as this: he had money that the black man wanted' (p. 20). Nick is mugged twice in the story and these attacks provide a parallel with the violent invasion of Karen's personal autonomy represented by his construction of her. Nick takes from Karen her personal sovereignty and the power to make her own judgments. He is shocked to find that Karen's evaluation of her relationship with her friend Stephanie differs from his, and when he objects to her decision to sell the Thunderbird she asks him accusingly, 'How come your judgments are always right and my judgments are always wrong?' (p. 20). Nick's relationship with Karen dissolves under the pressure of the conflict between his class inferiority and his gender superiority. As a man, he assumes that his perceptions are correct, that he has the right to legislate on matters of judgment; but he is Karen's financial and social inferior with no right to dictate how she disposes of her wealth. These conflicts are never spoken; the narrative uses the imagery of violent mugging to represent the hidden conflicts within this relationship as it breaks up.

In the story 'Weekend', the relationship between the primary characters Lenore and George is structured by conflict; it is a power struggle. He uses his illness, his silence, his drunkenness, his infidelity, his vulnerability and anger and alienation to keep Lenore in a subordinate position. He tells her she is 'simple' and she believes him. He uses his superior talent for words against her, to keep her inferior and pliable to his will. This ability to use words effectively, though in written not verbal ways, has benefited him in the past: by writing regularly to an aunt, he impresses her with the appearance of care which gets him his inheritance. The inheritance then is something for nothing; his letters are part of his posturing and lack any emotional significance; Lenore observes that '[s]he could never get him to admit that what he said or did was sometimes false' (p. 121). But the inheritance means a great deal to George because the money lends him financial security and liberates him from the need to work for a salary. In this way, George is placed in a quite different social and economic position from that of his partner. Lenore, in turn, uses her own relative powerlessness, her capacity for self-sacrifice, against him. She uses the conventional feminine qualities of nurturance, patience, humility to keep him with her in the power struggle with younger and more attractive women. 'I'm the only one you can go too far with' (p. 127), she tells him. As a result, their relationship is one of truce shot through with conflict:

> He says things over and over so that she will accept them as truths. And eventually she does. She does not like to think long and hard, and when there is an answer – even his answer – it is usually easier to accept it and go on with things. She goes on with what she has always done: tending the house and the children and George, when he needs her (p. 113).

Lenore's compromise, however, is less voluntary than she makes out – as George's common-law wife and mother of his young children, she is dependent upon him for financial security, and risks destitution for herself and her children if they separate. She is not married to George (though she thinks she might as well be, since she has all the pain and disadvantage with few of the benefits) though explaining why they have not married is less important within the context of the story than explaining why Lenore stays with him.

Of the two young women who are the latest in a regular string of weekend guests, Julie is bothered by the fact that George and Lenore are not married but live in a relationship the terms of which she cannot understand. Julie is baffled by Lenore's apparent acceptance of George's infidelity which, it appears, is usually played out with his female guests; Lenore, however, refuses to see the signs of George's unfaithfulness and claims that she cannot understand Julie's concerns. Of course, the significance of the weekend portrayed in this story is revealed when in this encounter with Julie and Sarah, Lenore and George must acknowledge, at least partially, the hidden dynamics of their relationship. The gradual uncovering of the power dynamic between George and Lenore happens by non-verbal means; the first time this happens, Sarah fails to play her part in the story George is spinning for the others:

> He is all smiles. Sarah lets him down. She looks embarrassed. Her eyes meet Lenore's quickly, and jump to Julie. The two girls stare at each other, and Lenore, left with only George to look at, looks at the fire and then gets up to pile on another log (p. 120).

The communication is not verbal, but the power relationships that determine the situation in which the characters find themselves cannot easily be verbalised. These power relationships are deeply embedded in the network of class and gender relationships in which the characters are engaged. George and Sarah keep disappearing upon the flimsiest pretext; Lenore keeps believing their stories and Julie keeps questioning the nature of the situation in which she has unexpectedly found herself. It is Julie's refusal to provide legitimation for Sarah's behaviour that reveals Lenore's habitual legitimation of George's behaviour. The informal nature of their relationship is repeated several times in the narrative, until Julie raises the issue of marriage as security. Considering her own failed marriage, Julie reflects, 'I'd never have the courage to live with a man and not marry. [...] I mean, I wish I had, that we hadn't gotten married, but I just don't have that kind of ... I'm not secure enough' (Beattie's ellipsis, p. 125). Julie lacks the emotional security to forego marriage; Lenore has swapped the contractual security of legal marriage for faith in her own ability to control and keep George with her. She resists the advice of her brother – who is a lawyer – to end the relationship with George for the same reason. Lenore has no financial independence but she has emotional autonomy; George depends upon her for his emotional security yet his compromise with her is fragile because, in contrast to her weak financial standing, he does have the financial security represented by his inheritance. It is in this context that the narrative offers conflicting views of the status of their relationship. Lenore explains why she stays with George – she has a comfortable life, he needs her in manifold ways, she has not married him because she feels it would be wrong to marry someone who thinks her 'simple' – but the narrator reveals that George simply has not asked her to marry him. Lenore is unable to do the asking because she knows from experience that she will be beaten down by George's powerful use of words, and that she will finally accept what he tells her; she thinks 'he can weasel out of any corner. At best, she can mildly fluster him' (p. 112). Their relationship is a constant tug of wills; Lenore recalls one of their rare male visitors telling her, 'Whatever this sick game is, I don't want to get involved in it' (p. 114). In important respects, Lenore and George do play out their relationship as a game which neither can win. Lenore wonders whether during her time living with George 'she has caught his way of playing games, along with his colds, his bad moods' (p. 125). But as a consequence of her femininity, Lenore plays for higher stakes than George; constant emotional conflict is the price she pays for a comfortable material life for her children and herself.

George's attitude towards and treatment of Lenore repeats his attitude towards the female students who visit and, by implication his attitude towards his work. In this way, a parallel is created between the domestic and professional worlds. He is a failure in both; yet he wants to believe that in both he is powerful and successful. Sarah flatters him by remarking that he was fired from his teaching post because he was ' "in touch" with everything, that they were afraid of him because he was so in touch' (p. 115). It is George's image of himself as an intellectual that links his private and professional worlds. When Lenore attempts to engage him in conversation, and questions his reluctance to talk with her, he responds that since he is no longer a professor he doesn't have to spend time talking any more. However, he talks incessantly with the young female students who are their weekend guests. He uses them to sustain his illusion that he is still engaged in the intellectual life, and that he is still young, attractive and clever – 'in touch'. Lenore, who is twenty-one years his junior, helps George to sustain the same illusion of youth. But George does more than simply use these women to flatter his own self-image; his domination of Lenore through the manipulation of words and sophisticated arguments reflects his domination of students like Sarah, who is placed in a position where she must play a role in the drama that is of George's creation. George does not dominate any of these women physically; but his power over them is exercised emotionally and socially. In this way, Beattie suggests that the internal relationships that become clear as the four are trapped indoors by the driving rain exist in parallel with the external public relationships in which these individuals are involved, and that both the domestic and the public gender relations are fundamentally political in nature.

All of these emotional and sexual currents are hidden; they are apparent in the nuances of the text: for example, the dinner party scene where Julie becomes increasingly lost in the dynamic developing among George, Sarah and Lenore. A power struggle develops between Sarah and Lenore as they fight for George. It is here that Lenore reveals the extent of her command of the situation. While George is out of the room, she takes advantage of Sarah's polite small talk to suggest that George would be flattered by a comparison between the hosts and Sarah's parents. Naively, Sarah does liken George to her father and George is barely able to disguise his displeasure: ' "Your father", George says. "I won't have that analogy" ' (p. 115). And as Sarah stumbles to rescue herself from the awkwardness of the situation, the suggestion that she and Julie should leave early is raised. Lenore has won. Eventually, both Sarah and Julie take refuge from a situation that neither comprehends: first in tears and then in escape from the house. The subtleties of the situation mirror those of the text itself – the knowing reader who is able to pick up the nuances and subtle ironies of the narrative is placed in a position like that of Lenore; the undiscerning reader however is placed in a position akin to Julie's. Beattie represents the experience of isolation, entrapment, alienation and emotional impoverishment among the educated white upper-middle classes. Why this is so, is less important than the ways in which it is so. The invisible currents of normal life and the ways in which social manners both disguise and reveal more fundamental, primal motives that are gender based – this is Beattie's dominating theme. In her representation of 'woman' as a gender category, Beattie demonstrates the differences that divide even women of the same class – especially differences of age but also experience, personality, cleverness – but within a context that shows how all women are still subject to male power. George dominates all the women in the story, even his young child Maria, and controls their potential for action. It is George's comment that she is 'simple' that causes Lenore to look at her daughter critically: 'when he recently remarked on their daughter's intelligence ... she found that she could no longer respond with simple pride; now she feels spite as well, feels that Maria exists as proof of her own good genes' (p. 112). Relations among all the women in the story are controlled by George.

Public and private worlds intersect in Beattie's fiction through the relationships and events within the home that repeat and mirror the external public world. The characters are trapped inside, sitting before the fire, out of the pouring rain; it is the weekend – time set apart from the working week and working world – yet work does not cease for Lenore, in fact it increases. The division of labour in this household clearly falls along gender lines. The story begins with Lenore kneeling before the grate, lighting a fire while everyone else still sleeps; she cooks and cleans and tends to the children. The public world intrudes in manifold ways: Sarah talks of the university and George's work, Julie confesses her marriage break up, Lenore reflects upon her brother's view of her lifestyle; even more than this, though, the subordination of women to masculine power, the fragility or insecurity of feminine existence, the division of women against each other by men, these influences from the patriarchal world operate powerfully to affect the way individuals behave even at the dinner table as Sarah and Lenore struggle to compete for George's attention and approval.

Beattie offers us a number of perspectives upon the reading of the social text with which she presents us. Lenore offers a limited model of the resisting reader – she refuses to accept the interpretation of events that are offered by others (the visiting lover, Sarah, or Julie). But she remains identified with George's interests because she knows too well the extent to which her interests are tied to his. Thus, she uses her insight into the unfolding drama to fight the person who threatens her (Sarah). She uses her considerable emotional and intellectual talents to protect what is hers and to maintain the situation as it is. George is doomed because he cannot value these talents: she thinks, 'If he thinks she's simple, what good would her simple wisdom do him?' (p. 127). At this point, the reader must make a distinction between their own response to the story and Lenore's. It is we whom Beattie expects will be able to see the subtle ways in which his own domination of Lenore is destroying George; she admits that she is less and less able to sleep, that George walks much of the night, most nights. We have to resist the temptation to adopt Lenore's point of view and instead see that she remains identified with the male interests that demean her. As the story concludes, George bitterly blames the departed guests but Lenore points out to him the special nature of their relationship: that he went too far with Sarah, that she is 'the only one you can go too far with' (p. 127). As she says this, she 'slides over closer to him, puts her hand on his shoulder and leans her head there, as if he could protect her from the awful things he has wished into being' (p. 128). Lenore knows that she is exploited and dominated by George, yet she remains identified with his perspective, his values and his interests.

Beattie typically treats characters of the baby-boom generation – individuals like Lenore who are 'thirty-something', alienated from their lives, who are both idealistic and cynical though they often have no self-consciousness. This characterisation contributes to the pervasive sense of meaninglessness. Children are unsentimental; they live unsettled and uncertain lives with the awareness of their parents' alienation. The narrator tells us that while the baby enjoys company, Lenore's daughter prefers to be left alone with her mother, she has 'given up being possessive about her father' (p. 118). In this way, Maria mirrors the attitude of her mother, but Lenore seems not to notice. Parents invest a lot of emotional value and energy into peripheral objects and activities – houseplants, cooking, pictures – at the expense of their children. Maria plays with the box of postcards Lenore has collected, carefully arranging the pictures on the floor.

Sarah absent-mindedly plays with objects like the bowl of stones and shells, which George has carefully arranged to produce a particular effect upon his guests. Lenore is able to tell Julie more about her relationship with George and the reason why she stays with him despite his behaviour by showing Julie the box of photographic self-portraits that George has taken. Words are worth very little except as a means of manipulating others, especially women, to George's masculine will; objects contain more meaning than the conversations in which the characters engage and are more revealing of their true relations.

In 'A Reasonable Man' Beattie focuses to such an extent upon these hidden relations between her characters that they are not even named; he remains 'the man', she is simply 'she', only their young son Robby who lives with 'the man's mother' is named. By removing the veneer of individual personality from these characters, the story tells not only of the hidden power relations between them but of the wife's alienation from herself as her fragile sense of self crumbles under the pressure of patriarchal gender relations. The motif that is repeated to lend the story coherence, among the otherwise disparate fragments of the wife's daily experiences, is her waiting for the telephone to ring. This motif underlines her confinement within the domestic space of the house; she leaves the house only when it is necessary, to shop or to run errands for her husband or to attend the craft lessons for which his mother has paid. She fears that her husband has had the telephone disconnected. Within the domestic world, she is very effective; for instance, the narrative details the nutritionally balanced meals she prepares. But her effectiveness in the domestic space is undermined by her husband's refusal to make love with her. She connects this refusal with the failure of the telephone to ring; she speculates that perhaps if she were to seduce her husband then the telephone would ring.

Her husband undermines her femininity in two ways: first, by his refusal to engage in a sexual relationship with his wife, secondly by his insistence that their son is taken from her, to live with his grandmother rather than his mother.

She *does* understand why he is with the man's mother, but she does not like it, or want to accept it. She has been very honest with the man, has told him her feelings about this, and has not been converted to his way of thinking. She never did anything to Robby. He agrees with this. And she does not see why she can't have him. There they disagree. They disagree, and the man has not made love to her for months – as long as the disagreement has gone on (p. 44).

In this way, he rejects her as a mother and a lover; his rejection is carefully aimed at the twin pillars of her feminine identity – the reproductive and the sexual services she brings to the marriage. The division of labour is divided sexually: she provides labour and services within the domestic space of the house, his labour is expended in the public world of business. The only effort she exerts outside the home is directed at the craft activities she is required to do three times per week. Even then, the instructor interprets her condition according to the stereotype of the tortured female artist. He lends her books by Sylvia Plath and asks her repeatedly whether she writes poetry. In fact, when she does write it is to keep a journal which she hopes will enable her to identify the causes of her unhappiness. But her husband and her instructor both encourage her to look inward, to herself, for the cause of her troubles. Rather than encourage her to seek the cause of her sadness and anger in the network of patriarchal relationships in which she lives, these men promote the idea that her experience is individual rather than social or cultural. The false image of feminine subjectivity offered by her instructor and her husband's rejection of her attempts to conform to patriarchal definitions of femininity, expose the difficulty encountered by women who try to live on their own terms in a male-dominated culture. This is the cause of the wife's anger and frustration; she cannot forge a relationship with the world on her own terms; the telephone will not ring for her.

Beattie reveals these conflicting layers of social experience, the private and the political, the domestic and the public, by representing a woman's mental breakdown in terms that are stripped of individual uniqueness. In this way, the causes that are deeply embedded in the values and terms of patriarchal culture become apparent to the reader. By viewing these characters as types, we can see the gender stereotypes that confine and constrain them, limiting their thoughts and behaviour to established forms. We can see the conflict between individual identity and socially prescribed gender identity that is promoted by the sexual division of labour, the collective oppression of women, and the patriarchal power relationships.

Socialist feminism helps us to get beyond the overwhelming personal, psychological interest of Beattie's stories to perceive the invisible power relationships that determine how the characters respond to each other. Beattie has been criticised as a mannerist, a stylist, whose range is very limited. But socialist feminism enables us to analyse the political dimension of her work, focusing on how personal life is shaped by the power structures that determine the nature of everyday life.

References and Selected Further Reading

Beattie, Ann, 1978. *Secrets and Surprises*, New York: Random House, 1991.

Berch, Bettina, 1982. *The Endless Day: The Political Economy of Women and Work*, New York: Harcourt Brace Jovanovich.

Centola, Steven R., 1990. 'An Interview with Ann Beattie', *Contemporary Literature*, vol. 31, no. 4 (Winter), pp. 405–422.

Delphy, Christine, 1984. *Close to Home: A Materialist Analysis of Women's Oppression*, trans. and ed. Diana Leonard, Amherst: University of Massachusetts Press.

Eisenstein, Zillah, ed., 1979. *Capitalist Patriarchy and the Case for Socialist Feminism*, New York: Monthly Review Press.

Epstein, Joseph, 1983. 'Ann Beattie and the Hippoisie', *Commentary*, vol. 75, no. 3 (March), pp. 54–58.

Foreman, Ann, 1977. *Femininity as Alienation: Women and the Family in Marxism and Psychoanalysis*, London: Pluto Press.

Hansen, Karen & Ilene J. Philipson, eds, 1990. *Women, Class and the Feminist Imagination: A Socialist-Feminist Reader*, Philadelphia: Temple University Press.

Hartsock, Nancy, 1979. 'Feminist Theory and the Development of Revolutionary Strategy', in Zillah R. Eisenstein, ed., *Capitalist Patriarchy and the Case for Socialist Feminism*. New York: Monthly Review Press, pp. 56–77.

Jaggar, Alison M., 1983. *Feminist Politics and Human Nature*, Totowa, NJ: Rowman & Allenheld.

Martin, Gloria, 1978. *Socialist Feminism: The First Decade, 1966–1976*, Seattle: Freedom Socialist Publications.

McKinstry, Susan Jaret, 1987. 'The Speaking Silence of Ann Beattie's Voice', *Studies in Short Fiction*, vol. 24, no. 2 (Spring), pp. 111–117.

Mitchell, Juliet, 1971. *Woman's Estate*, New York: Pantheon Books.

Montresor, Jaye Berman, ed., 1993. *The Critical Response to Ann Beattie*, Westport, CT: Greenwood.

Murphy, Christina, 1986. *Ann Beattie*, Boston: Twayne.

Nicholson, Linda J., 1986. *Gender and History: The Limits of Social Theory in the Age of the Family*, New York: Columbia University Press.

Plath, James, 1993. 'Counternarrative: An Interview with Ann Beattie', *Michigan Quarterly Review*, vol. 32, no. 3 (Summer), pp. 359–379.

Porter, Carolyn, 1985. 'Ann Beattie: The Art of the Missing', in Catherine Rainwater & William J. Scheick, eds, *Contemporary American Women Writers: Narrative Strategies*, Lexington: University Press of Kentucky, pp. 9–28.

Rowbotham, Sheila, 1973. *Woman's Consciousness, Man's World*, New York: Penguin.

Rowbotham, Sheila, Lynne Segal & Hilary Wainwright, 1979. *Beyond the Fragments: Feminism and the Making of Socialism*, London: Merlin Press.

Sargent, Lydia, ed., 1981. *Women and Revolution: A Discussion of the Unhappy Marriage of Marxism and Feminism*, Boston: South End Press.

Schapiro, Barbara, 1985. 'Ann Beattie and the Culture of Narcissism', *Webster Review*, vol. 10, no. 2 (Fall), pp. 86–101.

Tong, Rosemarie, 1989. *Feminist Thought: A Comprehensive Introduction*, Boulder, CO: Westview Press.

Tuana, Nancy & Rosemarie Tong, eds, 1995. *Feminism and Philosophy: Essential Readings in Theory, Reinterpretation, and Application*, Boulder, CO: Westview Press.

Vogel, Lise, 1983. *Marxism and the Oppression of Women: Towards a Unitary Theory*, New Brunswick: Rutgers University Press.

Weinbaum, Batya, 1978. *The Curious Courtship of Women's Liberation and Socialism*, Boston: South End Press.

Wyatt, David, 1992. 'Ann Beattie', *The Southern Review*, vol. 28, no. 1 (Winter), pp. 145–159.

Young, Iris Marion, 1990. *Throwing Like a Girl and Other Essays in Feminist Philosophy and Social Theory*, Bloomington: Indiana University Press.

Gender and Race: Feminism of Colour and Alice Walker, Denise Chávez, Leslie Marmon Silko, Maxine Hong Kingston

This chapter begins with a survey of the theoretical issues highlighted by feminists of colour, focusing upon Angela Davis's *Women, Race and Class* (1981), bell hooks's *Feminist Theory: From Margin to Center* (1984), Paula Gunn Allen's *The Sacred Hoop* (1986) and Gloria Anzaldúa's *Borderlands/La Frontiera* (1987) and *Making Face, Making Soul: Haciendo Caras* (1990). The primary theoretical concepts explored here include: the critique of mainstream feminism by women of colour in terms of the historical relationship between white feminism and racism, the theoretical focus upon activism (by women of colour) versus self-aggrandisement (by white middle-class feminists) and the consequent aim of redistributing cultural power equitably rather than struggling for increased access (by white women) to the existing power hierarchy. This critique of the aims and methods of the mainstream Women's Movement involves the theorising of women of colour as 'the other' in mainstream feminist discourse. Feminists of colour point to the emergence of Black Feminism, Chicana/Hispana Feminism, Native Feminism and Asian Feminism as distinct theoretical perspectives upon the oppression of women by virtue of their racialised sexuality. This racialised feminist perspective recognises the feminist issue of 'double consciousness': the perceived contradiction between what one is in oneself and the cultural image imposed by the racism of others, a contradiction that prevents women of colour achieving full subjectivity or selfhood. In literary terms, these issues make urgent the problem of constructing a feminist 'voice' with which women of colour can articulate their experiences both in literary and theoretical discourses. In the section that follows, I turn to the analysis of Alice Walker's *The Color Purple*, Denise Chávez's *The Last of the Menu Girls*, Leslie Marmon Silko's *Storyteller* and Maxine Hong Kingston's *The Woman Warrior*.

Survey of Feminism of Colour

Principles of Feminism of Colour

Feminism of colour has directed attention to the historical relationship between white feminism and racism. The first wave of American feminism supported the anti-slavery cause but threatened the withdrawal of its support for abolition if black men should be enfranchised before white women. Leaders like Elizabeth Cady Stanton did not perceive any relationship between racial prejudice and gender discrimination. Angela Davis, in *Women, Race and Class* (1981), quotes Elizabeth Cady Stanton's 1865 letter to the *New York Standard*:

Although this may remain a question for politicians to wrangle over for five or ten years, the black man is still, in a political point of view, far above the educated white women of the country. The representative women of the nation have done their uttermost for the last thirty years to secure freedom for the negro; and as long as he was lowest in the scale of being, we were willing to press his claims; but now, as the celestial gate to civil rights is slowly moving on its hinges, it becomes a serious question whether we had better stand aside and see "Sambo" walk into the kingdom first. ... If two millions of Southern black women are not to be secured the rights of person, property, wages and children, their emancipation is but another form of slavery. In fact, it is better to be the slave of an educated white man, than of a degraded, ignorant black one ... (Davis, 1981, p.70).

The second wave of feminism in America did little to recognise the interdependence of racism and sexism as symptomatic of a culture of oppression. Coloured women were excluded from positions of public influence in both the black male-dominated Civil Rights movement and the Women's Movement which was dominated by white women. In *Feminist Theory: From Margin to Center*, bell hooks [sic] criticises the colour (and class) blindness embedded in one of the resurgent feminist movement's canonical texts: Betty Friedan's *The Feminine Mystique* (1963). hooks points out:

> Friedan's famous phrase, 'the problem that has no name', often quoted to describe the condition of women in this society, actually referred to the plight of a select group of college-educated, middle and upper class, married white women – housewives bored with leisure, with the home, with children, with buying products, who wanted more out of life. ... That 'more' she defined as careers. She did not discuss who would be called in to take care of the children and maintain the home if more women like herself were freed from their house labor and given equal access with white men to the professions. She did not speak of the needs of women without men, without children, without homes. She ignored the existence of all non-white women and poor white women. She did not tell readers whether it was more fulfilling to be a maid, a babysitter, a factory worker, a clerk, or a prostitute, than to be a leisure class housewife (hooks, 1984, pp.1–2).

Not only black feminists like Davis and hooks, but all feminists of colour insist upon recognition of the relationship between class and race as they crucially affect the experience of gender and sexualised power relationships.

Feminists of colour promote activism as opposed to self-aggrandisement; they work towards the redistribution of cultural power rather than increased access (by white women) to the existing power hierarchy, which is how theorists like bell hooks represent the reform efforts of liberal feminism. Feminists of colour criticise the liberal or 'bourgeois' feminist struggle for equality with men, and in so doing they raise the problematic issue that not all men are equal in our exploitative society. In her writing, bell hooks discusses those cultural trends that have meant that ethnic groups have benefited by equal opportunity and affirmative action programmes but the institutionalised racism, classism and male supremacy of American culture remain unchallenged by liberal feminism. Plenty of women were working in exploitative and dehumanising jobs at the same time as Friedan was claiming that freedom for women means paid work outside the home. Work is not liberating for the poor, be they men or women. hooks explains: 'As workers, poor and working class women knew from their experiences that work was neither personally fulfilling nor liberatory – that it was for the most part exploitative and dehumanizing' (hooks, 1984, p. 97).

Further, when white women were grouped with non-white women and men, employers found that they could satisfy equal opportunities requirements while maintaining white supremacy by employing white women at the expense of non-whites. A closely associated issue brings this problem right to the heart of academic feminism and that issue is this: feminist 'careerism' has been bought at an extremely high price. The emphasis upon getting women into positions of power and prestige has meant preserving the existing socio-economic system, and the result has been continuing and increased poverty for the majority of women – women as a social class – whilst only select individuals have 'made it' to the top of the exploitative hierarchy. By addressing the problem of sexism in isolation from the network of oppressive relationships that include racism and classism as well, feminists have alienated working class and coloured women from the liberation struggle.

A feature of contemporary American culture is the emergence of Black Feminism, Chicana/Latina Feminism, Native Feminism, Asian Feminism as distinct theoretical perspectives upon the oppression of women by virtue of their racialised sexuality. Referring specifically to the experience of Chicanas, Yvonne Yarbro-Bejarano remarks, 'Perhaps the most important principle of Chicana feminist criticism is the realization that the Chicana's experience as a woman is inextricable from her experience as a member of an oppressed working-class racial minority and a culture which is not the dominant culture' (Yarbro-Bejarano, 1987, p. 140). Racism is experienced differently by each group; each group has a distinct historical experience as a racialised community within the United States. Blacks interpret their experience in terms of the historical context of slavery. For Chicanos, this historical context is shaped by annexation & the Treaty of Guadalupe Hildago. For Native Americans the experience of dispossession and genocidal violence shapes that racial history, while for Asian Americans, immigration and the history of indentured labour underlie a distinctive historical experience. For women, the experience of feminine sexuality is different according to ethnic or racial identity: to take the example of religion, Chicanas may be subject to the traditional gender constraints of Catholicism, some Asian American women to those of Oriental Confucianism, Native American women to those of native religions, and Black women to the constraints placed upon women by evangelical Christianity. In *Borderlands / La Frontera*, Gloria Anzaldúa explains that there are very few cultural roles available for Chicanas; women were confined to the roles of 'wife', 'prostitute' or 'nun'. Only recent access to education has opened up teaching as a profession to Hispanic women, providing an alternative to traditional, sexually-defined feminine roles. In patriarchal Chicano culture, femininity is identified with the carnal body and so women must be protected against the power of their own sexuality. First, the Catholic Church places controls upon feminine sexuality by forbidding birth control and abortion; then the traditional Hispanic family structure strictly regulates feminine behaviour, especially sexual behaviour. Correspondingly, masculinity is constructed differently according to each racial or ethnic group – for example, Chicanos invented the term 'machismo' – and femininity is defined in opposition to these dominant images of masculine gender identity. Both Alice Walker and Maxine Hong Kingston, among other ethnic women writers, have been criticised by men within their racial group for portraying the oppression of women not by white men but by men of colour and thus for representing racialised masculinity in negative terms. This means that women in each racial group need to express the ways in which their individual experience of their sexuality is mediated by their racial identity.

The phrase 'double consciousness' or double stigma describes the oppression of the individual both as a woman and as a member of an ethnic minority; or in other words, the divergent experience of what one is in oneself versus the cultural image imposed by the racism of others. In her introduction to *Making Face, Making Soul: Haciendo Caras*, Gloria Anzaldúa addresses this need to wear a protective appearance which for many women of colour is a survival strategy: 'like a chameleon, to change color when the dangers are many and the options are few' (Anzaldúa, 1990, p. xv). She describes this disguise as the masks that have been created by a racist culture, masks that are 'steeped with self-hatred and other internalized oppressions' (p. xv). Historically this has described the experience of blacks who are placed in a fixed subject position by the racist white culture they inhabit. However, Black women describe the same mechanism in operation when they deal with white feminists. White women place themselves in a position of domination over subordinate coloured women and speak of their own condition as if issues of race and class were invisible. The Native American poet Joy Harjo has explained in an interview that mainstream feminism just does not translate into tribal terms: 'The word "feminism" doesn't carry over to the tribal world, but a concept mirroring a similar meaning would. Let's see what would it then be called – empowerment, some kind of empowerment' (Harjo in Coltelli, 1996, p. 65).

One of the most prominent Native theorists of this kind of feminine empowerment, which she explores in terms of Native spirituality, is Paula Gunn Allen. In the essay, 'Who is your Mother? The Red Roots of White Feminism' published in *The Sacred Hoop*, Allen describes the importance accorded to women in tribal society:

Femaleness was highly valued, both respected and feared, and all social institutions reflected this attitude. Even modern sayings, like the Cheyenne statement that a people is not conquered until the hearts of the women are on the ground, express the Indians' understanding that without the power of woman the people will not live, but with it, they will endure and prosper (Allen, 1990, p. 212).

Allen contrasts this traditional valuation of femininity with what she sees as the mainstream feminist tendency to reject tradition and history in favour of the new. She sums up the difference between white American and Native attitudes thus: 'Indians think it is important to remember, while Americans believe it is important to forget' (p. 210). It is important then for white feminists to understand that there have existed societies that empower women, that historical precedents for the empowerment of women exist. But the Anglo-Saxon focus of American history, including the history of the feminist movement, keeps white feminists apart from the Native women who could teach them new ways of thinking about empowerment.

The construction of a feminist 'voice' for women of colour, a voice with which to speak to white women as well as men, is therefore an urgent issue. Gloria Anzaldúa explains the manner in which Chicanas are oppressed by the cultural imperative that women remain silent, unquestioning, invisible, within traditional Chicano culture; even the language that is available to these women expresses masculine rather than feminine consciousness: 'Chicanas use *nostros* whether we're male or female. We are robbed of female being by the masculine plural' (Anzaldúa, 1987, p. 54). Maxine Hong Kingston makes the same point in *The Woman Warrior* when she explains that the word for 'female' is also the word for 'slave': 'There is a Chinese word for the female *I* – which is "slave". Break the women with their own tongues!' (Kingston, 1975, p.49). Some of the most pressing questions facing ethnic women writers are: how to speak in such a way as to be listened to seriously by white women and by men within one's own racial group? How can one speak from a discredited cultural position? How can one write when established literary forms have been devised to express the lives and thoughts of men (coloured and white) and white women? Among the strategies designed to respond to these questions are: the construction of ethnic women's literary traditions; the rediscovery of earlier modes of articulation; the challenge to conventional distinctions among forms of literary expression. The subversion of conventional forms of literary expression can require that the writer fracture traditional literary forms to make them express coloured women's experience. Examples of this strategy include Alice Walker's use of the epistolary form in *The Color Purple*; the use, by Sandra Cisneros in *The House on Mango Street* and Denise Chávez in *The Last of the Menu Girls*, of the twin techniques of discontinuous narrative and the *kunstleroman* or portrait of the young artist; Maxine Hong Kingston's variation of the memoir in *The Woman Warrior*; Leslie Marmon Silko's challenge to the distinction between poetry, prose and fiction in *Storyteller*. Such texts are characterised by the insistence that the reader work hard to understand the specialised racial or ethnic references included in the text: Chinese mythology, tribal ritual, phraseology (especially Spanish), cross-cultural references, and the like.

Third-World Feminism in Praxis

The discussion that follows takes four key texts of American ethnic women's writing, representing four important areas of American ethnic literature: Black, Chicana, Native and Asian writing. These texts are Alice Walker's *The Color Purple*, Denise Chávez's *The Last of the Menu Girls*, Leslie Marmon Silko's *Storyteller* and Maxine Hong Kingston's *The Woman Warrior*. This discussion focuses upon two areas: first, the development of a distinctive feminine ethnic or racial voice in these texts, and secondly the strategies by which elements of an ethnic cultural tradition are reworked so that they become expressive of a feminist voice instead of expressing traditional patriarchal values. These writers also engage with the oppressive aspects of Black, Chicano, Native and Asian cultures, and attempt to express an analytic perspective from which the opportunity for liberation becomes possible without the denial of ethnic heritage.

Alice Walker, The Color Purple *(1983)*

I begin by establishing a context for reading Alice Walker's work in terms of Black feminist issues and the particularities of Black American feminist thought. Turning then to *The Color Purple*, the narrative structure of a feminist epistolary novel provides a starting point for a consideration in feminist terms of Walker's dominant themes: the concept of God; the interconnectedness of race and gender oppression; racial politics; sexuality: incestuous rape, lesbianism, 'womanism' versus feminism; writing and self-expression.

Alice Walker was actively involved in the Civil Rights Movement, particularly the fight against segregation and the restriction of voting rights to the literate, and also the Women's Movement. She writes of her experiences, though in fictional form, in the early novel *Meridian* where she shows herself to be especially opposed to male domination of 'the Movement'. The essays gathered in the collection *In Search of Our Mothers' Gardens* (1984) tell how she was inspired by Martin Luther King Jr to join SNCC (Students Non-violent Coordinating Committee), but she was inspired to continue writing a literature of protest by the continuing disempowerment of women within the Black nationalist movement and by what she saw as the selling-out of the civil rights struggle by middle class blacks when the fight is only half won:

I think Medgar Evers and Martin Luther King, Jr., would be dismayed by the lack of radicalism in the new black middle class, and discouraged to know that a majority of the black people helped most by the Movement of the sixties has abandoned itself to the pursuit of cars, expensive furniture, large houses, and the finest Scotch. That in fact the very class that owes its new affluence to the Movement now refuses to support the organizations that made its success possible, and has retreated from its concern for black people who are poor ("Choosing to Stay

at Home: Ten Years After the March on Washington",
Walker, 1984, p.168).

Walker continues to write in support of equality for Blacks
and women. The important social and political role of the
woman writer is defined in the graduation address Walker
delivered at Sarah Lawrence College in 1972, where she
stresses that the task confronting educated women is nothing
less than the transformation of the world: 'the world is not
good enough; we must make it better' ('A Talk: Convocation
1972', Walker, 1984, p. 37). So the writer has to change the
world. But how? Most importantly, by opening people's eyes:
to the proud self-consciousness of Black achievement and
Black potential, to the strategies of self-denial and racial
shame promoted by a racist culture, to the innate powers
available to all women. In the course of describing her work
with Black women in Mississippi, Walker asks, 'How do you
teach earnest but educationally crippled middle-aged and
older women the significance of their past? How do you get
them to understand the pathos and beauty of a heritage they
have been taught to regard with shame? How do you make
them appreciate their own endurance, creativity, incredible
loveliness of spirit? It should have been as simple as handing
them each a mirror, but it was not' ('But Yet and Still the
Cotton Gin Kept on Working ...', Walker, 1984, p. 28).

In 'Duties of the Black Revolutionary Artist' (1971), Walker
explains that these duties of the Black artist include working
with and being with the people: 'The real revolution is always
concerned with the least glamorous stuff. With raising a
reading level from second grade to third. With simplifying
history and writing it down (or reciting it) for the old folks.
With helping illiterates fill out food-stamp forms – for they
must eat, revolution or not. The dull, frustrating work with
our people is the work of the black revolutionary artist. It
means, most of all, staying close enough to them to be there
whenever they need you' ('Duties of the Black Revolutionary
Artist', Walker, 1984, p. 135). Being a Black revolutionary
artist means she must be 'the voice of the people, but she is
also the People' (p. 138). Through literature, the writer

engages with, and continues into the future, the tradition of African-American struggle.

As a revolutionary artist, Walker faces the problem of how to represent a complex Black woman when all available literary forms mitigate against this. There are two related formal problems: first, distrust of a predominantly white readership which may misinterpret the text and read it on white terms rather than its own African-American terms; second, the available literary forms belong to the Anglo-American literary tradition and so whilst they can convey black subject matter, that substance is placed in conflict with the structural properties of the form. In *The Color Purple*, Walker's solution is to create a feminist epistolary mode, adapted to Black women's experience. The autobiographical or diary element of the form places the self in a prominent position, it asserts the self, and so it is an effective strategy for the foregrounding of black female subjectivity. The letter, as the basic structural element of the narrative, anticipates the responses of the reader and so explains potential misunder-standings or misinterpretations before they occur. However, in the first half of the novel the reader is God and so Celie adopts a self-effacing stance in relation to the projected (non-human or trans-human, or divine) reader. This changes when Celie leaves Mr – to travel to Memphis with Shug and she is able to address Nettie directly:

> I don't write to God no more, I write to you. ... All my life I never care what people thought bout nothing I did, I say [to Shug]. But deep in my heart I care about God. What he going to think. And come to find out, he don't think. Just sit up there glorying in being deef, I reckon. But it ain't easy, trying to do without God. Even if you know he ain't there, trying to do without him is a strain (Walker, 1983, pp. 151–152).

This substitution of God with Nettie represents the revolution that has happened in Celie's life and a redefini-tion of her projected image of God follows. Her image of God as a patriarchal figure, 'big and old and tall and graybearded and white' is replaced with Shug's perception of God as a power that is inherent in everything: 'God is inside you and inside everybody else' (p. 166), she tells Celie.

Celie begins with a conventional patriarchal image of God but this image changes as a result of her relationship with Shug and begins to approach Walker's description in *The Temple of My Familiar*:

> It is actually your own spirit that is the familiar. Untampered with. And its 'temple' is freedom. It is not somebody else's idea of what your temple should be. Your spirit's temple is freedom. ... The ultimate 'temple' has to be freedom. ... And it is only with freedom of the spirit that we can claim as we are, in any sense, free (p. 139).

Celie seeks through God to transcend her material circumstances and to free her spirit; Celie's God is her soul's refuge. But where God is a way to understand and explain the significance of what is happening to herself, it is actually Shug Avery who brings salvation in the form of personal sovereignty.

Nettie finds God in her adopted family and she follows this family as she follows God. She too discovers an understanding of her situation, but in Nettie's case it is her ethnic or racial situation rather than her gender experience that requires clarification. She comes to realise that repatriation is not a viable solution to the race problem in America; Africa is not home for African-Americans. Freedom must be defined in America, within the context of her own personal and racial origins. The reconstituted family (when her sister returns and her children are restored to her) becomes Celie's refuge, and at the end of the narrative her letters are addressed to Nettie rather than to God. In the absence of her real family, Celie finds that it is only possible with God to experience an expanded consciousness, a sense of being that is greater than her individual self. At the end of the novel, her frustrations have been satisfied, she exists as a complete woman, and her final letter, which begins 'Dear God. Dear stars, dear trees, dear sky, dear peoples. Dear Everything. Dear God' (p. 242), expresses this sense of belonging to the world, where the world is a place that has been put right and made complete.

The Color Purple offers a parable of change through the agency of poor Black women and so challenges the complicity of white feminism (past and present) with racism. It also contests earlier representations of Black women as powerless or repressive or hostile to Black masculinity. Walker shows how dominant images of masculinity lead to oppression in Black families where women suffer multiple repressions; until she escapes to Memphis, Celie's suffering is a consequence of her family roles. Walker creates emblematic female characters: Celie, Shug, Sophia, and dramatises their capacity to assess and affect social relations, to survive the exploitation of their bodies and minds both by the dominant Anglo-American society and by their own community.

The reader is required to share the novel's resistance of cultural imperialism by trying to understand the story within its Black context and not in white or race-neutral terms. A basic assumption of the text is that individuals are not all essentially the same, that racial and gender differences are fundamental and require separate understanding. Black women cannot be treated like white men; 'equality' on those terms is unacceptable. The understanding of Black women's position is only possible within the context of Black women's historical experience.

The record of this historical experience is corrected in *The Color Purple* where Walker takes issue with the view that Black men suffered more under slavery and its aftermath. For example, imagery of the emasculation of Black men dominates the popular imagination: white fears of Black sexuality are symbolised by the castration that often accompanied lynching and other forms of racialised murder. Women were lynched, though infrequently; commonly enslaved Black women were deprived of their humanity, treated as livestock and used for breeding purposes to provide children (often the children of their masters) for market. The systematic rape of Black women leads to dehumanisation and death of the spirit if not a physical death. Walker exposes the extent of female suffering under this regime, yet she distances her characters from violence and victimisation by whites and instead focuses upon the ways in which women are oppressed both by Black men, and white men and women. Celie suffers twenty years of rape and beatings from her husband, but she controls her violent rage and reacts in subtle ways to avoid losing her humanity, which would only brutalise herself and reduce her to acting as is expected of a 'nigger'.

If the oppression of Black women is related closely to the exploitation and control of their sexuality, then Walker uses sexuality as an avenue of liberation in *The Color Purple*. She achieves this within the context of incestuous rape, a motif that recurs throughout Black women's writing (in texts like Toni Morrison's *The Bluest Eye*, Gayle Jones's *Corregidora*, and Maya Angelou's *I Know Why the Caged Bird Sings*). The image has its origins in the forced breeding of slave women who were raped by their white owners who, in some cases, were the fathers of these women. As Angela Davis and bell hooks have pointed out, rape was used as an instrument of terror both on the plantation and as part of the enslavement process. Celie's response to this horrifying and dehumanising experience is typical – she turns inward the guilt and pain, transforming them into masochistic self-loathing. Loss of pride and self-respect follows; these feelings of worthlessness are heightened for Celie who believes that her children have been taken from her and killed.

Walker establishes a subtle contrast between the violence of heterosexual rape and lesbian sexuality. This is a relatively understated theme in the narrative. Lesbianism is represented as an icon of feminine individuality and sexual self-determination; a state of being as separate from men and as far removed from patriarchy as possible. Shug and Celie discover in their relationship respect, support, sisterhood and, above all, a kind of recognition that is not possible from the male gaze. Shug is proud of her sexuality, she lives through her body, and she is able to teach Celie the pride and self-respect that have been destroyed throughout the course of years of sexual and physical abuse. Through Shug, Celie finds that she is complete in herself; she is transformed from being the object of male ridicule and becomes the subject of female support. This is the dominant message that emerges from the book: apart from men, women can find dignity, spiritual sustenance and also sexual satisfaction. Women may remain second class citizens but they are no longer silent, invisible second class citizens. And that is a beginning.

The term 'womanism' is used by Walker to describe her commitment to ending the oppression of women, rather than the term 'feminism'. Feminism in America is too closely tied to racism for the comfort of many black women – bell hooks and Angela Davis write extensively about this, as mentioned above. In Walker's terms, a 'womanist' loves women and women's culture; a womanist is concerned to assert women's identity and independence on their own terms; being a womanist involves 'wanting to know more and in greater depth than is good for one', according to Alice Walker; a womanist represents women as complex undiminished human beings. The women of *The Color Purple* are liberated through pride in their gender, their 'womanness'. Celie's frailty and strength, her humility and pathos represent her as ordinary, representative of the mass of oppressed women, where Shug is strong, self-confident and exemplary of what women can become.

A key element of Black women's liberation is the acquisition of literacy. The twin issues of education and literacy have always been prominent in Black American writing. Slaves were strictly forbidden access to education, because whites saw education as potentially empowering; they were forbidden to read and write because these skills may enable slaves to communicate their stories to other slaves and to abolitionist whites. The slave narrative, an autobiographical account of real life under slavery, often dictated by an escaped slave to a white abolitionist, was a very popular literary form in the nineteenth century and an effective weapon in the fight to abolish slavery in America. (Slavery was abolished in America in 1864, in Britain in 1807, in Mauritania in 1980; we should note that the Anti-Slavery Society, based in London, is still active). The legacy of slave writings is still very much in evidence in contemporary African-American texts, like *The Color Purple*, and one element of this is the equation between literacy and freedom. To be able to write of one's life, to set down experience in words and thereby achieve a degree of intellectual distance from lived events, this enables oppressed

Blacks to begin the attempt to see their lives as determined by political and economic motives that are impersonal. So the reasons for suffering are identified not as personal inadequacy and worthlessness but political decisions that are made independently of the individuals who suffer as a consequence. This liberation from guilt is itself empowering; patriarchal society depends upon the internalisation of its values by its victims. The refusal to be made subordinate, to be belittled and demeaned, marks the beginning of resistance to patriarchal values.

The Color Purple describes a dual quest for literacy and freedom; this quest provides both the subject and the structure of the narrative. But the text also displays a pervasive distrust of language. This is expressed as a distrust of the white reader who may be illiterate in Black terms and who may then censor the text in the process of interpreting it, or otherwise misinterpret the text as the result of white inability to read accurately Black experience. But the narrative also responds to the possibility that white readers will distrust the truth of the story and the author's credentials to tell such a story. Walker herself has been attacked for representing all Black men as brutal and violent; she has been criticised for her activism on behalf of sexually mutilated women when she herself has not been mutilated; and, historically, the writers of slave narratives were accused of inventing horrors that did not exist under slavery. The attack on the writer, especially the Black American writer, who writes to expose the realities of life lived under a racist patriarchal regime is a common strategy to discredit not just the writer but the suffering of the oppressed people of whom she writes. Walker is acutely aware of this and takes steps to counter such allegations: the narrative is carefully crafted so that Celie tells her own story, in her own words, using her own dialect, and the presence of the writer is minimised throughout the telling of the story. In the postscript, Walker places herself in the position of medium in relation to her characters; she writes, 'I thank everybody in this book for coming', signing herself 'A.W., author and medium' (p. 245). Walker thus represents herself as enabling the story to be told, as a facilitator, not as the creator of the characters and their stories.

I have dwelt at some length upon Walker's achievement in *The Color Purple* because in this text Walker addresses the key issues for feminists of colour: the acquisition of an effective literary voice, the oppression of women within their own ethnic group as well as within the dominant patriarchal racist culture, the control of feminine sexuality and the exploration of alternative means of experiencing sexuality, the reception of mainstream feminism by feminists of colour, and the embeddedness of the work of writers of colour within the historical and traditional contexts of their racial identity. I want now to look more briefly at how these issues are taken up in a Chicana context by Denise Chávez, in a Native American context by Leslie Marmon Silko and in an Asian American context by Maxine Hong Kingston.

Denise Chávez, The Last of the Menu Girls *(1986)*

The discontinuous narrative form of *The Last of the Menu Girls*, which is a series of connected stories that can be read either individually or in series, represents a significant innovation in terms of creating literary structures that will express the consciousness of women of colour. In this narrative, Chávez represents the acquisition of an effective literary voice in the structure and in the thematic substance of the text. The opening story of the sequence is structured according to the headings on the employment form that is filled in by the protagonist, a young Chicana Rocío Esquibel, juxtaposed with vignettes of the hospital patients she serves. The imposition of an external form upon the representation of her life and experience represents the fragmented and discontinuous quality of life experienced by Chicanas, who are subject to a range of social and cultural gender prescriptions which prevent the exercise of personal sovereignty and agency. Thus, the structure of the narrative represents the fragmentation of identity under the twin pressures of racism and sexism.

Rocío is subject to the conflict between what she is expected to be within the confines of the patriarchal Chicano family and the microcosm of white supremacist society that she encounters at the hospital. Thus, she is caught between how she experiences her self subjectively and how others experience her. For example, the young woman with whom she works, Arlene, compliments Rocío for never losing her temper: 'You never get angry, do you?' she asks. Rocío replies: ' "Rarely," I said. But inside, I was always angry'. Rocío continues, 'I want to be someone else, somewhere else, someone important and responsible and sexy. I want to be sexy' (Chávez, 1986, p. 34). Rocío's internal experience is at odds with the stereotypes to which she is subjected by those, especially the whites, who surround her at the hospital.

The narrative represents, for example, a contrast between Rocío's sophisticated vocabulary and the barely articulate mumblings of her boss, Mr Smith. This white man, whose relationship to her Rocío clearly understands as determined by their ethnic, gender and class differences, treats her just as 'the new girl'; 'menus', he mumbles to himself, identifying her with the objects she is to deliver each day to the patients in their beds. This contrast is sustained by all those, in particular the patients, who see her simply as a functionary, a 'menu-girl'. She recalls one patient in particular, a young woman named Elizabeth Rainey who does not bother to be polite, and Rocío wonders, 'How many people yelled at me to go away that summer, have yelled since then, countless people, of all ages, sick people, really sick people, dying people, people who were well and still rudely tied into their needs for privacy and space, affronted by these constant impositions from, of all people, the menu girl!' (p. 27). This explains her sympathy for patients like the Hispanic man, nicknamed 'Juan the Nose' whose nose has been bitten off in a bar fight, who is perhaps an illegal immigrant, who is unconscious and in any case is unable to speak English. Rocío's sympathy contrasts with the attitude of the nurses who speculate about how 'human' these illegal immigrants can be; these nurses who themselves bear Hispanic names – Esperanza, Erminia, Rosario, Luciano – do not disguise their hostility towards 'aliens', especially those who do not speak English.

Chávez situates Rocío's experience within the context of the oppression of women within their own ethnic group as well as within the dominant patriarchal racist culture. One of the dominant themes of the narrative is the limited range of possibilities available within Chicano culture from which a young Chicana can choose when deciding how to live her life. Rocío visualises this choice in terms of a contrast first between her own situation and that of the white women she encounters; second, she contrasts her own aspirations and dreams with the reality of the women's lives she sees within her own family. Images of women appear in the narrative in succession; old and young, white and Hispanic, from the past and the present. These images of feminine destiny provide a gallery of portraits against which Rocío can measure her own potential. And she rejects them all.

These images of femininity are linked, negatively, with the imagery of the narrative which emphasises the body, especially the female body, but in terms of death, dying and disease. Rocío reflects that she 'never wanted to be like Great Aunt Eutilia, or Doña Mercedes with the holes in her back, or my mother, her scarred legs, her whitened thighs' (p. 17). But the proximity of feminine suffering and intense feminine experience has revealed to Rocío some basic truths about herself. She realises, 'I had made that awesome leap into myself that steamy summer of illness and dread – confronting at every turn, the flesh, its lingering cries' (pp. 35–36). There are two female figures that dominate this opening story – the mythical figure of La Llorona and the historical figure of Florence Nightingale. In Chicano mythology, La Llorona is the woman driven to distraction who has murdered her children in order to punish her husband for his infidelity. According to the legend, she hides the bodies, but too well so that when she returns to bury them she cannot find them. So La Llorona searches ceaselessly for her lost children, weeping and wailing as she searches. La Llorona represents an image of the dispossessed Hispanic woman, the victim of oppression and exploitation who bears the blame for her own suffering. Florence Nightingale, in contrast, is associated with the realisation of feminine suffering Rocío makes as a result of her experience in the hospital: Rocío gazes at her portrait and thinks, 'Her look encompassed all of the great unspeakable sufferings of every war' (p. 37), this knowledge of suffering and of the conflicts and struggles that are fought invisibly in women's lives is the knowledge that Rocío has acquired. The notion of women's lives as conflict and struggle, struggle to avoid the fate of La Llorona and the female relatives who follow in her image, is powerfully represented in *The Last of the Menu Girls* as Rocío seeks a way to live her own life that is of her own determination.

Leslie Marmon Silko, Storyteller

The use of traditional images such as La Llorona betrays the embeddedness of Chávez's work, like that of other writers of colour, within the historical and traditional contexts of their racial identity. This is the case with Leslie Marmon Silko's *Storyteller*, a text that combines memoir, photographs, poetry and fiction in the attempt to represent accurately the experience of Native American women. The story 'Lullaby' is narrated by a third-person narrator but the story is filtered through the consciousness and memory of the woman Ayah. The story describes the last few hours in the lives of Ayah and her husband. Dispossessed of everything they have had in their lives, old and unwanted even by each other, they surrender to despair and so die. The tone of the story is elegiac, as is suited to the subject matter – loss and death. Nostalgia for a lost tribal world where the human and non-human worlds were integrated, where life had meaning and where individuals understood their place within a larger scheme, permeates the story and adds a harsh edge to Silko's condemnation of Native genocide, which takes both physical and cultural forms.

The primary theme of this story is the contrast between tribal life and life under white male domination. This contrast is developed in a number of ways, like the difference between Ayah's memories of the cosy hogan of her childhood and of the stark shack in which the rancher permits them to live and from which she and Chato are evicted when they are too old to work. The effect of white contact is alienation from nature and each other; Ayah remembers a time 'when they had no black rubber overshoes; only the high buckskin leggings that they wrapped over their elkhide moccasins' (Silko, 1981, p. 44). The substitution of rubber for hide symbolises the separation from nature and from traditional ways that is the consequence of white domination of Native people.

Dispossession is represented in a number of ways. There is the repeated motif of their physical eviction: first from their shack, then from the bar, and then from the barn until they have only the icy arroyo in which to rest. Ayah recalls removal of their children by force to a government institution, and that when they return to visit they can no longer understand her. The conscription and death of their son Jimmie is recollected through the figure of the government official who comes to their door with the news of Jimmie's death. When she describes her first, successful, evasion of the white doctor and social workers who want to take her children away, Ayah makes reference to 'the high volcanic peak the Mexicans called Guadalupe' (p. 46), perhaps alluding to the Treaty of Guadalupe Hildago by whose terms Mexicans were simultaneously annexed to the United States and dispossessed of their land. The loss of her children Ayah blames partly upon Chato, who has taught her only enough English so that she can sign her name and thus sign away her children to the white government; but she also blames the government for having already taken her older son Jimmie who could have explained to her the significance of the papers she was signing.

Ayah is bitter as she recalls the exploitation of Indians by the white patriarchal government and the willingness of men like Chato to believe white lies. Chato is always prepared to believe what he is told, and who accepts the assumption of the supremacy of white men, which his wife does not. And so she has no sympathy for him; 'he should have known all along what would happen' (p. 50). But his ability to speak English and Spanish means that he has a limited acceptance in white society – he is permitted to enter the bar where other

Indians are not – but this does not alter the fact that he is Indian and is treated accordingly. It does mean that he expects a certain dispensation from racial prejudice which does not come about. His wife is more realistic in her expectations than he is, but this realism is borne of her complete exclusion from white masculine society.

Language, then, functions as an instrument of domination: the children learn English at the expense of the language of their parents and ancestors; Ayah knows enough written English to sign her children away; Ayah realises, 'it was like the old ones always told her about learning their language or any of their ways: it endangered you' (p. 2342). The narrative portrays a complex network of betrayals: of Indians by whites; Indians by other Indians (the interpreters) and women by other women (white social workers). The awareness of the dispossession, exploitation and betrayal of themselves and their people drives Indians like Ayah and Chato to despair and to alcoholism.

Silko uses the traditional activities of spinning and weaving as powerful sources of imagery. In the first sentences: 'The sun had gone down but the snow in the wind gave off its own light. It came in thick tufts like new wool – washed before the weaver spins it' (p. 2339), snow and nature are associated with wool, as are Ayah's memories of her family and tribal past. Gradually in the course of the story snow is associated with death and the destruction of native culture. In contrast, the deathly influence of whites is symbolised by dust and dryness. The link between dust and death is first made when Ayah describes covering her dead children's corpses with dust, sand and stones; she remembers this while describing the spiritual death she has endured when her children were forcibly taken from her by whites and so the association is made with white disruption of Indian life. Later, Ayah describes the life they live on welfare as a meaningless routine, like planting the garden in May 'not because anything would survive the summer dust, but because it was time to do this. The journey [to collect the government cheque] passed the days that smelled silent and dry like the caves above the canyon with yellow painted buffaloes on their walls' (p. 2344). Here is made the connection between the destruction of a living tribal culture, dust and white supremacy. Ayah is betrayed by her own husband, but he in turn is betrayed by the false promises made to him by white patriarchal society. As Paula Gunn Allen observes, without the women a tribe will not survive; Ayah has been destroyed not only by the invasion of her life by white male culture, represented by doctors, policemen and social workers, but also by the complicity of Chato with the forces of dispossession and destruction. White men and Indian men together destroy the tribal life she had enjoyed, they betray her faith and dispossess her of all that she holds valuable.

Maxine Hong Kingston, The Woman Warrior

Like *Storyteller* and *The Last of the Menu Girls*, *The Woman Warrior* represents a hybrid form, comprised of auto-biography, biography, myths and legends, historical reconstruction. In each of the five sections of the narrative, there is offered a feminine character or a feminine role (daughter, student, warrior, writer) which offers a model of feminine identity; but the effect of this multiplicity of roles is not to clarify but to render identity mysterious. The form of the narrative seeks to articulate the forces, and the disjunctions – between China and America, past and present, mythic and mundane, real and recollected – that have shaped Maxine's identity. She tries to find a voice with which to express her relationship with her mother, especially, and so reach an understanding of how women can relate to each other within the terms of a brutally misogynistic Chinese culture and an American culture comprised of conflicting gender values. Consequently, the narrative voice is complicated and confusing. It varies from subjective reconstruction (in the story of the No Name Aunt), to imaginative construction (as in the telling of Moon Orchid's story), or historical verisimilitude (when recounting her mother's experiences in the section entitled 'Shaman'). The fragmentation of narrative form, which shifts from first to third person narration, attempts to overcome the perception of cultural doubleness (Chinese and American) by creating the illusion of simultaneity within the reader's consciousness.

The themes of the narrative emphasise the position of women in Chinese and American patriarchal cultures. History and generational change are represented in terms of the periods pre- and post-Communist Revolution, which 'put an end to prostitution by giving women what they wanted: a job and a room of their own' (Kingston, 1976, p. 61), but poverty was still endemic and women suffered most intensely as a consequence. This poverty enabled Maxine's mother to become educated, but still she owned a girl slave (*mui tsai*). Maxine struggles to understand the contradictions that her mother represents – Brave Orchid tries to raise her daughter in the Chinese fashion of submissiveness and subordination but she herself represents a forceful and opinionated woman, independent and strong-willed.

The narrative necessarily explores the misogynistic practices that her mother has overcome in traditional Chinese patriarchy: institutionalised female servitude, infant betrothal, slavery, concubinage, prostitution. What emerges is a powerful image of gender relations that are organised according to Confucian patriarchy. Women owe obedience to the men in their family, it is the network of family relations that gives women their identity, and consequently marriage is both a woman's life and her fate. This feminine dependence upon the male dominated family unit is reinforced by the cultural attitudes that Maxine finds crystallised in degrading proverbs like 'Girls are maggots in the rice' and 'It is more profitable to raise geese than daughters' (p. 41). Under Chinese patriarchy, language itself embodies the assumption of feminine inferiority – 'There is a Chinese word for the female *I* – which is "slave". Break the women with their own tongues!' (p. 49). In Chinese terms, the words 'girl' and 'bad' are assumed to be synonymous. Maxine recalls that as a child, ' "I'm not a bad girl," I would scream. ... I might as well have said, "I'm not a girl" ' (p. 48).

Maxine tries to understand the conflicting demands made of her by her Chinese ancestry and American childhood. She is critical of China and the culture that belittles her for reason of her gender; it is from an American perspective that she hears Chinese voices: 'You can see the disgust on American faces looking at women like that. It isn't just the loudness. It is the way Chinese sounds, chingchong ugly, to American ears, not beautiful like Japanese sayonara words with the consonants and vowels as regular as Italian' (p.154). The effort to analyse and understand her cross-cultural experience is difficult but the alternative that is represented by Moon Orchid is unacceptable. She finds two different lifestyles impossible to deal with and loses her sanity. Maxine is torn between the two cultures: she is aware of her difficulties in understanding Chinese culture but she is also aware that she doesn't belong entirely to American culture. Only as a woman warrior can she imagine bringing the two together: 'Nobody in history has conquered and united both North America and Asia' (p. 50).

This triumph over the cultural conflicts she suffers can only be represented through the telling of it. This means that Maxine must overcome the patriarchal Chinese imperative of feminine silence. The ability of a woman to express herself is related to the narrative motif of mutilation. The narrative represents the figure of the woman warrior who bears the villagers' wrongs carved into her back and tells of Maxine's mother cutting her daughter's frenum – either to silence her and repress the 'ready tongue [that] is an evil tongue' (p. 148) or to free her to articulate her own thoughts and, as Brave Orchid claims, to learn many languages. The No Name Aunt is punished for her illegitimate child and is forced to give 'silent birth' (p.18), as a child Maxine bullies a classmate who refuses to talk; her aunt Moon Orchid, unable to talk about her confusion of fantasy with reality, finally goes mad. Maxine confesses, 'I thought talking and not talking made the difference between sanity and insanity. Insane people were the ones who couldn't explain themselves' (p. 166). In the final chapter, she makes a list of grievances to explain to her mother, and thus make her mutilated tongue work in the cause of her own liberation.

The title of the narrative points to the importance of the theme of resistance and rebellion. Various rebellions are interrelated in the text; such as Kingston's rebellion against conventional literary forms that are inadequate to express her cross-cultural position, her rebellion against her powerful mother; and her rebellion against the Chinese cultural influences to which she is subject as her inheritance. Hers is a rebellion against imposed racial and gender identities. These imposed identities are represented in part by the imagery of ghosts that recur throughout the narrative. The text is subtitled 'Memoirs of a Girlhood Among Ghosts'. Ghosts threaten Chinese traditions by drawing people away from Chinese culture, such as Taxi Ghosts, Police Ghosts, Grocery Ghosts, or by subverting traditional culture, which is the crime committed by the No Name Aunt who drowns herself and her child in the village well so that she might haunt her persecutors. Threats to traditional culture are rendered void, deprived of reality, when they are represented as ghosts. The most terrifying ghosts Maxine encounters are the dead and tortured Chinese images that her mother conjures up and which haunt her dreams.

The powerful influence that Maxine's mother exerts over her daughter comes primarily from the stories that she tells. This 'talk-story', as Maxine calls it, can sustain superstitions, embody warnings, but it can also offer chances to imagine unrealised possibilities. Saying can be a form of vengeance but it can also be a form of aspiration, a way of imagining what is possible. When she finally realises this, Maxine warns: 'Be careful what you say. It comes true. It comes true. I had to leave home in order to see the world logically, logic the new way of seeing. ... Shine floodlights into dark corners: no ghosts' (p.182). In important respects, the entire text of *The Woman Warrior* is a discontinuous talk-story, telling the story of how Maxine develops both as an artist and a woman. In this way, *The Woman Warrior* can be seen as a feminist *Kunstlerroman* that presents us with a portrait of the artist as a feminist of colour. At the end of the narrative, she is able to express a new view of herself as a translator or a mediator between cultures who transcends the imposed gender constraints of both Chinese and American patriarchy.

References and Selected Further Reading

Abbandonato, Linda, 1991. 'A View from "Elsewhere": Subversive Sexuality and the Rewriting of the Heroine's Story in *The Color Purple*', *PMLA*, vol. 106, no. 5 (October), pp. 1106–1115.

Allen, Paula Gunn, 1983. *Studies in American Indian Literature*, New York: MLA.

——, 1996. *The Sacred Hoop: Recovering the Feminine in American Indian Traditions*, Boston: Beacon Press.

——, 1998. *Off the Reservation: Reflections on Boundary-Busting, Border-Crossing, Loose Canons*, Boston: Beacon Press.

Ammott, Teresa L. & Julie A. Matthaei, 1991. *Race, Gender and Work: A Multicultural Economic History of Women in the United States*, Boston: South End Press.

Anderson, Douglas, 1995. 'Displaced Abjection and States of Grace: Denise Chávez's *The Last of the Menu Girls*', in Julia Brown, ed., *American Women Short Story Writers: A Collection of Critical Essays*, New York: Garland, pp. 235–250.

Anzaldúa, Gloria, 1987. *Borderlands / La Frontiera: The New Mestiza*, San Francisco: Aunt Lute Books.

——, ed., 1990. *Haciendo Caras: Making Face, Making Soul: Creative and Critical Perspectives by Feminists of Color*, San Francisco: Aunt Lute Books.

Arnold, Ellen, 1998. 'Listening to the Spirits: An Interview with Leslie Marmon Silko', *Studies in American Indian Literatures*, vol. 10, no. 3 (Fall), pp. 1–33.

Berlant, Lauren, 1988. 'Race, Gender, and Nation in *The Color Purple*', *Critical Inquiry*, vol. 14, no. 4 (Summer), pp. 831–859.

Bloom, Harold, ed., 1989. *Alice Walker*, New York: Chelsea.

Boynton, Victoria, 1996. 'Desire's Revision: Feminist Appropriation of Native American Traditional Sources', *Modern Language Studies*, vol. 26, no. 2–3 (Spring-Summer), pp. 53–71.

Browdy de Hernandez, Jennifer, 1994. 'Laughing, Crying, Surviving: The Pragmatic Politics of Leslie Marmon Silko's *Storyteller*', *A-B:-Auto-Biography Studies*, vol. 9, no. 1 (Spring), pp.18–42.

Bus, Heiner, 1993. 'Gender Roles and the Emergence of a Writer in Denise Chávez's *The Last of the Menu Girls* (1986)', in Renate von Bardelben, ed., *Gender, Self and Society: Proceedings of IV International Conference on Hispanic Cultures of the United States*. Frankfurt: Peter Lang, pp. 277–286.

Butler Evans, Elliott, 1989. *Race, Gender, and Desire: Narrative Strategies in the Fiction of Toni Cade Bambara, Toni Morrison, and Alice Walker*, Philadelphia: Temple University Press.

Callaloo, 1989. 'Alice Walker: A Special Section', *Callaloo*, vol. 12, no. 2 (Spring), pp. 295–345.

Carter, Nancy Corson, 1994. 'Claiming the Bittersweet Matrix: Alice Walker, Sandra Cisneros, and Adrienne Rich', *Critique*, vol. 35, no. 4 (Summer), pp. 195–204.

Castillo, Susan Perez, 1994. 'The Construction of Gender and Ethnicity in the Texts of Leslie Silko and Louise Erdrich', *Yearbook of English Studies*, vol. 24, pp. 228–236.

Castillo, Susan & Victor M. P. Da Rosa, eds, 1997. *Native American Women in Literature and Culture*, Porto, Portugal: Fernando Pessoa University Press.

Christian, Barbara, 1985. *Black Feminist Criticism*, Oxford: Pergamon.

——, ed., 1994. *Alice Walker: 'Everyday Use'*, New Brunswick: Rutgers University Press.

Collins, Patricia Hill, 1990. *Black Feminist Thought*, London: Unwin Hyman.

Coltelli, Laura, ed., 1996. *The Spiral of Memory: Interviews*, Ann Arbor: University of Michigan Press.

Cowart, David, 1996. 'Heritage and Deracination in Walker's 'Everyday Use', *Studies in Short Fiction*, vol. 33, no. 2 (Spring), pp. 171–184.

Danielson, Linda, 1989. 'The Storytellers in Storyteller', *Studies in American Indian Literatures*, vol. 1, no. 2 (Fall), pp. 21–31.

Davis, Angela Y., 1981. *Women, Race and Class*, New York: Random House.

Echoes from Gold Mountain: An Asian American Journal, 1978. Asian American Studies, Long Beach: California State University.

Evans, Charlene Taylor, 1996. 'Mother-Daughter Relationships as Epistemological Structures: Leslie Marmon Silko's *Almanac of the Dead* and *Storyteller*', in Elizabeth Brown-Guillory, ed., *Women of Color: Mother-Daughter Relationships in Twentieth-Century Literature*, Austin: University of Texas Press, pp. 172–187.

Evans, Marie, 1985. *Black Women Writers*, London: Pluto.

Eysturoy, Annie, 1996. *Daughters of Self-Creation: The Contemporary Chicana Novel*, Albuquerque: University of New Mexico Press.

Fifer, Elizabeth, 1985. 'Alice Walker: The Dialect and Letters of *The Color Purple*', in Catherine Rainwater & William J. Scheick, eds, *Contemporary American Women Writers: Narrative Strategies*, Lexington: University Press of Kentucky, pp. 155–171.

Fisher, Dexter, ed., 1980. *The Third Woman: Minority Women Writers of the United States*. Boston: Houghton Mifflin.

Froula, Christine, 1986. 'The Daughter's Seduction: Sexual Violence and Literary History', *Signs*, vol. 11, no. 4 (Summer), pp. 621–644.

Giddings, P., 1984. *When and Where I Enter: The Impact of Black Women on Race and Sex in America*, New York: Wm Morrow.

Gonzalez, Maria, 1996. 'Love and Conflict: Mexican American Women Writers as Daughters', in Elizabeth Brown Guillory, ed., *Women of Color: Mother-Daughter Relationships in Twentieth-Century Literature*, Austin: University of Texas Press, pp. 153–171.

Graulich, Melody, ed., 1993. *'Yellow Woman', Leslie Marmon Silko*, New Brunswick: Rutgers University Press.

hooks, bell, 1981. *Ain't I a Woman: Black Women and Feminism*, Boston: South End Press.

——, 1984. *Feminist Theory: From Margin to Center*, Boston: South End Press.

——, 1990. *Yearning: Race, Gender and Cultural Politics*, Boston: South End Press.

Howard, Lillie P., ed., 1993. *Alice Walker and Zora Neale Hurston: The Common Bond*, Westport, CT: Greenwood.

Hull, Gloria T., Patricia Dell Scott & Barbara Smith, eds, 1982. *But Some of Us Are Brave*, Old Westbury, NY: Feminist Press.

Islas, Arturo, 1983. 'Maxine Hong Kingston' in Marilyn Yalom, ed., *Women Writers of the West Coast: Speaking of Their Lives and Careers*, Santa Barbara: Capra, pp. 11–19.

Joseph, Gloria & Jill Lewis, 1981. *Common Differences: Conflicts in Black and White Feminist Perspectives*, New York: Anchor.

Juhasz, Suzanne, 1985. 'Maxine Hong Kingston: Narrative Technique and Female Identity', in Catherine Rainwater & William J. Scheick, eds, *Contemporary American Women Writers: Narrative Strategies*, Lexington: University Press of Kentucky, pp. 173–189.

Kelley, Margot, 1997. 'A Minor Revolution: Chicano/a Composite Novels and the Limits of Genre', in Julia Brown, ed., *Ethnicity and the American Short Story*. New York: Garland, pp. 63–84.

Kingston, Maxine Hong, 1976. *The Woman Warrior*, London: Picador, 1981.

——, 1982. 'Cultural Mis-Reading by American Reviewers' in Guy Amirthanayagam, ed., *Asian and Western Writers in Dialogue: New Cultural Identities*, London: Macmillan, pp. 55–65.

——, 1998. 'Finding a Voice' in Virginia P. Clark, Paul A. Eschholz & Alfred F. Rosa, eds, *Language: Readings in Language and Culture*, New York: St Martin's, pp. 13–18.

Krumholz, Linda J., 1994. ' "To Understand This World Differently": Reading and Subversion in Leslie Marmon Silko's "Storyteller"', *ARIEL*, vol. 25, no. 1 (January), pp. 89–113.

Krupat, Arnold, 1989. 'The Dialogic of Silko's *Storyteller*' in Gerald Vizenor, ed., *Narrative Chance: Postmodern Discourse on Native American Indian Literatures*, Albuquerque: University of New Mexico Press, pp. 55–68.

Lappas, Catherine, 1994. ' "The Way I Heard It Was . . .": Myth, Memory, and Autobiography in *Storyteller* and *The Woman Warrior*', *CEA Critic*, vol. 57, no. 1 (Fall), pp. 57–67.

Lee, Robert A., 1990. 'Ethnic Renaissance: Rudolfo Anaya, Louise Erdrich, and Maxine Hong Kingston', in Graham Clarke, ed., *The New American Writing: Essays on American Literature Since 1970*, New York: St Martin's, pp. 139–164.

Light, Alison, 1987. 'Fear of the Happy Ending: '*The Color Purple*', Reading and Racism', Essays and Studies, vol. 40, pp. 103–117.

Lim, Shirley Geok-Lin & Amy Ling, eds, 1992. *Reading the Literatures of Asian America*, Philadelphia: Temple University Press.

Ling, Amy, 1990. 'Chinese American Women Writers: The Tradition behind Maxine Hong Kingston', in A. LaVonne Brown Ruoff & Jerry W. Ward, eds, *Redefining American Literary History*, New York: MLA, pp. 219–236.

——, 1995. 'Maxine Hong Kingston and the Dialogic Dilemma of Asian American Writers', *Bucknell Review*, vol. 39, no. 1, pp. 151–166.

Lorde, Audre, 1984. *Sister Outsider*, rpt. in *The Audre Lorde Compendium: Essays, Speeches and Journals*, London: Pandora, 1996.

Madsen, Deborah L., 1994. '(Dis)Figuration: The Body as Icon in the Writings of Maxine Hong Kingston', *Yearbook of English Studies*, vol. 24, pp. 237–250.

Moraga, Cherríe & Gloria Anzaldúa, eds, 1981. *This Bridge Called My Back: Writings of Radical Women of Color*, Watertown, MA: Persephone Press.

Nelson, Robert M., 1995. *Place and Vision: The Function of Landscape in Native American Fiction*, New York: Peter Lang.

Nishime, LeiLana, 1995. 'Engendering Genre: Gender and Nationalism in *China Men* and *The Woman Warrior*', *MELUS*, vol. 20, no. 1 (Spring), pp. 67–82.

Omolade, Barbara, 1980. 'Black Women and Feminism', in Hester Eisenstein & Alice Jardine, eds, *The Future of Difference*, Boston: G. K. Hall, pp. 247–257.

Pellerin, Simone, 1997. 'Death and the Power of Words in Leslie Marmon Silko's Storyteller', in Susan Castillo & Victor M. P. Da Rosa, eds, *Native American Women in Literature and Culture*, Porto, Portugal: Fernando Pessoa University Press, pp. 119–126.

Rabinowitz, Paula, 1987. 'Eccentric Memories: A Conversation with Maxine Hong Kingston', *Michigan Quarterly Review*, vol. 26, no. 1 (Winter), pp. 177–187.

Rebolledo, Tey Diana, 1995. *Women Singing in the Snow: A Cultural Analysis of Chicana Literature*, Tuscon & London: University of Arizona Press.

Rich, Adrienne, 1978. 'Disloyal to Civilization: Feminism, Racism and Gynephobia', *Chrysalis*, vol.7, pp.9–27.

Rocard, Marcienne, 1993. '*The Last of the Menu Girls* by Denise Chávez: The Emergence of Self as a Woman Writer', in Renate von Bardelben, ed., *Gender, Self and Society: Proceedings of IV International Conference on Hispanic Cultures of the United States*, Frankfurt: Peter Lang, pp. 87–96.

Rosaldo, Renato, 1991. 'Fables of the Fallen Guy', in Héctor Calderón & José David Saldívar, eds, *Criticism in the Borderlands: Studies in Chicano Literature, Culture, and Ideology*, Durham, NC: Duke University Press.

Ross, Daniel W., 1988. 'Celie in the Looking Glass: The Desire for Selfhood in *The Color Purple*', *Modern Fiction Studies*, vol. 34, no. 1 (Spring), pp. 69–84.

San Juan, E., Jr, 1991. 'Beyond Identity Politics: The Predicament of the Asian Writer in Late Capitalism', *American Literary History*, vol. 3, no. 3 (Fall), pp. 542–565.

Schueller, Malini, 1989. 'Questioning Race and Gender Definitions: Dialogic Subversions in *The Woman Warrior*', *Criticism*, vol. 1, no. 4 (Fall), pp. 421–437.

Schweninger, Lee, 1993. 'A Skin of Lakeweed: An Ecofeminist Approach to Erdrich and Silko', in Barbara Frey Waxman, ed., *Multicultural Literatures through Feminist/ Poststructuralist Lenses*, Knoxville: University of Tennessee Press, pp. 37–56.

Schwenk, Katrin, 1994. 'Lynching and Rape: Border Cases in African American History and Fiction', in Werner Sollors & Maria Diedrich, eds, *The Black Columbiad: Defining Moments in African American Literature and Culture*, Cambridge, MA: Harvard University Press, pp. 312–324.

Selzer, Linda, 1995. 'Race and Domesticity in *The Color Purple*', *African American Review*, vol. 29, no. 1 (Spring), pp. 67–82.

Silko, Leslie Marmon, 1981. 'Language and Literature from a Pueblo Indian Perspective', in Leslie A. Fiedler & Houston A. Baker Jr, eds, *English Literature: Opening Up the Canon*, Baltimore: Johns Hopkins University Press, pp. 54–72.

——, 1981. *Storyteller*. New York: Little, Brown & Co.

——, 1996. 'Landscape, History, and the Pueblo Imagination', in Cheryll Glotfelty & Harold Fromm, eds, *The Ecocriticism Reader: Landmarks in Literary Ecology*, Athens: University of Georgia Press, pp. 264–275.

Skenazy, Paul & Tera Martin, eds, 1998. *Conversations with Maxine Hong Kingston*, Jackson: University Press of Mississippi.

Smith, Barbara, 1990. 'The Truth That Never Hurts: Black Lesbians in Fiction in the 1980s', in Joanne M. Braxton & Andrée Nicola McLaughlin, eds, *Wild Women in the Whirlwind: Afra-American Culture and the Contemporary Literary Renaissance*, New Brunswick: Rutgers University Press, pp. 213–245.

Smith, Patricia Clark & Paula Gunn Allen, 1987. 'Earthly Relations, Carnal Knowledge: Southwestern American Indian Women Writers and Landscape', in Vera Norwood & Janice Monk, eds, *The Desert Is No Lady: Southwestern Landscapes in Women's Writing and Art*, New Haven: Yale University Press, pp. 174–196.

Smith, Sidonie, 1997. 'Maxine Hong Kingston's Woman Warrior: Filiality and Woman's Autobiographical Storytelling', in Robyn R. Warhol & Diane Price Herndl, eds, *Feminisms: An Anthology of Literary Theory and Criticism*, New Brunswick: Rutgers University Press, pp. 1117–1137.

Spelman, Elizabeth, 1980. '"Theories of Race and Gender: The Erasure of Black Women', *Quest*, vol. 5 no. 4, pp.36–62.

Spillers, Hortense J., 1989. '"The Permanent Obliquity of an In(pha)llibly Straight": In the Time of the Daughters and the Fathers', in Cheryl A. Wall, ed., *Changing Our Own Words: Essays on Criticism, Theory, and Writing by Black Women*, New Brunswick: Rutgers University Press, pp. 127–149.

St Clair, Janet, 1994. 'Uneasy Ethnocentrism: Recent Works of Allen, Silko, and Hogan', *Studies in American Indian Literatures*, vol. 6, no. 1 (Spring), pp. 82–98.

Talpode, Chandra, Ann Russon & Lourdes Torres, eds, 1991. *Third World Women and the Politics of Feminism*, Bloomington: Indiana University Press.

Tate, Claudia, ed., 1983. *Black Women Writers at Work*, New York: Continuum.

Tucker, Lindsey, 1988. 'Alice Walker's *The Color Purple*: Emergent Woman, Emergent Text', *Black American Literature Forum*, vol. 22, no. 1 (Spring), pp. 81–95.

Velie, Alan R., 1982. *Four American Indian Literary Masters: N. Scott Momaday, James Welch, Leslie Marmon Silko, and Gerald Vizenor*, Norman: University of Oklahoma Press.

Wall, Cheryl A., ed., 1989. *Changing Our Own Words: Essays on Criticism, Theory and Writing by Black Women*, New Brunswick & London: Rutgers University Press.

Walker, Alice, 1983. *The Color Purple*, London: The Women's Press, 1986.

——, 1984. *In Search of Our Mothers' Gardens: Womanist Prose*, London: The Women's Press.

——, 1988. *Living by the Word: Selected Writings, 1973–1987*, London: The Women's Press.

——, *The Temple of My Familiar*, London: Penguin.

Wong, Sau-ling Cynthia, 1988. 'Necessity and Extravagance in Maxine Hong Kingston's *The Woman Warrior*: Art and the Ethnic Experience', *MELUS*, vol. 15, no. 1 (Spring), pp. 4–26.

Woo, Deborah, 1990. 'Maxine Hong Kingston: The Ethnic Writer and the Burden of Dual Authenticity', *Amerasia Journal*, vol. 16, no. 1, pp. 173–200.

Yarbro-Bejarano, Yvonne, 1987. 'Chicana Literature from a Chicana Feminist Perspective', in María Hererra-Sobek & Helena María Viramontes, eds, *Chicana Creativity and Criticism: Charting New Frontiers in American Literature*, special issue, *Americas Review*, vol. 15, no. 3-4, pp. 139–145.

Index